SERVING LATINO COMMUNITIES

A How-To-Do-It Manual for Librarians®, Second Edition

CAMILA ALIRE
JACQUELINE AYALA

HOW-TO-DO-IT MANUALS
FOR LIBRARIANS

NUMBER 158

NEAL-SCHUMAN PUBLISHERS, INC.
New York   London

Published by Neal-Schuman Publishers, Inc.
100 William St., Suite 2004
New York, NY 10038

ISBN-13: 978-1-55570-606-7
ISBN-10: 1-55570-606-1

CONTENTS

LIST OF FIGURES

PREFACE

Latinos are the fastest-growing ethnic group in the United States. There are now over 40 million Latinos in this country, and they are no longer concentrated in just the South and Southwest. Given these numbers, it is more vital than ever for librarians to reach out to this underserved group. All libraries today need to have a plan for Latino-focused services.

Many librarians are willing to make changes but have no idea how to implement the necessary programs. In addition, staff members may be insecure about their ability to work with people who are culturally, ethnically, and racially different from themselves. *Serving Latino Communities* provides a step-by-step approach that addresses questions and issues in the order in which a library will most likely encounter them.

For more than ten years, we have been leading conferences and workshops on how to develop services for Latinos. We have worked with librarians all over the country and have supplemented our research with visits to institutions that are noted for their exemplary programs. In our preparation for this new edition, we discovered, to our delight, that many libraries have made great progress in the past few years. *Serving Latino Communities* focuses on these success stories and incorporates their wisdom as well as examples of their materials. The ideas in this book will help librarians in all settings attract Latino users and keep them coming back. Many of the resources can also be adapted for service to minorities of any race or ethnicity.

If you are forming a plan from scratch, *Serving Latino Communities* shows you how to back up your convictions with facts and convince others of the benefits of this new service direction. Some decision makers still resist focusing on this group. An argument bolstered by statistics and hard evidence can make the difference between a program that flourishes and one that never even happens. If your library is already reaching out to Latinos, the updated ideas, hints, and tips will help you improve and expand your services.

Since information technology is an increasingly important aspect of librarianship, our resources and references now include many online information sources. Throughout the book, we highlight sophisticated library Web sites that promote services, resources, and special programming for Latino patrons.

ORGANIZATION

Serving Latino Communities outlines a sequential, systematic process for service development. Each chapter also addresses potential problems. Real life dictates that any institution trying to reach Latinos may meet challenges from many sides.

- Chapter 1, "Understanding the Latino Community," gives background on the broad social differences between Anglo and Latino culture. It also introduces the potentially confusing issue of ethnic terminology.

- Chapter 2, "Investigating Latino Demographics," provides statistics regarding the American Latino population as well as compelling evidence for the importance of service to this group.

- You may already be committed to reaching this community, but before making changes, you will need to convince others, from the board of trustees to existing patrons. Chapter 3, "Building a Case for Serving Latinos," will help you build a strong argument based on economic, political, and social benefits.

- Because Latinos have traditionally fallen into the nonuser category, it's important to find out what they want from your library. Chapter 4, "Conducting a Community Needs Assessment," explores how to use surveys, interviews, and focus groups to identify Latinos' needs. Because focus groups are by far the most popular method, we have significantly expanded that section.

- Chapter 5, "Starting Out: Programs, Services, and Partnerships," offers creative ways to implement your plans. Many of the libraries we studied had partners who were instrumental to the success of their outreach to Latino residents. We have also added programming ideas for the new nationwide program *Día de los niños / Día de los libros*, which in the past five years has expanded exponentially and has found a home at the ALA's Association of Library Services to Children.

- How will potential patrons find out about your new services? Chapter 6, "Reaching the Latino Community," discusses effective outreach, marketing, and public relations and provides examples of promotional materials from various libraries.

- Chapter 7, "Establishing a Latino Collection," gives practical advice to selectors and addresses management issues such as reviewing and rewriting collection development policies and practices. We have completely revised and expanded the information on Latino distributors and publishers.

- Chapter 8, "Latinos: Planning for a Skilled, Competent Workforce," confronts a topic of concern for many libraries. We discuss the realities of training a non-Latino staff and outline strategies for recruiting Latino professionals, paraprofessionals, volunteers, and trustees.

- Funding for new programming is another pressing issue for many library administrators. Chapter 9, "Obtaining Funding," examines both internal and external sources of financial support. We provide a sample proposal format and share some innovative and successful ideas for grant writing.

- We have been amazed at the growth of relevant Web sites in the past few years. The Resource Directory in Chapter 10 now includes an expanded listing of electronic and Web resources. This chapter also provides a list of books, periodicals, library organizations, and conferences.

We hope that this manual will help ease the frustrations you might experience while trying to reach Latinos. The advice and examples we provide will assist you in this extremely important effort. This revised edition gives you current information that takes into account the many changes that have occurred in the past few years. What you are preparing to do is what our profession is all about-providing equal information access to all, regardless of ethnicity or race. All members of our communities deserve our best efforts to meet their information needs.

ACKNOWLEDGMENTS

We want to acknowledge all the dedicated library staff who work so hard to provide library services to Latino communities globally. We are grateful to all those who agreed to be interviewed and provided us with material for this publication.

Thanks to Judith A. Castiano, who introduced us. Judith served as the first American Indian (Laguna Pueblo) President of National REFORMA. She retired from a career of service to library customers and communities in December 2005.

We also want to honor, acknowledge, and thank Dr. Ron Baza and Alan Radcliffe for their support, patience, and understanding of our efforts and commitment.

1

UNDERSTANDING THE LATINO COMMUNITY

> *The Latino community is a very diverse population. One of the hottest topics continues to be how to address those of the same or similar ethnic background without offending anyone by your choice of term.*

Because Latinos have not traditionally been a part of the public library's clientele, we want to introduce you to our community. It is important that you know the basic elements of this underserved community. Learning these elements is no different than learning about any new, nontraditional clientele. For example, if a large number of military personnel and their families were being relocated owing to the opening of a newly built military base in your service area, there would be a significant impact on your community's population and tax base, and you would have to prepare your library to attract and serve those active military residents.

Serving this new military clientele with a different outlook and tradition, varying socioeconomic backgrounds, and special information needs would be a challenge for your library. You and your staff would be busy learning all you could learn about the military culture in general—values, attitudes, needs, and so forth. The same process applies to your discovering the Latino community. To help prepare you, we thought it necessary to provide in this chapter a general flavor of the cultural and social characteristics of Latinos, along with a discussion of ethnic terminology.

APPRECIATING LATINO CULTURE AND SOCIETY

> Latino culture is a lens through which the hardships and contradictions of our long journey from Latin America and the Caribbean ought to be pondered. We come with a set bag of archetypes, a difficult view of our collective past, and a hopeful sense of the future. (Stavans, 1995: 190)

What do we know about the social and cultural framework of Latinos? For one thing, there are many countries of origin and many different reasons for persons from those respective countries to have entered the United States. In the fall of 2005, an enforcement-only piece of legislation aimed at immigration reform (H.R. 4437) was passed in the House of Representatives. Early in 2006, a strong showing by immigrant people and their supporters in cities including but not limited to Chicago, Los Angeles, San Diego, Denver, and Washington, D.C., made some facts very clear: Latinos want to be respected and recognized for their contributions made daily to the United States.

The Latino culture consists of a set of collective prototypes, each belonging to a specific subculture. For example, the Argentine American subculture is somewhat different from the subculture of Latinos of Salvadoreño descent, which is different from the Nicaragüense subculture, and so forth. Whatever brought them to this country, Latinos have struggled first to leave their motherland and second to adapt to a new way of life once they arrive here. Although they may come from different socioeconomic classes, there is a strong sense of patriotism for their motherland, or *la madre patria*. Recent immigrants have a strong association with their country of origin and will preserve as many rituals as possible to counteract the homesickness they or their family members experience. Central to their migration, Latinos hold a powerful hope for a different and better life in the United States, for themselves and for their future generations. Second-, third-, or fourth-generation Latinos will seem more confident in their dual ability of relating to their relatives in native countries and rearing children in American schools, speaking fluently their native Spanish as well as the acquired language of English. These individuals are embracing their biculturalism; but even if a Latino in this country grows up monolingual in English, that does not deny the historical and cultural importance of the Spanish language for that person. The Spanish language is one commonality among all the subgroups of Latinos. Another commonality is the role of religion in Latino culture. Not all Latinos are Catholics, but many have either been raised Catholic or come from families that have a historical affiliation with Catholicism. Regardless of religious affiliation, Latinos tend to have a strong religious background. The similarities among the Latino subgroups are greater than the differences.

From a social perspective, other common elements among Latinos deserve mention. First of all, *la familia* (the family) is a very important social institution. The nuclear family—husband, wife, children, grandparents—is, in general, responsible for rearing children. There is also an extended family that includes all the other relatives who provide an important economic and social support system. Latino families are usually hierarchical, with the male being the dominant and authoritarian figure and the female, as the more nurturing parent, maintaining the major role of childrearing. Consequently, today's generation of Latinos faces variations of the roles played by nuclear family members. You may be serving males who have left family members behind in their countries of origin, or female, single head of households supporting school-age children. The younger members of the family entering your community branches may be interacting with you in English while the adult family members stand at a distance conversing in Spanish or are right behind the children observing in silence. Although the Latinas who visit the library may be conversant with English, the children they bring into the library for lapsit or toddler storytimes may not be their own, but those of their employers. The matriarchal Latino household, present since the 1860s in California (Camarillo, 1979), in reality has increased in everyday life. Whether matriarchal or patriarchal, the institution of *la familia* continues to be tantamount for Latinos in your community.

Another important characteristic of the Latino culture is machismo. Although many Latinos would consider the macho Latino to be more stereotypical than real, machismo is still prevalent today, much to the chagrin of some more-liberated Latinas.

It is at this point that we need to help clarify for you what stereotypes are and how to combat them as a library worker.

> Stereotypes are generalizations, or assumptions, that people make about the characteristics of all members of a group, based on an image (often wrong) about what people in that group are like. (Burgess, 2003)

What is important for you to remember is that only through experiencing a person or persons from a different culture can you make your own judgments. Experience is the best way to dispel any stereotypes or generalizations about another group.

Latino males are stereotypically depicted as demonstrating excessive aggression and sexual vigor and having little regard for some women. (Stavans, 1995) However, machismo also historically and traditionally connotes bravery, courage, and protection of and respect for family. This goes hand in hand with the idea of the male as the dominant figure. With the Latino male traditionally being the authority, do not be surprised if Latino family members act differently when they visit the library with the father than when they are in the library without him. When the entire family visits the library, respect demonstrated to the father will go a long way toward making the family feel welcomed and valued.

The Latino culture has an enduring tradition of *compadrazgo*, which is a system of godparent relationships. Normally, the godparents are chosen at the baptism of a child and their influence on the family may be socioeconomic. If they remain strong co-parents, *compadres* usually assist in aspects encompassing childrearing, finances, and religion.

> Compadrazgo established bonds between families that transcended class and racial lines and went beyond mere religious significance. The rites of baptism established kinship

networks between rich and poor—between Spanish, mestizo, and Indian—and often carried with them political loyalty and economic-occupational ties. (Camarillo, 1979: 12–13)

Today *compadres* are considered to be important members of the Latino family. Still largely chosen for the baptismal ritual, it is the duty of the *compadres* to take over the upbringing of their *ahijados* (godchildren) should the birth parents be unable to do so. Additionally, *compadre* (or *comadre*) is a term of endearment. It is important for you to understand the overall Latino culture and devote some time to learning a little more as your resources and timetable allow.

RESPECTING TERMINOLOGY

What term do we use to address the "growing population of Spanish-speaking people" we serve? If you were speaking Spanish, the answer would be less difficult. But the terminology that service professionals are seeking is English-language terminology. An acceptable way to conduct library business and yet not demean the customer is a challenge, especially if you are not fluent in the native language of the user. We have been in this situation many times ourselves. During your first encounters, rely on the "Four A's" method: **A**lways **A**cknowledge politely **A**nd **A**ddress with respect. Once you have read this book, performed your community needs assessment, and interacted many times with your customers, the terms will be familiar. Right now, you may be fearful of embarrassment or of making a negative first impression. To complicate matters a bit, there are regional differences in the choice of terms: Latino seems to be gaining popularity on the east and west coasts and in major urban centers, while Hispanic (or the Spanish *Hispano*) tends to be the preferred term in many areas of the Northeast or some states in the American Southwest, such as New Mexico. We are providing you with very broad generalizations, and there are always exceptions. The single most important lesson to learn in this section is that no one, universally accepted term describes the incredibly diverse Latino population.

GENERAL TERMS

For the overall population that is the focus of this book, the most popular terms currently in use are Latinos, *Hispanos*, Hispanics, Hispanic-Americans, Spanish, and Spanish-speaking. As you will see later, each smaller cultural group within the larger umbrella group has its own terms to describe itself.

For libraries and other service-oriented organizations, the variety of terms can be problematic. As employees of successful service-oriented organizations that strive to be responsible, helpful, culturally sensitive, and responsive to users, librarians do not want to offend someone unintentionally by using the wrong term. So naturally, we, as caring individuals, take cues about the right words to use from the minority group members themselves. The problem is that there is little agreement as to terminology within the Latino community. In this section we will describe the most popular terms and indicate our own personal preferences and the reasons for our choices.

Why are there so many terms for this group? Why can't there be just one universally accepted term that everyone can use? In answering this question, it may help to remember that this is not a new phenomenon. For example, we saw (and continue to see) a variety of terms used in the black community; many of the terms came about during the civil rights movement when feelings of black pride changed the way many African Americans thought and felt about themselves. New terms, such as Afro-Americans, blacks, African Americans, and so forth, came into existence as individuals in black communities redefined their identities based on the new realities or expanded visions of their lives. Accordingly, some terms came into vogue, some remained, some changed meaning, some were adopted by certain members, and some terms that were originally imposed from outside the black population were totally rejected by others. No one term could encompass all the variations in life experience. Because the life experience for blacks in this country has changed so dramatically since the civil rights movement, so too have the terms used to describe this population.

Ethnic terminology is in a constant state of flux because of individual self-examination, group identification, and personal preference. Because people's lives are always changing and because language is always evolving, many terms may be used at any one time. The term that a person of color uses to refer to himself or herself is a very personal, intimate choice. This term may change several times during the person's lifetime as this individual examines and reexamines his or her own identity.

This pattern is currently taking place within the Latino community. As individuals reexamine and redefine their identities based on new realities or hoped-for possibilities, new words and phrases are on their way in. They coexist with other, more established terms that may be on the way out. Terms that may have been imposed from the outside may give way to terms of choice.

Hispanic and Latino are the two most prevalent ethnic terms in use today. They are similar in that both refer to the composite group that includes individuals from a wide variety of culturally related, though distinct, groups. Both terms are broadly interpreted to include individuals with Spanish-language or Spanish-heritage backgrounds from the Americas (American Southwest, Mexico, and Central and South America); the Caribbean areas with Spanish influence (primarily the Dominican Republic, Puerto Rico, and Cuba); and Spain.

While both terms are attempts to describe the same population, the terms can be, but are not necessarily, quite different in attitude. One obvious and major difference is that Hispanic is an English word while Latino is a Spanish word meaning Latin, as in Latin America. Another major difference between the terms has to do with the issue of acculturation. Very generally speaking, Hispanic tends to connote acceptance of majority cultural values, integration into the majority culture, and political traditionalism; while Latino tends to connote the acceptance, preservation, and promotion of a unique cultural heritage as well as political activism. A third major difference is that the terms emphasize different racial and cultural backgrounds. Individuals who use Hispanic generally are emphasizing European Spanish heritage, while those who use Latino are acknowledging and celebrating indigenous or mestizo (mixed European and Indian) backgrounds.

There are also generational differences to consider. Most young adults, for example, may prefer the term Latino. As an example, the music that is increasing in popularity today is referred to as Latino music, never Hispanic music. Generally speaking, older generations may not be comfortable with the term Latino. Thus, within the same family there can be a variety of terms used, with parents and grandparents using Spanish or Hispanic and adolescents using Latino.

Terms such as Latin, Spanish-speaking, or Spanish were popular during the late 1960s and early 1970s. Used by persons who are from this era or when speaking to groups that might be conservative owing to age or politics and by many organizations created in the late 1960s and early 1970s in their official names, the terms are less frequent in appearance today. An example in the library field is the national organization REFORMA, founded in 1971, and originally referred to as the National Association of Spanish-Speaking Librarians in the United States. Its subtitle was changed in 1984 to National Association to Promote Library Services to the Spanish-Speaking, and again in the late 1990s to National Association to Promote Library and Information Services to Latinos and the Spanish-Speaking. These changes reflect an attempt by REFORMA to acknowledge its mission and membership, which encompasses many non-Latinos, as well as its presence globally.

SPECIFIC TERMS

Up to this point, we have only addressed the multiplicity of pan-ethnic terms that attempt to describe a very large, composite group. In addition to these terms, other terms refer to specific cultural groups within this larger population. Among Latinos, there are three major cultural groups: Mexican Americans, Cuban Americans, and Puerto Ricans. However, in addition to these three cultures, the United States has recently experienced a large number of immigrants (both documented and undocumented) from Central America, South America, and the Caribbean. Although individuals from each of these many cultural groups can and do use a number of different terms to refer to themselves, it is not necessary for us to provide all the terms here.

We can illustrate this multiplicity of terms within a cultural group by examining the terminology used by one such group, those with a Mexican heritage. One finds a variety of terms to describe this population: Chicano, Mexicano, Mexican American, and Hispano, to name the most popular ones. Usage may vary from one region to another, from one generation to another, and from one income class to another. As previously mentioned, there may even be variation within the same family. The same is true for each of the cultural groups noted above; there will always be a number of terms for each distinct group.

From the title of our book, it is apparent that we prefer to use Latino to describe the population that is the focus of this book. What follows is a brief explanation of this term and our rationale for choosing it.

For both practical and philosophical reasons, when referring to the overall larger population group, we use the term Latino. For practical reasons, it would be too difficult to refer to Latinos/Hispanics/Spanish-speaking/Hispanic Americans; so we decided to settle on one term. We also have philosophical reasons for choosing this term. It is a self-chosen term that is used widely, especially along both coasts and in larger urban centers, and it is increasingly being used by youth and by those who acknowledge and emphasize their indigenous and mestizo backgrounds. Occasionally we may have to use the term Hispanic, because of its use in official census publications. When referring to the current majority population in this country, we use the term *white*.

To summarize, there are two broad categories of terms with which you should be familiar. First, several ethnic terms are used when referring to the entire Latino population. Second, other terms are used when referring to specific cultural groups within the Latino population. None of these terms enjoy universal acceptance among people within the Latino community. The usage of a specific term reflects a personal choice that may change over one's lifetime. While we personally use different terms to describe ourselves politically and as professional librarians, there is consensus by both authors on the term *Latina librarians*. In Spanish, the word *bibliotecarias* succinctly describes this professional term. Our choice, for both practical and philosophical reasons, is to use the term Latino.

TERMINOLOGY HINTS

There is one challenge for any person who is sensitive to and respects the differences of others: that of trying not to offend others. In the case of ethnic terminology, the potential problem lies in using a different term from the one used by a Latino individual. We want to offer you a few hints on how to handle this.

First of all, if you are unsure about the terminology to use for the Latino group you have in your community, we recommend that you ask one of your formal or informal Latino leaders. If you have Latino friends or acquaintances, ask them what they prefer being called.

Also, check the media. If you have a local or area newspaper or radio station, pay attention to the ethnic terminology they use. You can bet that if they use the wrong term, someone will set them straight.

If you have several Latino subgroups, we suggest you investigate each of them. Let's say you know that your community has residents who are second- and third-generation Mexican American. Most recently, your community has also experienced an influx of *Salvadoreño* and *Guatemalteco* immigrants. It is important to ask representatives from each Latino subgroup which ethnic term they prefer. More than likely, they will use either Latino or Hispanic, or they will choose a term that applies only to their specific cultural background.

Second, we must accept that we all make mistakes. If you or a staff member uses the wrong term, and someone informs you that he or she is not Hispanic, Latino, or whatever, then apologize and ask the individual what he or she prefers being called.

Third, inform your staff about the terminology preferred by your Latino residents and why. Our suggestions are not necessarily directed at making you politically correct but at ensuring that your Latino customers will return to the library.

Do you want your underserved Latinos to enter a new and different establishment—your library—which is perceived as a traditionally white institution? Understand that they will come with some apprehension. We offer one last piece of advice for you and your staff: Body language and tone of voice are very important when addressing anyone, and the way in which your library personnel treat your new Latino users and interact with them will be the most important factor in generating return customers.

LEARNING MORE

We have provided a general introduction to Latino culture and traditions, which lays the foundation for the rest of the book. We thought it necessary to discuss ethnic terminology in this chapter, since confusion can result from the many terms used when referring to this cultural group.

If you did not know much about Latinos, you now have a basic head start in understanding the dynamic culture of this growing group. Since Latinos come from such diverse backgrounds, we strongly recommend that you learn more about the Latinos in your community. Chapter 2 will help you get started.

2 INVESTIGATING LATINO DEMOGRAPHICS

> *As information professionals, we need to look at Latino demographic data to search for patterns of change that affect our libraries and the services we will provide in the future.*

DEFINING DEMOGRAPHICS

Why should you try to attract and serve Latinos or any underserved minority in your community? Businesses, government agencies, and nonprofit organizations rely on this country's demographic data to analyze trends and to help them make strategic decisions concerning the development of products and services for customers of the future. Libraries should be no different. One of the great tenets of our profession is that libraries should provide equal access to information for all people. We can serve as a role model for other institutions by trying to reach all people with our services and assisting the public in grasping why this marketing and connection is so vitally important.

According to Webster's dictionary, *demography* is defined as the "statistical study of populations." Demographers use statistics or data to ascertain the characteristics of a population. When doing this, they look for any patterns of change within that population and then make future projections based on those changes.

If you have not heard the term *NIMBY* (Not In My Back Yard), you still might be familiar with the concept of how difficult it can be for a halfway house, a casino, or perhaps an airport to be built in a portion of town where vocal residents protest against it. Some of these residents might even agree with all the reasons why an airport expansion, for example, is necessary—it is the *location* that they are against—simply because the location proposed is close enough to them to affect their daily routines. Similarly, we use a term that we would like to introduce to you: CHIMBY (Change In My Back Yard), referring to a process of preparing yourself, your co-workers, and your library systems and information centers to better respond to the needs of Latino constituents in your community. Acknowledging the Latino community and educating one another about its needs are necessary pieces of meeting the challenge of delivering top-notch service. As previously stated, how your library personnel treat your new Latino users and interact with them will be the most important factor in generating return customers.

The national data we have compiled in this chapter present a very complex portrait of Latinos in the United States. This rapidly growing segment of the population is made up of a variety of culturally related, though distinct groups. When compared to the general population, Latinos are significantly younger, are disproportionately represented in lower income groups, have a relatively high level of bilingualism, and lag behind the general population with respect to educational attainment. The challenge for public libraries involved in developing services and collections for Latinos, or in maintaining these services, is to be proactive about meeting the demand.

The solution, for any business faced with change in its backyard, is to analyze as much data on their city and county as possible. The review or analysis allows the business to respond accordingly to the changes. This same approach can be utilized when it comes to library service. Our purpose here is to highlight demographic and socioeconomic factors and trends that impact delivery of services, programs, and materials to Latinos.

CHARACTERIZING THE LATINO POPULATION

In this section, the data presented come primarily from the 2000 census, tables, and reports and from recent projections provided by the U.S. Bureau of the Census. The major demographic and socioeconomic statistics that provide an overview of Latinos in the United States are highlighted.

The Census Bureau used the term Latino for the first time on the 2000 census (Guzman, 2001), and it is now included in official census publications. The bureau also designed and administered a nationwide survey entitled the *American Community Survey* in 2005. Along with its counterpart, entitled *The Puerto Rico Community Survey*, it provides a fresh look as to how communities are changing and provides data on a yearly basis by conducting monthly surveys in every community. This powerful census tool results in up-to-date statistics for businesses, local leaders, and decision makers rather than relying on a community snapshot prepared only every ten years. *American Community Survey (ACS)* may be accessed at www.factfinder.gov and serves to facilitate access to data on major characteristics (for example, how many people are employed; what proportion of families speak a language other than English at home) of a community. A program to streamline the census in 2010 will make improvements and result in many changes, including the more frequent release of data for areas as small as census tracts, which are small, relatively permanent statistical subdivisions of a county. More information is available at http://www.census.gov/geo/www/cen_tract.html.

POPULATION GROWTH

The 2000 census showed that there were 35.3 million Latinos in the United States, totaling 12.5 percent of the American population. (Guzman, 2001) Population growth rates in recent years have been very high. Between 1980 and 1990, the number of Latinos grew by an amazing 53 percent, approximately seven times the growth rate for the general population. Between 1990 and 2000, the number of Latinos grew by 57.9 percent compared with 13 percent for the general population. (Guzman, 2001) In July 2005, approximately 42.7 million Latinos were in the United States, constituting 14 percent of the nation's total population. (U.S. Census, 2006: CB06-FF) Latinos are now the largest ethnic or racial minority in the United States.

Data obtained on race in the 2000 census is not directly comparable to data obtained in earlier censuses, such as the 1990 census. We want to caution readers, especially those who are familiar with our first edition, of this fact. The reason is simply that the question on race has changed from a self-identification to one that asks individuals to report if they belong to one or more races. In some instances, going back to update a statistic from 1980 would not be possible since different data was collected on the 2000 census.

Among the population counted in 2000, Asians numbered 11 million or 4.2 percent; Native Hawaiian or Pacific Islanders numbered 874,000 or 0.3 percent; the larger African American (black) population totaled 36.4 million or 12.9 percent; and Native Americans (American Indian and Alaskan native) numbered 4.1 million or 1.5 percent. The total population grew from 248.7 million people in 1990 to 281.4 million in 2000, or by 13 percent, but each of these groups experienced dramatic increases in their respective populations during the same period that surpassed the growth rate of the total population.

When you combine a large and growing Latino population with the very high population growth rate among the ethnic groups mentioned, it is important to plan for diverse collections and services in our academic and public libraries. The Bureau of the Census periodically issues forecasts for various racial and ethnic groups. According to the bureau's projections, there will be 73 million Latinos in the year 2030, growing to 102.6 million by mid-century and making up 24 percent of the total U.S. population. (U.S. Census, 2004) It is estimated that people of color will make up the majority of the American population sometime around the middle of the 21st century. Since racial and ethnic groups are fast-growing segments of the population, they can no longer be ignored as minority groups. Library professionals who are prepared to serve ethnically diverse populations will be better positioned to be effective in light of the dramatic impact on libraries and other service agencies providing services to Latinos.

SUBGROUPS

The cultural diversity within the Latino population is astonishing. Latinos come from culturally related but distinct groups. Sometimes the reality of how many countries Latinos represent in either North, Central, or South America and the variety of our traditions is confounding even to Latinos.

In the U.S., two-thirds of the Latino population are Mexicanos. (Ramirez & de la Cruz, 2002) Three cultural groups (Mexican, Puerto Rican, and Cuban) make up 72.5 percent of the total Latino population. *Puertorriqueños* and *Cubanos* are the second and third largest groups, making up 9.7 percent and 3.5 percent of Latinos, respectively. *Dominicanos* are another major cultural group, accounting for 2.3 percent of all Latinos. (Guzman, 2001)

Latinos who are from Central American backgrounds make up 5.1 percent of the Latino population. This Central American category includes *Salvadoreños, Guatemaltecos, Nicaragüense, Hondureños, Panameños*, and *Costarricense* (Salvadorans, Guatemalans, Nicaraguans, Hondurans, Panamanians, Costa Ricans). (Guzman, 2001) South Americans, including *Colombianos, Ecuatorianos, Peruanos, Argentinos*, and *Chilenos* (Colombians, Ecuadorians, Peruvians, Argentinians, and Chileans), make up 4.0 percent of the Latino population. (Guzman, 2001)

Planning library services for Latinos who may come from quite different cultural backgrounds will be discussed in a subsequent chapter. For public libraries in medium-size to large urban centers it will be particularly challenging to offer services, programs, and materials where Latino populations are more likely to be heterogeneous.

AGE DISTRIBUTION

The 2000 census shows that the Latino population has a higher proportion of young adults and children than the general population. This age group (youth) is a rapidly growing segment of the Latino population. Nearly 35 percent of Latinos are under the age of 18, compared with 25.7 percent for the general population. The median age of Latinos is 25.9 years as compared with the median age of 35.3 for the general population. (Guzman, 2001)

Recently released Census Bureau figures indicate that Latino preschoolers (those under five years of age) continue to outnumber their African American counterparts. (U.S. Census Bureau, *Census 2000, Summary File 3 [SF 3]*; generated by Jacqueline Ayala using American Factfinder; www.factfinder.census.gov; [August 8, 2006]). Now and in the future, children's services librarians, school library media specialists, and teen (young-adult, or YA) librarians should strive to become culturally competent in meeting the needs of linguistically and ethnically diverse Latino children and their families. Clearly, Latinos who are younger than the general population will need to be responded to creatively.

EDUCATIONAL ATTAINMENT

While Latinos have made great strides in educational attainment over the last 30-odd years, they lag behind the attainment of the general population. As evidence of improvement, in 1970 less than one-third of Latinos 25 years old and over completed at least four years of high school; the 2000 census shows that of those Latinos 25 years old and over, at least 52.4 percent completed high school. Further evidence of progress can be seen in the number of college degrees awarded to Latinos. The 2000 census shows that 10.4 percent of Latinos 25 years old and over completed four years or more of college. Though still low when compared with non-Latinos (21.2 percent completed four or more years of college), this is a significant improvement from 1970, when only 4.5 percent of Latinos 25 years old and over completed four years or more of college. Educational attainment levels among Latinos are improving, yet there are still significant and disturbing differences between Latinos and non-Latinos. A little over half (52.4 percent) of Latinos in 2000 (or 18,270,377) had at least a high school diploma, as compared with 83.6 percent (or 143,085,659) of the non-Latino population. (Ramirez and de la Cruz, 2003)

SOCIOECONOMIC STATUS COMPARISONS

Poverty levels are high and the income levels are low for Latinos. In 2000, 22.6 percent of all Latinos were living in poverty as compared with 12.4 percent of non-Latinos. A total of 27.8 percent of Latino children (under age 18) lived in poverty in 2000.

Latino women and the elderly have disturbingly high poverty rates when compared with the population in general. In 2001, 23.2 percent of Latino women (or 4,243,000) lived in poverty, compared with 12.9 percent (or 18,580,000) women who are not Latina. Latinos aged 65 and older, or *la tercer edad*, are twice as likely (19.6 percent) as non-Latinos (9.9 percent) to live in poverty. (U.S. Census Bureau, *Census 2000, Summary File 3 [SF 3]*; generated by Jacqueline Ayala using American Factfinder www.factfinder.census.gov; [August 8, 2006])

The 2000 statistics on median income (using 1999 dollars) also show a disturbing picture. The median income for all American families in 2000 was $50,046. For Latino families the median income was $34,397. For Latino families headed by a female with no husband present (17 percent of all Latino families), the median income plummeted to $23,809. Compare this figure with the total population of female heads of household with no husband present (12 percent of all households), whose median income was $25,458. (U.S. Census Bureau, *Census 2000, Summary File 3 [SF 3]*); generated by Jacqueline Ayala using American Factfinder www.factfinder. census.gov; [August 8, 2006])

Since poverty is a fact of life for a significant number of Latino families, it should come as no surprise that employment patterns vary significantly between Latinos and non-Latinos. Here are but a few statistics from 2000 to illustrate these labor force disparities:

- 21.9 percent of Latino adult males work in construction, extraction, and maintenance, compared with 17.1 percent of non-Latino males.

- 25.6 percent of Latino adult females are employed in service occupations, compared with 18.0 percent of non-Latino females.

- Only 22.9 percent of Latino adult females are employed in managerial or professional positions, compared with 36.2 percent of non-Latino females.

- Only 14.6 percent of Latino males held management and professional jobs, while 31.4 percent of non-Latino adult males held such positions. (U.S. Census Bureau, *Census 2000, Summary File 3 [SF 3]*); generated by Jacqueline Ayala using American Factfinder; www.factfinder. census.gov; [August 8, 2006])

NATIVE-BORN LATINOS

The 2000 census indicates that a very large majority (59.8 percent) of Latinos are born in the United States. An additional 11.2 percent of Latinos are foreign-born, naturalized citizens. The remaining 29 percent of Latinos are foreign-born, noncitizens. (Guzman, 2001) The majority of Latinos residing in the United States are native-born. (See Figure 2.1)

IMMIGRATION: A HEATED TOPIC

In 2000, the nation's population showed a 57 percent increase in the foreign-born population from 1990 census figures; the 1990 figure of 19.8 million foreign-born rose to 31.1 million in 2000. (Lyman, 2006) Of foreign-born, noncitizens (29 percent), a large percentage are undocumented immigrants as well as relatively recent and large numbers of Latino immigrants who have not had time to go through the normal naturalization process.

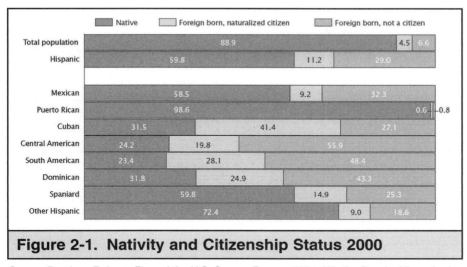

Figure 2-1. Nativity and Citizenship Status 2000

Source: Ramirez, Roberto R., and the U.S. Census Bureau. 2004. *We the People: Hispanics in the United States.* Available: www.census.gov/prod/2004pubs/censr-18.pdf

Almost 4 million foreign-born Latinos (or half of all 7.8 million foreign-born Latinos) arrived in the United States between the years 1980 and 1990. Some 52.1 percent of foreign-born Latinos entered the United States between the years 1990 and 2002. Immigrants from Mexico, Cuba, and Central and South America, who had traditionally come to the United States, were now immigrating in greater numbers than ever before. Figures from Census 2000 show there were 655,165 *Salvadoreños*, 764,945 *Dominicanos*, 470,684 *Colombianos*, 372,487 *Guatemaltecos*, 177,684 *Nicaragüense*, 260,559 *Ecuatorianos*, 233,926 *Peruanos*, 217,569 *Hondureños*, and 100,864 *Argentinos* residing in this country. (Guzman, 2001) When combined with the already large and still growing numbers of Latinos of Mexican, Puerto Rican, and Cuban origin, these new arrivals have helped to make Latinos a presence in the country.

One dynamic that has made the immigration of Latinos an issue is that they are choosing to live outside the states of California, Florida, New York, and Texas, home to two out of every three foreign-born persons born in Latin America. Traditionally, Latinos have settled in Illinois and New Jersey as well. But since 2000, increasing numbers of Latinos have immigrated to the southeastern states of Georgia and North Carolina in addition to Indiana, Ohio, South Dakota, Delaware, Missouri, Colorado, and New Hampshire. Immigrants are being seen in schools, at the workplace, and in hospitals, and the impact of their presence is being felt in more and more communities. (Lyman, 2006)

Public libraries have long served as places where immigrants can become educated and find resources about democracy, English, and American society. In March 2006, the Office of Citizenship released "Library Services for Immigrants: A Report on Current Practices," offering ideas for libraries that wish to serve immigrants living in their community.

LANGUAGE

A fairly large number of Latinos are bilingual. The 2000 census shows that although some 78.5 percent of Latinos speak Spanish at home, 37.9 percent of Latinos that speak Spanish at home report that they also speak English very well. Libraries that seek to provide services and collections for this population will need to keep in mind that options should include both languages or bilingual materials as the opportunity arises. (U.S. Census Bureau, *Census 2000, Summary File* 3[SF3]); generated by Jacqueline Ayala using American Factfinder www.factfinder.census.gov; [August 8, 2006]

KEEPING STATISTICS IN PERSPECTIVE

The demographic information in this chapter will assist you in understanding why libraries with a service area that includes the Latino community should proactively develop outreach services to raise the status of the underserved Latino community from information-poor to information-rich. The demographics of this country are quickly changing, revealing a very diverse population.

A word of advice: When you look at data like these, it is tempting to simplify things by focusing solely on the population segment that is highlighted instead of examining the full range of the entire Latino community's needs. For example, we have seen that the Latino population is generally younger than the population as a whole, so a seemingly rational strategy for public libraries would be to funnel large amounts of resources into children's services and collections. However, to do so would neglect the needs of Latino teenagers and adults. Similarly, since 78.5 percent of Latinos speak Spanish at home, it might be tempting to put all of a library's resources into Spanish-language materials, but this approach would neglect the needs of a very large number of individuals seeking bilingual or English-language materials. As is the case with most things in life, balance is the key!

3 BUILDING A CASE FOR SERVING LATINOS

> *As with any presentation, knowing your audience is as important as delivering your message.*

It is a library's responsibility to know its community makeup and to provide services that are appropriate to the needs of the population. With the growing population of Spanish-speaking minorities, these statements increasingly point to the need for libraries to serve the Hispanic community by providing bilingual and multicultural information. (Buck et al., 2004: 23)

It is our purpose in this chapter to provide a framework to help you defend your position of service. Using the tips provided, you will need to add the necessary local information that best supports and complements your position. We also provide a framework for organizing your presentation.

Different lines of reasoning can be used depending on your audience. For example, you may use all of them when addressing your staff or board of trustees or funding body. On the other hand, you may want to concentrate on only some of them when addressing a group of educators. As with any presentation, knowing your audience is as important as delivering your message. Remember that your goal is to convince your audience—supporters, neutral folks, and your opposition—that providing library services to your Latino community must happen.

We have already presented in Chapter 2 some national demographic data about Latinos. Obtaining and using more pertinent local data coupled with presenting a strong rationale is the place to start. The reality of trying to provide services to the underserved Latinos in your community and being a part of CHIMBY (Change In My Backyard) will expose you to some harsh realities. Attitudes will not change overnight. You will find yourself repeating your data and rationale over and over, because you are committed to serving your entire community. As it becomes second nature to present and/or defend to any audience your goal of serving Latinos in your community, so too will your message spread.

Most of you have already determined that something has to be done to provide library services for Latinos in your community. Having realized that is the first step in meeting the challenge ahead of you. The bigger challenge is convincing your library staff, board of trustees, government officials, and sometimes the general public that library resources—human, time, and financial—need to be expended to reach out and serve your Latino community.

FINDING AND USING STATE AND LOCAL DEMOGRAPHICS

As a planner of library services, you already know how important demographic data are. In this section, we will give you step-by-step instructions on how and where to obtain local Latino demographic data easily from the U.S. Census Bureau. Of course, obtaining all the data in the world will not help much if the data just sit on the shelf. But if it is relatively easy to obtain this information, you should have more time to analyze and understand what you find, and you will benefit in a number of ways:

- You will gain a better understanding of your target Latino audience.
- You will be better prepared to identify and define your goals.
- You will be better prepared to develop strategies to meet Latino user needs.
- Most important, you will be able to demonstrate to others (staff, the community in general, and funding authorities) that there is a need for your library to initiate or improve library services to Latinos.

We highly recommend that you or a colleague (perhaps a member of your library staff) commit to learning how to research demographic data from the U.S. Census Bureau. The resources that we will briefly highlight here are Web-based and can be accessed from the census Web page (www.census.gov). This is the quickest way to obtain local Latino demographic data.

We are using the term Latino—and so is the U.S. Census Bureau as of 2000. In the various searches that you perform, you will notice that a global adoption of the term has not yet occurred, and many tables and data sets will use both Hispanic and Latino or just Hispanic.

Some data is from the 2000 census and some has been updated as of 2005. This is due to the introduction of the *American Community Survey*, an ongoing survey of U.S. communities and neighborhoods. Look for the

2005 data whenever possible and try to determine if there is data for the same calendar year in which you are performing your search. This is normally done in the form of a report or brief and always announced by a press release. The Census Bureau also makes predictions as to how the population will grow, so you may want to refer to those figures if they pertain to Latinos and to use the most realistic numbers when developing your rationale. They can be found easily under the "People & Households" category.

Although there are products (both print and CDs) that contain the data tables and graphs that we were familiar with and used to seeing, they are not all being purchased by our libraries. With the trend moving toward data retrieval by way of the Internet, the series that we described in depth in the first edition is available in both print and PDF format on the Internet. The name of the series is "PHC-2 Census 2000 Summary Social, Economic, and Housing Characteristics." It contains a printed report on each state, the District of Columbia, and Puerto Rico. A United States summary is available as well. The URL <http://factfinder.census.gov/servlet/Product-BrowserServlet?id=103779&product=PHC-2%20Census%202000%3A%20Summary%20Social%2C%20Economic%20and%20Housing%20Characteristics&_lang=en> will point you to a product summary.

POPULATION

- Data Finders

On the Census Bureau home page locate the heading for "Data Finders." In that column, there is a "Population Finder" search box. Plug in your city or town and your state and you can link to a table with population figures.

LATINOS AND OTHER RACIAL/ETHNIC POPULATIONS

- Minority Links (Facts on the Hispanic or Latino Populations)

On the Census Bureau home page locate the heading for "Newsroom." In that section, choose the title "Minority Links." Facts on the Latino population are organized under the headings "American Community Survey/Decennial Census," "Social and Economic Characteristics," "Profiles," "News Releases and Multimedia," and "Additional Resources." (See Figure 3.1) Under "Profiles," you can obtain briefs such as *Hispanic Population in the United States* and *We the People: Hispanics in the United States*.

If you want a convenient way to get general information on Latinos, this is the only location you will need. Refer to it frequently to update your data profiles. Data is available as well for blacks or African Americans, Asians, Native Americans, Native Hawaiians and other Pacific Islanders, and American Indians and Alaska Natives through this feature.

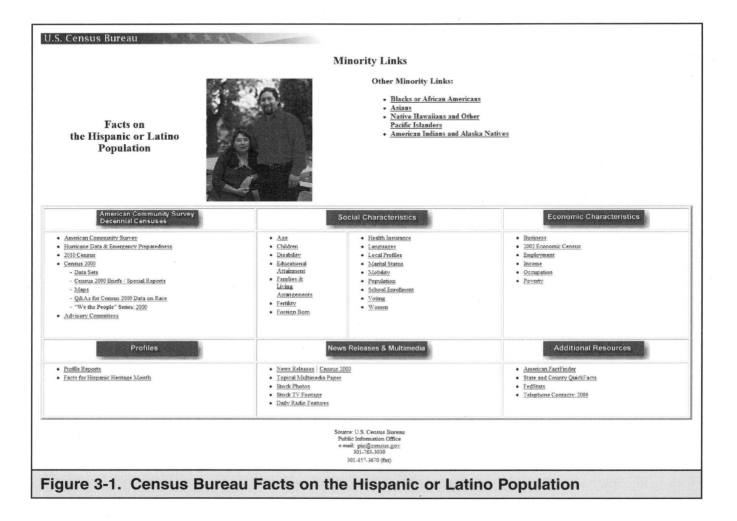

Figure 3-1. Census Bureau Facts on the Hispanic or Latino Population

SOCIAL AND ECONOMIC CHARACTERISTICS OF LATINOS

- American Factfinder

From the Census Bureau "Minority Links" facts on Latinos, go to the "Additional Resources" column. Select "American Factfinder" and you will be linked to a source where your searches for population, housing, economic, and geographic data can be easily performed. You can be as specific as your census tract, and you will be able to obtain a fact sheet for your community.

One disclaimer: We have found that not all data is accessible on the Internet for our smaller and more rural communities. But although you might not be able to find a detailed statistic for your demographic, you can confer with your census staff expert (remember you designated one earlier) on searching strategies or other methods of obtaining the statistic. Our local regional planning agency has a Web site that provides census data and more local demographics. Perhaps you can find such a resource in your county or state government Web pages as well.

You can obtain a useful demographic profile of Latinos in your community at a very low cost, which will help you to complete the following Latino demographics worksheet. (See Figure 3.2) With data obtained from the appropriate tables covering your service area, you can begin to develop your rationale for providing services to Latinos.

LATINO DEMOGRAPHICS WORKSHEET

20 _____ Latino Demographics for _____
(city or county)

To complete this chart for your service area, obtain the appropriate data from the U.S. Census Web page. We suggest trying factfinder.gov.

Population Overview

 Total population of service area _____
 Total Latino population _____
 Latino population as a percentage
  of total population _____

Latino Subcultural Groups

 Total Latinos (of any race) _____
 Mexican _____
 Puerto Rican _____
 Cuban _____
 Other Latino _____
  Dominican Republic _____
  Central American _____
   Costa Rican _____
   Guatemalan _____
   Honduran _____
   Nicaraguan _____
   Panamanian _____
   Salvadoran _____
   Other Central American _____
  South American _____
   Argentinean _____
   Chilean _____
   Colombian _____
   Peruvian _____
   Venezuelan _____
   Other South American _____

Latino Age Distribution

 Total Latinos
  Under 3 years of age _____
  3 and 4 years _____
  5 to 9 years _____
  10 to 14 years _____
  15 to 17 years _____

(cont'd.)

Figure 3-2. Latino Demographics Worksheet

Latino Age Distribution *(cont'd.)*

        18 and 19 years   _____
        20 to 24 years   _____
        25 to 29 years   _____
        30 to 34 years   _____
        35 to 39 years   _____
        40 to 44 years   _____
        45 to 49 years   _____
        50 to 54 years   _____
        55 to 59 years   _____
        60 to 64 years   _____
        65 to 74 years   _____
        75 years and older   _____
Mean Age   _____

Foreign-Born Latinos

    Total Number of Latinos   _____
    Percentage of Total Number of Latinos
        who are foreign-born   _____

Language Spoken by Latinos and Ability to Speak English

    Number of Latinos 5 years of age and over   _____

    Speak a language other than English   _____
        5 to 17 years of age   _____
        18 to 64 years   _____
        65 to 74 years   _____
        75 years and over   _____

    Do not speak English very well   _____
        5 to 17 years of age   _____
        18 to 64 years   _____
        65 to 74 years   _____
        75 years and over   _____

Latino Educational Attainment

    Latinos 18 to 24 years of age   _____
        High school graduate (includes equivalency)   _____
        Some college or associate degree   _____
        Bachelor's degree or higher   _____

    Latinos 25 years of age and over   _____
        Less than 5th grade   _____
        5th to 8th grade   _____
        9th to 12th grade, no diploma   _____
        High school graduate (includes equivalency)   _____
        Some college, no degree   _____
        Associate degree, occupational program   _____
        Associate degree, academic program   _____
        Bachelor's degree   _____
        Graduate or professional degree   _____

    Latinos 25 years of age and over   _____
        Percent less than 5th grade   _____
        Percent 5th to 8th grade   _____
        Percent high school graduate or higher   _____
        Percent some college or higher   _____
        Percent bachelor's degree or higher   _____

(cont'd.)

Figure 3-2. Latino Demographics Worksheet *(continued)*

Latino Educational Attainment *(cont'd.)*

    Latino Males 25 to 34 years

        Percent high school graduate or higher   _____

        Percent bachelor's degree or higher   _____

    Latino Females 25 to 34 years

        Percent high school graduate or higher   _____

        Percent bachelor's degree or higher   _____

Latino Income in 1999 Dollars

    Household median income   _____

    Family median income   _____

    Per capita income   _____

Latinos Below Poverty Level

    Percent of Latino families below poverty level   _____

Income Levels in 1999

	White, of Latino origin	Latino	White, not of Latino origin
Total Households			
Less than $5,000	_____	_____	_____
$5,000 to $9,999	_____	_____	_____
$10,000 to $14,999	_____	_____	_____
$15,000 to $24,999	_____	_____	_____
$25,000 to $34,999	_____	_____	_____
$35,000 to $49,999	_____	_____	_____
$50,000 to $74,999	_____	_____	_____
$75,000 to $99,999	_____	_____	_____
$100,000 or more	_____	_____	_____
Median (dollars)	_____	_____	_____
Mean (dollars)	_____	_____	_____
Total Families			
Less than $5,000	_____	_____	_____
$5,000 to $9,999	_____	_____	_____
$10,000 to $14,999	_____	_____	_____
$15,000 to $24,999	_____	_____	_____
$25,000 to $34,999	_____	_____	_____
$35,000 to $49,999	_____	_____	_____
$50,000 to $74,999	_____	_____	_____
$75,000 to $99,999	_____	_____	_____
$100,000 or more	_____	_____	_____
Median (dollars)	_____	_____	_____
Mean (dollars)	_____	_____	_____

Latino Labor Force in 2000

    Latinos 16 years of age and over, percent in labor force   _____

    Latino civilian labor force, percent unemployed   _____

Occupation of Employed Latinos

    Employed Latinos 16 years and over   _____

        Managerial or professional positions   _____

        Technical, sales, and administrative support   _____

        Service occupations   _____

        Farming, forestry, and fishing   _____

        Precision production, craft, and repair   _____

        Operators, fabricators, and laborers   _____

        Construction, extraction, and maintenance   _____

Figure 3-2. Latino Demographics Worksheet *(continued)*

SUPPORTING THE CASE

Changing demographics is only one of many reasons for providing services to Latinos in your area. Much of what we will share is just common sense, but you should be prepared to approach your rationale systematically. The rest of this chapter focuses on the main points to consider for preparing your rationale, including the development of Latino human potential from an economic perspective; the development of Latino children as library users; the development of a future political base; and the development of a social responsibility perspective.

Additionally, we will discuss the need to change mindset from aiming library services predominantly to your white majority users to integrating library services for Latinos in your community. You will also need to consider developing a library policy statement that reflects services to your minority community. This statement can be part of your library's mission statement, or it can be attached to your mission statement.

Last, but not least, we recommend that you consider using several documents relating to equality of access that have been endorsed by the American Library Association (ALA); these documents will help build and support your rationale.

ECONOMICS

One of the most effective ways to convince a group of people, no matter their socioeconomic background, of the importance of a service is to tell them how it will affect their wallets. Without fail, this method gets everybody's attention.

If you were to record all the services, programs, and materials—along with the rationale for each item—that your library currently provides that could develop any individual's potential, you could come up with a long list. If you were to try making the same list of services or potential services for Latinos in your community, you would probably find that the reasons are basically the same.

Like other groups, Latinos want to improve their economic well-being and the well-being of their families. We like to think of it as developing human potential. One way Latinos can do that is to be able to compete for higher-paying jobs. What role can the library play here? Providing bilingual materials on job search strategies, such as resumé writing, and providing bilingual programming on the same subject are just two ideas. The more informed Latinos are, the better they will be at preparing for, applying for, and interviewing for jobs.

Libraries already successfully serving their Latino communities maintain that the more popular materials for Latino adults are self-help materials, such as those on resumé writing and other job search strategies. Decision-makers will listen when you tell them that outreach to Latinos in your community has the potential to make those residents even more economically productive in the community. Latinos, like all other residents, already contribute to your community's economy. Latinos pay taxes—sales, income, and/or property—which in turn support public services such as police, fire, and the library.

If you have any anecdotal information that could support any of the rationales we have mentioned, note and share them with your audience. Telling a real-life story that illustrates your point is an effective persuasion technique. For example, let us say that a Latino middle-aged gentleman, who was just laid off from his job, came into your library for the first time as a referral and requested help in getting information on job search strategies and preparing a resumé. Your librarian was able to assist in meeting his information needs. Several weeks later, the gentleman returned to thank the librarian and let her know that he got a job right away and was told that his resumé was the best one submitted to the employer. That is good, solid anecdotal information that you can use to your advantage.

Libraries can position themselves with their decision-makers and others by becoming involved in literacy development efforts. If developing a literacy program as an outreach effort to the Latino community and to the community as a whole is not a possibility, then the library needs to position itself as an effective partner with already-established literacy programs. Libraries are in the best position to link literacy programs with relevant library services and library programming.

Illiteracy is endemic among the lower socioeconomic groups, and most national and state data will show that it is most prevalent among minority groups. The important point is that libraries are in the position to tie literacy with libraries and with the economic success of the community's residents.

There are no direct illiteracy data available at the local level; such information is often inferred from other data, such as measurements of educational attainment. The most common way to determine illiteracy rates is to ascertain the percentage of adults, ages 18 and over, or ages 25 and over, who do not *start* or do not *finish* high school. Researchers working on the national adult literacy survey (NALS) have confirmed that people who do not start or finish high school score very low on functional literacy tests. You can determine your local illiteracy rates by using educational attainment data for your community.

Public libraries can indirectly affect Latino student achievement by involving Latino parents in literacy and reading. Once Latino parents learn to read, they will also understand the importance of reading often to their children. Public library programs that promote parents' reading to children can become "extremely helpful tools in developing literacy by involving parents and the community in the schooling process and creating a link between home and school." (Constantino, 1994)

Remember that linking library services for Latinos with developing their human potential and providing opportunities for them to improve their economic status in the community is a strong rationale. All of this, in turn, contributes to the community's economy. Remember to use whatever demographic data are available and to include anecdotal information that supports your points. You can incorporate visual aids (PowerPoint charts, posters, graphics) to show your point and improve your presentation.

Last but not least, we want to make sure we do not leave you with the wrong impression about Latinos and their contributions to the economy. The Hispanic unemployment rate reached a historic low of 5.2 percent in the second quarter of 2006. The gap between the seasonally adjusted un-employment rates for Latinos and non-Latinos was just 0.6 percentage points—the smallest since 1973, when employment data on Latinos first became available. (Kochhar, 2007) In 2004, 68 percent of Latinos age 16 and older were in the civilian labor force. In 2002, Latino-owned busi-nesses numbered 1.6 million, which between the period of 1997 and 2002 showed a growth rate of 31 percent compared with the national average of 10 percent during the same time span. (U.S. Census Bureau, Press Release, generated by Jacqueline Ayala using Facts for Hispanic Heritage Month; www.census.gov/Press_Release/www/releases/archives/facts_for_fea-tures_special_editions/index.html; [August 8, 2006]). Such information can also be used to help dispel the stereotype some people have of Latinos' being lazy and on welfare. The bottom line is that the more informed your Latino residents become, the more they will be able to make good eco-nomic decisions throughout their lifetime.

LATINO CHILDREN

Everyone agrees that children are our future. This future will affect many "Baby Boomers" who already find themselves holding onto and protecting their wallets more and more. How we adults assist in the development of the full potential of our children is vitally important and does not rest solely with the educational system. Libraries also should play a significant role in developing our children and young adults regardless of their color, because Latino children have the same potential (but not necessarily the same op-portunities) as other children to become productive members of our society.

Most children, including Latino children, will eventually contribute fi-nancially to the retirements of your community's decision-makers. Let them know that! It makes sense to support any effort that will allow chil-dren to achieve their potential. The benefit of this investment—providing library services to Latino children—far outweighs the initial cost of these services. The future economic success of Latino children will affect every-one's future economic well-being.

We cannot say enough about how important libraries are in developing the human potential of children, and in this case Latino children. Children are our future small-business owners, government officials, artists, corporate executives, military personnel, public safety employees, politicians, teachers, and other white- and blue-collar workers. You will need to convince your decision-makers that everyone in the community has a personal stake in the success of Latino children.

It is never too early to start involving preschool Latino children in libraries. This involvement is the critical first phase in combating illiteracy in children and young adults. Again, you can use data in your rationale that compares high school dropout rates of whites to those of Latinos.

One other message about Latino children as library users that can be made, which will be further elaborated in the next section, deals with children as a future political base in the community. These children are the voters of the future. Of course, that is assuming that they will be literate enough to vote and will have learned the importance of voting. Libraries can play a major role in achieving these goals.

Shape the rationale in the preceding paragraphs to fit your local situation. Again, if you can think of any local anecdotes to illustrate and support your rationale, incorporate them into your presentation.

FUTURE POLITICAL BASE

Libraries should always be cognizant of the potential effect their users can have on their library's future fiscal well-being. Latinos who use their public library to meet their information needs—personal, professional, and recreational—will be the same folks who will learn the importance of registering to vote, and they will learn how to find the necessary information to help them decide how to vote.

This rationale employs the same reasoning used by libraries for the development of Latino human potential. That is, how can Latino library users assist the library in the future? By serving a segment of the community that has never been served before—the Latino community—the library is indirectly developing another strong political base. This rationale is most effective with your library staff, your board of trustees, and other library users.

A satisfied customer is an ardent supporter. By serving a segment of the community that has never been served before, the library is developing an additional support group that can possibly make the voting difference on a mill levy or a bond issue. This same informed Latino community can lobby its local city officials, state legislature, and national congressional representatives on issues that affect community library services. Again, this is a rationale hard to argue against.

We found that libraries in the United States are able to develop some of their Latino users into overall library advocates—board of trustees members, Friends of the Library members, employees, and/or volunteers. It is that advocacy we are talking about. Most libraries usually do not underestimate the role of white library users as advocates; but many do not think of Latinos (and other minorities) as potential advocates, only because Latinos are traditionally not part of their library user base.

This advocacy potential is available to public libraries once they develop their Latino library user base. Using this rationale of developing the library's political base is most effective with library staff. Developing another political base of support affects their library jobs because the Latino community can help pass bond issues for a new building or mill levies to increase materials, services, and salaries.

The challenge many libraries face is that of convincing staff members that library services must be extended to serve another nonuser group in the community—Latinos. When you explain that expanding services to the Latino community affects them in the long run, the staff is more willing to listen and support changes in services.

SOCIAL RESPONSIBILITY

The fourth rationale for developing library services to reach the Latino community deals with social responsibility. Recently, there seems to be a backlash within the library profession against the role of librarians and libraries in dealing with social issues, because many of these issues supposedly have nothing to do with libraries and library services. There should be no misunderstanding, however, about the issue of providing library services to your Latino community.

If libraries assume the role of serving a culturally diverse society, then they are fostering a climate for racial harmony among all groups within their communities. People tend to fear the unknown; consequently, we all have a tendency to fear those who may not look, speak, or live as we do. Libraries can play an important role in developing healthy race relationships among people who are different ethnically and socially. How do they do this? They can purchase materials and promote programming that can educate and enlighten their majority users. Knowledge and understanding of and respect for the Latino culture will help reduce that fear. (Talbot, 1990)

This rationale, which is more philosophically based than it is pragmatic, could be the least effective of all the rationales you present. Nonetheless, it can still be a valuable approach built around the needs of your local environment and using examples or anecdotes for support.

CHANGING THE LIBRARY SERVICES MINDSET

The realities of your local situation might suggest that your local decision-makers may not recognize their community as a multicultural community relative to library services or any other public services offered by the local government. You will need to develop and present a shift in your library services mindset. Such a shift incorporates library services for Latinos as an integral part of your library's existing services. The sooner you can do this in your efforts to serve Latinos in your community, the better. This approach will help lay to rest the funding opposition from others who do understand the need to reach out to Latino residents.

It is not the fault of Latino communities that libraries have not chosen to reach out to and provide services for them as they have for their white populations. Providing services to Latinos should not be viewed as a funding issue. That is, finding the funds to tailor services to attract Latinos to the library should not be more important than serving them.

Remember to point out to your audience that the Latinos in your community pay taxes—sales, property, and/or income. Their taxes already support the library and other public services. It is important to remember that Latino information needs are as important as the needs of others but they will probably also differ from your non-minority current users' needs. The services offered to your current clientele will not necessarily work for a Latino clientele. Other people may not understand this difference, which is why advocating for the development of such services will be an issue. You need to anticipate this potential opposition and be prepared to address or respond to those issues.

One way to initiate this change in services to Latinos is through a library policy statement that describes a service your library provides or a position it holds. That is why it is necessary that your policies address the importance of and need for your library to develop and provide library services to your minority community (in this case, Latinos).

USING AMERICAN LIBRARY ASSOCIATION DOCUMENTS

Four documents endorsed by the American Library Association (ALA) can help you develop your rationale. You may want to refer to any or all of them; you may want to make any or all of them available to your audience. Together, these documents express our profession's highest principles as they relate to the provision of equal access to library and information services for everyone in the community.

Adopted in 1988 by the Reference and Adult Services Division (RASD, now known as the Reference and User Services Association) of the ALA, the "RUSA RSS Guidelines for Library Services to Hispanics" is a policy statement issued by a nationally recognized library organization that affirms the responsibilities of libraries to provide library services to

Latinos in every community. For your convenience, the text appears in Appendix 3A at the end of this chapter. Also sponsored by RUSA are the "Guidelines for the Development and Promotion of Multilingual Collections and Services," reproduced in Appendix 3B. These documents were both revised in 2006.

The "Library Bill of Rights" was originally adopted by the ALA in 1948, and has been amended several times since then. This document is one of the cornerstones of our profession, affirming that all libraries should provide resources for the interest, information, and enlightenment of all people in the community. The text of this document is included in Appendix 3C. A Spanish translation is included in Appendix 3D.

The "Freedom to Read" statement was originally adopted in 1953 by the ALA and the American Book Publishers Council, which later consolidated with the American Educational Publishers Institute to become the Association of American Publishers. The "Freedom to Read" statement has subsequently been endorsed by many national organizations. The statement affirms the proposition that it is in society's best interest for publishers and librarians to make available a diversity of opinion and thought, including materials that may not be popular with the majority. If the presence of Spanish books in your library is challenged, you can use this document to support Latinos and their freedom to read. The text of this document is included in Appendix 3E.

PRESENTING THE RATIONALE

We will leave you with a simple framework to organize your presentation—the five "W's" (who, what, why, when, where) and one "H" (how). Do not forget to include whatever demographic data you have collected to support your rationale when you use this framework. The six questions need not necessarily be used in the same order; place them in the order that will most benefit you in your presentation.

1. WHO is involved in this library proposal?
   (a) Your public library (name); and (b) Latinos in your community.
2. WHAT is involved in this proposal?
   Providing library services for Latinos in your community. Use some general demographic data for your service area or city/county area to support your rationale. Start with getting your board to adopt a policy statement regarding library services to your multicultural community and then proceed from there.

3. WHY is it important for the library to be involved? Design and build your rationale here using the topical areas presented earlier. Remember to gather and use any local and relevant anecdotal information.

4. HOW will the library be involved? Explain what services you plan to offer; how you plan to provide those services (methodology); what costs are involved (optional); and what you plan for outreach efforts. Also, you may need to design an implementation plan with a phase-in component.

5. WHEN does the library propose implementing these actions? Offer a time line that reflects all of the above.

6. WHERE will the library provide these services for Latinos? This information is dependent on where your Latino community is located in your library service area. You may only have one main library, which would make this section easy; or, if you have several branches with Latino residents in their service areas, you may want to start in one of the branches and then phase the others in. Again, your decision will depend on your local service area and funding situations.

CONCLUSION

Building a rationale may not be as important for some librarians because they already have a solid base of support from staff and governing bodies. Others may need to plan carefully what is in their rationale, what supporting materials are needed to sustain it, and how they are going to present it—and this will not be an easy task.

After reading this chapter, it is our intent that you will have a solid foundation from which to start building a rationale. Try to adapt the concepts to fit your local situation and determine what demographic data will be helpful. You may even come up with additional lines of reasoning specific to your situation. Remember that if you use national data, you also need to use local data to make your rationale more relevant to your audience. In addition, anecdotal material draws the picture for your audience and will help clarify and strengthen your rationale.

When you are demonstrating the need for your library to initiate or improve library services to Latinos, it is crucial to keep your audience in mind. Your presentation needs to be tailored to the audience, whether they are staff, the community in general, government officials, the board of trustees, funding authorities, or representatives of these groups combined.

APPENDIX 3A: RUSA RSS GUIDELINES FOR LIBRARY SERVICES TO SPANISH-SPEAKING LIBRARY USERS

Revised in 2006 by the Library Services to the Spanish-Speaking Committee, Reference Services Section (RSS) of the Reference and User Services Association (RUSA), American Library Association. Adopted by the Reference and Adult Services Division Board of Directors, January 1988, and submitted to the ALA Standards Committee for review. Permission to reproduce granted by Susan Beck, Chair, RUSA, RSS.

Introduction

Library services to Spanish-speaking users can be complex: nationality, regional differences, and culture provide myriad combinations within that community. As an example, there are significant linguistic and cultural differences reflected in the varieties of Spanish spoken by Mexicans, Puerto Ricans, Cubans, and other Spanish-speaking groups. To recognize and respond correctly to these differences is a major theme within these guidelines. Although the committee is aware of numerous terms for this target population, it has chosen to use the term "Spanish-speaking" in order to encompass the many users that make up this diverse community instead of the outdated and limiting term of "Hispanic."

REFORMA, the National Association to Promote Library and Information Services to Latinos and the Spanish Speaking, has taken a role in the production of this document: one committee member served as liaison to REFORMA, and the organization has given input throughout the revision process.

Although these guidelines were written by persons with professional interest in service to Spanish-speaking library users, they were written consciously for all library personnel who see a need to initiate service to this population. In that sense, the guidelines are a basic beginner's manual intended for a hypothetical librarian serving as an administrator of a medium-to-small institution having become aware of the needs of Spanish-speaking communities within its service area. As with any guidelines, these are designed to aid in the development of that service and to remind readers of professional concerns regarding the target population.

1.0 Collection and Selection of Materials

Spanish-speaking communities in the United States have varying language skills and competencies in English and Spanish. The members of these communities have diverse needs and are entitled to access to materials that meet those needs. Use standard criteria to aid in the selection of library materials. In order to best carry out a systematic focus for collection development for these communities, develop and regularly update a Spanish Language Collection Development Policy.

1.1 Relevancy

1.1.1 Library materials for Spanish-speaking library users should meet the educational and recreational needs of the communities served. Libraries should provide appropriate and culturally relevant materials at a level that meets the needs and interests of the various user groups represented in the communities.

1.2 Language

1.2.1 The collection should also contain bilingual materials. Emphasize titles from publishers in the countries represented by the major user groups in these communities. The collection should also contain standard Spanish-language titles from Spanish-speaking communities and countries. When purchasing translated works, carefully examine the languages used to ensure accuracy and faithfulness to the original work.

1.3 Bibliographic Access

1.3.1 Bibliographic access to the library's collection should include Spanish-language subject headings in the public catalog to facilitate the location of Spanish-language and bilingual materials. Also provide any locally produced access and identification aids, including lists, bibliographies, and point-of-use bibliographic instructional materials in Spanish.

1.4 Formats

1.4.1 Collect all formats including both print and non-print materials. Include all reading levels, whether educational or recreational. Supplement traditional print and audiovisual materials with electronic resources available on the Internet.

1.5 Selection

1.5.1 Selection of Spanish-language materials should follow the established procedures for collection development. Consult general and specialized evaluation tools.

1.5.2 In addition to Spanish review publications and popular Spanish periodicals, regularly review Spanish-language resources, listservs, Web sites, and other Internet resources to identify potential materials to include in the collection.

1.6 Use of vendors in acquiring Spanish-language titles

1.6.1 Carefully select and evaluate vendors that supply Spanish-language materials. Take into consideration the country of origin and communities served. As part of the process for acquiring Spanish-language materials, develop good professional relationships with vendors and continually explore different options and services. Support local Spanish-language bookstores and consider them important sources of information and materials. Select and evaluate bookstores and their services on an ongoing basis.

1.7 Promoting support for the Spanish-language collection through gifts and donations

1.7.1 Work with local community groups in selecting, acquiring, evaluating and weeding Spanish-language collections. Encourage local support through gifts, exchanges, and donations to the collection. When evaluating these items, consider the formally established criteria included in a gifts and donations policy statement. Apply normal selection criteria when determining whether to add gifts and donations to the collections. Include those materials not appropriate for the collection in book sales, exchanges, or donations to other libraries or organizations that serve Spanish-speaking communities.

1.8 Evaluating Spanish-language collections

1.8.1 Criteria used in evaluating Spanish-language collections should be consistent with review and maintenance policies of the library.

2.0 Programs, Services, and Community Relations

In keeping with the ALA policy supporting multilingual services, carefully select the language used for programming and services (bilingual or Spanish only) as well as regional linguistic characteristics of vocabulary, accent, and nuance. Choices should reflect the characteristics of the local community.

2.1 Diversity of Culture

2.1.1 To understand the composition and needs of the target populations, develop a profile of the Spanish-speaking communities the library intends to serve. Federal census data, state government statistics, and interviews with local leaders, local residents, and other community organizations will assist in the development of the community profile. A meaningful community profile will include such information as gender, age, level of education, language skills, and country of origin.

2.2 Programs

2.2.1 Traditional and non-traditional creative programming effectively attracts and meets the needs of Spanish-speaking communities. Because of limited resources available for services to the Spanish-speaking community within any given institution, libraries serving the target population should cooperate with local community groups. Such cooperation may include the sharing of program costs, cooperative acquisitions, or joint (reciprocal) borrowing privileges, to name but a few.

2.2.2 Programs developed to provide library orientation or service should recognize bias by social and economic forces present among this group, such as immigration or transient aspects of labor.

2.2.3 The Spanish-speaking populations served may consist of a mix of economic and social factors that combine to form a very diverse culture. Each represented culture must be considered in the development of programming and should be accurately reflected in the program content.

2.3 Outreach Services

2.3.1 Continually assess and analyze the community in order to aid in the planning and delivery of library services to meet community needs. Further these aims by: participating in the work of local community organizations that serve the Spanish-speaking; establishing partnerships with such organizations in the development and presentation of library programs and services; using local radio and cable programs, public service announcements, newspapers, and regional Internet providers as a means of communicating with the targeted populations.

2.3.2 Also consider library nonusers. Use programs, literature, and publicity in creative ways and in a variety of settings to attract those for whom libraries are not part of their life experience.

2.4 Intercultural Understanding

2.4.1 As part of its activities in working with local populations representing a multiplicity of cultures, the library should actively promote intercultural communication and cooperation.

2.4.2 Schedule cultural events such as exhibits of art, dance, music, etc. in appreciation of the contributions and heritages of Spanish-speaking cultures during traditional festivals and holidays.

2.5 Bibliographic Instruction

2.5.1 Offer library instruction in Spanish that highlights bilingual or language-specific formats.

2.6 Electronic Resources

2.6.1 Provide the target community with access to, and training in, the use of electronic resources, including full-text databases, online resources, and Internet access.

2.6.1.1 Provide bilingual written policies for access to public terminals with Internet connection.

2.6.2 Provide access to, and bilingual training in, the use of electronic resources to Spanish-speaking communities.

2.6.2.1 Provide access to digital format, Spanish-language, government publications when available. Provision of access to electronic resources in all formats is an especially important service that must be provided to users who may have had limited experience in the use of computer technology.

3.0 Personnel

3.1 Recruitment

3.1.1 Recruit Spanish-speaking library personnel in all job classifications, i.e., librarians, paraprofessionals, clerical workers, and volunteers.

3.1.2 Contact Spanish-speaking graduates of library education programs accredited by the American Library Association.

3.1.3 Make extensive use of hotlines, minority recruiting services, local Spanish-language media, and services provided by Latino library organizations.

3.2 Compensation

3.2.1 Recognize and financially compensate bilingual employees in positions where job specifications or actual conditions require the knowledge of Spanish.

3.3 Staff Development

3.3.1 Encourage staff development at all job levels.

3.3.2 Provide diversity training for all staff. Include workshops on library services to Spanish speakers such as: collection development for Spanish-language materials or classes on different aspects of Spanish/Hispanic/Latino cultures, i.e., music, authors, etc.

3.3.3 Make educational opportunities available to non-Spanish-speaking staff to learn the language. This could include: providing a teacher for basic Spanish classes offered for all library staff; developing a professional collection of language-learning materials such as books, cassettes, videos, or computer software for staff use; providing benefits or encouraging staff to make use of already existing benefits such as educational reimbursement for community college classes and flextime to allow staff to take classes that fit into their work schedule.

4.0 Facilities

The library building, through its location, signage, architecture, and appearance, should be an attraction, not a barrier, to members of the Spanish-speaking communities that it serves.

4.1 Interior and Exterior

4.1.1 Choose decorations and graphics to modify interior and exterior to create an ambience suitable to the clientele served. Multicultural posters and displays help create a welcoming environment. Take care that the alterations made will conform to the culture of the community.

4.2 Location

4.2.1 Locate new library buildings conveniently and strategically in order to attract the target population to the library. Determine the location of the library in terms of its proximity to local schools and public transportation.

4.2.2 Place comfortable seating near the Spanish collection for those patrons who prefer to use the materials in the library.

4.2.3 Make meeting rooms equally accessible to the Spanish-speaking communities and promote them by creating a bilingual flyer that details how to reserve and use the rooms. Distribute these flyers to Spanish-speaking groups in your community.

4.3 Signage

4.3.1 Display bilingual signs prominently and visibly. Display a "welcome" sign at the entrance in Spanish. Pay attention to the particular dialect of Spanish used so that the wording, phraseology, and connotation of the language conform to the cultures of the community.

4.3.2 Use international, non-verbal symbols whenever possible, such as the

i symbol for "information."

4.4 Collection Placement

4.4.1 When space is allocated within existing structures, make collections both visible and accessible to patrons as they enter the library.

4.5 Access

4.5.1 Create bilingual or Spanish translations of library literature that assist in accessing the library and its collections. Examples include: welcome brochures, library maps, guides to using the library, and lists of library resources. Allow Spanish-speaking users to provide input before materials are disseminated. Distribute this library literature to local organizations that serve the Spanish-speaking in your community.

Appendix

Persons of Spanish/Hispanic/Latino origin or descent are those who classified themselves in one of the specific Hispanic or Latino categories listed on the Census 2000 or American Community Survey questionnaire. Categories listed on the 2000 questionnaire include Mexican, Mexican American,

Chicano, Puerto Rican, Cuban or other Spanish/Hispanic/Latino group. According to the US Census Glossary the definition also extends to "people whose origins are from Spain, the Spanish-speaking countries of Central or South America, the Caribbean, or those identifying themselves generally as Spanish, Spanish-American, etc." [Source: U.S. Department of Commerce, U.S. Census Bureau. "American FactFinder Glossary." Available: www.census.gov (accessed January 23, 2006).]

Origin can be viewed as the ancestry, nationality group, lineage, or country of birth of the person or the person's parents or ancestors before their arrival in the United States. Persons who identify themselves as Spanish, Hispanic, or Latino origin may be of any race. [Source: U.S. Department of Commerce, U.S. Census Bureau. "American FactFinder Glossary." Available: www.census.gov (accessed January 23, 2006).]

RUSA RSS Library Services to the Spanish-Speaking Committee members and document authors as of publishing date

Adam Davis, Co-Chair
Head of Reference
Delray Beach Public Library

Maria Villanueva, Co-Chair
Librarian II
Collection Development Specialist
Adult Materials Selection Department
Chicago Public Library

Dr. Ivan E. Calimano, REFORMA Liaison
Universidad Interamericana de San German
Escuela Graduada de Ciencias de la Información

Jane Phalen Currie
Hope College / Van Wylen library

Mark McKinley Sanders
East Carolina University

John Bruce Upchurch
Doctoral Student
University of Tennessee

APPENDIX 3B: RUSA RSS GUIDELINES FOR THE DEVELOPMENT AND PROMOTION OF MULTILINGUAL COLLECTIONS AND SERVICES

Prepared by the Library Services to the Spanish-Speaking Committee, Reference Services Section (RSS) of the Reference and User Services Association (RUSA), American Library Association. Permission to reproduce granted by Susan Beck, Chair, RUSA, RSS.

1.0 Introduction

Traditionally, the United States has been a country that attracts large numbers of immigrants from all over the globe. While some libraries have established collections and programs to serve the needs of library-users whose native language is not English, little has been done on a national scale to systematically address these needs. In addition, the multilingual needs of library patrons who are language students, foreign students, or bilingual citizens have been under-served by traditional library services.

It is the responsibility of libraries to provide an equitable level of service to all members of their communities regardless of ethnic, cultural, or linguistic background. Providing library materials for ethnic, cultural, and linguistic groups should not be seen as an "additional" or "extra" service, but as an integral part of every library's services. Libraries should establish goals, objectives, and policies that integrate multilingual services into their overall work plan. These guidelines should serve as models with which to assess the provision of services and materials.

2.0 Collection and Selection of Materials

Provide an effective, balanced, and substantial collection for each ethnic, cultural, or linguistic group in the community. Purchase materials in the languages, dialects, etc. of the groups served.

Consider the demand and availability of materials as important factors in establishing a level of collection development. The low volume of publishing in some languages or difficulty in obtaining publications may make it impossible to provide the same amount of material in all languages. Bindings and paper quality of the materials may not be equal to the quality of materials typically purchased in the United States, Canada, and elsewhere. Libraries may find it necessary to purchase from small presses, publishers and bookstores outside the country, neighborhood bookstores, conferences, and book fairs.

2.1 Levels for Selection

2.1.1 Provide library materials related primarily to the population of the targeted ethnic, linguistic, or cultural groups served.

2.1.2 Base materials selection on community analyses, needs assessments, and statistical data such as the U.S. Census. Appropriate aids include focus groups, interviews, and questionnaires.

2.1.3 Provide a cross-section of subjects, literary genres, geographic areas, and time periods appropriate to the users' interests and needs. In order to provide information and to promote intercultural awareness and understanding, it is also desirable that library materials reflecting the interests and experiences of the various cultural groups of the community be available in both English and the original language, by authors from each national, linguistic, and cultural group represented in the community.

2.2 Formats

2.2.1 Acquire materials in a variety of formats, which may include print, audio, audio-visual, and computer software as appropriate to diverse patron needs. When print materials are scarce, or when literacy materials are in high demand, place an emphasis on acquiring non-print materials, such as audio recordings and videos.

2.2.2 Provide literacy materials, including computers with literacy software, in the native languages of their non-English speaking patrons.

2.2.3 Provide language-learning materials to encourage heritage language retention and to provide all members of the community with an opportunity to learn or review other languages. Also provide materials of all types to aid in learning English as a second language, including materials oriented toward learners of specific language backgrounds.

2.3 Bibliographic Access

2.3.1 Catalog all materials in the original language and script. Provide bibliographic access in both English and the original language.

2.4 Physical Access

2.4.1 Ensure that multilingual collections housed separately are visible and accessible to the community.

2.4.2 Display highly visible directional signage in the languages of the major linguistic groups that use the library's multilingual collection.

2.4.3 Provide forms, notices, information pamphlets, and other printed materials in targeted languages.

2.4.4 Provide access, signage, and appropriate technology for accessing the materials in all formats with clear instructions and librarian assistance available when necessary for the hearing, visually, and physically impaired members of the community.

2.5 Collection Maintenance

2.5.1 Collection polices should allow for the purchase of multiple copies of items so that the physical stock for all languages is adequate.

2.5.2 Evaluate out-of-date and worn-out materials on a regular basis, then discard it or offer to community organizations' archives or special collections, or other appropriate groups.

2.5.3 Maintain preservation measures, such as rebinding, to repair worn-out materials that are heavily used and still relevant. Also facilitate, encourage, and sponsor the preservation of original materials that relate to the heritage of local ethnic, linguistic, and cultural groups.

2.5.4 Demand should not be used as the sole determining factor in collection development. Low demand for multilingual materials may be the result of inadequate collections, services, or publicity in the past.

3.0 Programs, Services, and Community Relations

Provide and actively promote multilingual services and programming for the various ethnic groups in the community.

Provide multilingual services at the same levels according to the same standards as for the general public. Library card applications, interlibrary loan information, welcome brochures, and other information should be in the preferred language of the library user.

Develop contacts with the community leaders of the targeted ethnic, linguistic, and cultural groups. In the case of small or widely scattered groups, a central or cooperative library effort is the best means to provide materials and services in order to maximize efficiency and reduce costs and still provide adequate materials and services.

3.1 Cultural Diversity

3.1.1 Because the population served may be comprised of various cultures, each specific culture must be considered in the development of programming and services.

3.1.2 The degree of bilingualism and the retention of linguistic cultural identity by particular groups, as well as the level of social integration/assimilation, will also determine the level of service to a particular ethnic group. Some members of these groups may wish to be regarded as Americans only, rather than as members of an ethnic group.

3.2 Programming and Marketing

3.2.1 Direct social and cultural community activities toward the targeted ethnic, linguistic, and cultural groups. Programs such as concerts of ethnic music, exhibitions, and demonstrations of traditional arts and crafts may be considered appropriate examples.

3.2.2 Provide programming and publicity in the preferred languages of the ethnic groups as well as in English. Take into account the sensibilities and expectations of the targeted group when promoting library services.

3.2.3 Provide facilities, promote, and offer English-as-a-second-language, literacy classes, and programs for English learners.

3.2.4 Make the library's Web presence known to its patrons who have limited English abilities. A mirror site of the library's home page should exist, translating the contents into the preferred language of the library user. Important community events should also be available on the library's Web site in the preferred language of the library user.

3.3 Outreach Services

3.3.1 Provide multilingual services and materials to those patrons not able to use the library personally, including homebound patrons and those in correctional institutions and hospitals.

3.3.2 Present outreach activities in non-library, but familiar, alternative locations, such as factories, meeting rooms of ethnic organizations, and places of worship.

3.3.3 Participate in the life of the community by becoming involved with or initiating local events such as festivals, commemorations, and other cultural activities related to the various ethnic, linguistic, and cultural groups in the area. Entertain non-traditional partnerships with media, social service agencies, and community-based organizations. Produce and disseminate information about the various ethnic, linguistic, and cultural groups in the community.

3.4 Information and Reference Services

3.4.1 Provide reference and information services in the most commonly used languages. In addition, special effort must be made to provide service to recently arrived immigrant groups.

3.4.2 Provide the same level of service for interlibrary loan in all languages as for the English-speaking patrons.

3.4.3 Provide reference and referral services about multicultural and multilingual local resources.

3.4.4 Provide bibliographic instruction in appropriate languages as necessary.

4.0 Staffing

4.1 Library staff working with patrons who have limited English abilities should be multilingual in order to provide effective service.

4.2 Offer continuing education or staff development programs that promote sensitivity and cultural, ethnic, and linguistic awareness of the staff and enhance their abilities in dealing with ethnically different patrons.

4.3 Library staff with expertise in languages and cultures should share their expertise with other staff and other libraries and be recognized and financially compensated for these abilities.

4.4 Schools of library science should advertise the need for multicultural and multilingual librarians and actively recruit people of linguistic and ethnic minorities. They should offer courses that deal with the issues involved in serving an ethnically, culturally, and linguistically diverse society.

RUSA RSS Library Services to the Spanish-Speaking Committee members and document authors as of publishing date

Adam Davis, Co-Chair
Head of Reference
Delray Beach Public Library

Maria Villanueva, Co-Chair
Librarian II
Collection Development Specialist
Adult Materials Selection Department
Chicago Public Library

Dr. Ivan E. Calimano, REFORMA Liaison
Universidad Interamericana de San German
Escuela Graduada de Ciencias de la Información

Jane Phalen Currie
Hope College / Van Wylen library

Mark McKinley Sanders
East Carolina University

John Bruce Upchurch
Doctoral Student
University of Tennessee

APPENDIX 3C: LIBRARY BILL OF RIGHTS

The American Library Association affirms that all libraries are forums for information and ideas, and that the following basic policies should guide their services:

1. Books and other library resources should be provided for the interest, information, and enlightenment of all people of the community the library serves. Materials should not be excluded because of the origin, background, or views of those contributing to their creation.

2. Libraries should provide materials and information presenting all points of view on current and historical issues. Materials should not be proscribed or removed because of partisan or doctrinal disapproval.

3. Libraries should challenge censorship in the fulfillment of their responsibility to provide information and enlightenment.

4. Libraries should cooperate with all persons and groups concerned with resisting abridgement of free expression and free access to ideas.

5. A person's right to use a library should not be denied or abridged because of origin, age, background, or views.

6. Libraries which make exhibit spaces and meeting rooms available to the public they serve should make such facilities available on an equitable basis, regardless of the beliefs or affiliations of individuals or groups requesting their use.

Adopted June 18, 1948. Amended February 2, 1961; June 27, 1967; and January 23, 1980, by the ALA Council. Permission to adapt and reproduce granted by Mary Ghikas, Associate Executive Director, ALA.

APPENDIX 3D: DECLARACIÓN DE LOS DERECHOS DE LAS BIBLIOTECAS

La Asociación de Bibliotecas de los Estados Unidos de America (American Library Association) afirma que todas las bibliotecas son foros abiertos para la información y las ideas, y que las siguientes normas basicas deben dirigir sus servicios.

1. Con el fin de satisfacer el interés de sus usuarios y darles acceso a todo tipo de información, toda bibloteca debe poner sus libros y otros recursos a la disposición de todos los integrantes de la comunidad a la cual sirve.

2. Toda biblioteca debe proveer información y materiales que representen todos los puntos de vista sobre temas históricos y de actualidad. Ningun material debe ser prohibido ni retirado de circulación por motivos doctrinarios o partidistas.

3. En su misión de proveer información sin restricciones, toda biblioteca debe enfrentarse a todo acto y tipo de censura.

4. Toda biblioteca debe cooperar con todos los individuos y grupos interesados en oponerse a cualquiera restriccion a la libre expresión y el libre acceso a las ideas.

5. No se le debe negar a ninguna persona el derecho de usar la biblioteca por motivos de origen, edad, antecedentes personales o punto de vista.

6. Toda biblioteca que cuente con espacio disponible para exhibiciones o reuniones publicas, debe ofrecerlo en forma equitativa, sin tener en cuenta la creencia o afiliación de los individuos o grupos que soliciten su uso.

Adoptado el 18 de junio 1948. Enmendad el 2 de febrero de 1961 y el 23 de enero de 1980 por el Consejo de la Asociación de Bibliotecas de los Estados Unidos de America (Council of the American Library Association). Permission to adapt and reproduce granted by Mary Ghikas, Associate Executive Director, ALA.

APPENDIX 3E: FREEDOM TO READ

The freedom to read is essential to our democracy. It is continuously under attack. Private groups and public authorities in various parts of the country are working to remove books from sale, to censor textbooks, to label "controversial" books, to distribute lists of "objectionable" books or authors, and to purge libraries. These actions apparently rise from a view that our national tradition of free expression is no longer valid; that censorship and suppression are needed to avoid the subversion of politics and the corruption of morals. We, as citizens devoted to the use of books and as librarians and publishers responsible for disseminating them, wish to assert the public interest in the preservation of the freedom to read.

We are deeply concerned about these attempts at suppression. Most such attempts rest on a denial of the fundamental premise of democracy: that the ordinary citizen, by exercising critical judgment, will accept the good and reject the bad. The censors, public and private, assume that they should determine what is good and what is bad for their fellow-citizens.

We trust Americans to recognize propaganda, and to reject it. We do not believe they are prepared to sacrifice their heritage of a free press in order to be "protected" against what others think may be bad for them. We believe they still favor free enterprise in ideas and expression.

We are aware, of course, that books are not alone in being subjected to efforts at suppression. We are aware that these efforts are related to a larger pattern of pressures being brought against education, the press, films, radio, and television. The problem is not only one of actual censorship. The shadow of fear cast by these pressures leads, we suspect, to an even larger voluntary curtailment of expression by those who seek to avoid controversy.

Such pressure toward conformity is perhaps natural to a time of uneasy change and pervading fear. Especially when so many of our apprehensions are directed against an ideology, the expression of a dissident idea becomes a thing feared in itself, and we tend to move against it as against a hostile deed, with suppression.

And yet suppression is never more dangerous than in such a time of social tension. Freedom has given the United States the elasticity to endure strain. Freedom keeps open the path of novel and creative solutions, and enables change to come by choice. Every silencing of a heresy, every enforcement of an orthodoxy, diminishes the toughness and resilience of our society and leaves it the less able to deal with stress.

Now as always in our history, books are among our greatest instruments of freedom. They are almost the only means for making generally available ideas or manners of expression that can initially command only a small audience. They are the natural medium for the new idea and the untried voice from which come the original contributions to social growth. They are essential to the extended discussion which serious thought requires, and to the accumulation of knowledge and ideas into organized collections.

We believe that free communication is essential to the preservation of a free society and a creative culture. We believe that these pressures towards conformity present the danger of limiting the range and variety of inquiry and expression on which our democracy and our culture depend. We believe that every American community must jealously guard the freedom to publish and to circulate, in order to preserve its own freedom to read. We believe that publishers and librarians have a profound responsibility to give validity to that freedom to read by making it possible for the readers to choose freely from a variety of offerings.

The freedom to read is guaranteed by the Constitution. Those with faith in free people will stand firm on these constitutional guarantees of essential rights and will exercise the responsibilities that accompany these rights.

We therefore affirm these propositions:

1. It is in the public interest for publishers and librarians to make available the widest diversity of views and expressions, including those which are unorthodox or unpopular with the majority.

   Creative thought is by definition new, and what is new is different. The bearer of every new thought is a rebel until that idea is refined and tested. Totalitarian systems attempt to maintain themselves in power by the ruthless suppression of any concept which challenges the established orthodoxy. The power of a democratic system to adapt to change is vastly strengthened by the freedom of its citizens to choose widely from among conflicting opinions offered freely to them. To stifle every nonconformist idea at birth would mark the end of the democratic process. Furthermore, only through the constant activity of weighing and selecting can the democratic mind attain the strength demanded by times like these. We need to know not only what we believe but why we believe it.

2. Publishers, librarians, and booksellers do not need to endorse every idea or presentation contained in the books they make available. It would conflict with the public interest for them to establish their own political, moral, or aesthetic views as a standard for determining what books should be published or circulated.

   Publishers and librarians serve the educational process by helping to make available knowledge and ideas required for the growth of the mind and the increase of learning. They do not foster education by imposing as mentors the patterns of their own thought. The people should have the freedom to read and consider a broader range of ideas than those that may be held by any single librarian or publisher or government or church. It is wrong that what one can read should be confined to what another thinks proper.

3. It is contrary to the public interest for publishers or librarians to determine the acceptability of a book on the basis of the personal history or political affiliations of the author.

   A book should be judged as a book. No art or literature can flourish if it is to be measured by the political views or private lives of its creators. No society of free people can flourish which draws up lists of writers to whom it will not listen, whatever they may have to say.

4. There is no place in our society for the efforts to coerce the taste of others, to confine adults to the reading of matter deemed suitable for adolescents, or to inhibit the efforts of writers to achieve artistic expression.

   To some, much of modern literature is shocking. But is not much of life itself shocking? We cut off literature at the source if we prevent writers from dealing with the stuff of life. Parents and teachers have a responsibility to prepare the young to meet the diversity of experiences in life to which they will be exposed, as they have a responsibility to help them learn to think critically for themselves. These are affirmative responsibilities, not to be discharged simply by preventing them from reading works for which they are not yet prepared. In these matters taste differs, and taste cannot be legislated; nor can machinery be devised which will suit the demands of one group without limiting the freedom of others.

5. It is not in the public interest to force a reader to accept with any book the prejudgment of a label characterizing the book or author as subversive or dangerous.

   The idea of labeling presupposes the existence of individuals or groups with wisdom to determine by authority what is good or bad for the citizen. It presupposes that individuals must be directed in making up their minds about the ideas they examine. But Americans do not need others to do their thinking for them.

6. It is the responsibility of publishers and librarians, as guardians of the people's freedom to read, to contest encroachments upon that freedom by individuals or groups seeking to impose their own standards or tastes upon the community at large.

   It is inevitable in the give and take of the democratic process that the political, the moral, or the aesthetic concepts of an individual or group will occasionally collide with those of another individual or group. In a free society individuals are free to determine for themselves what they wish to read, and each group is free to determine what it will recommend to its freely associated members. But no group has the right to take the law into its own hands, and to impose its own concept of politics or morality upon other members of a democratic society. Freedom is no freedom if it is accorded only to the accepted and the inoffensive.

7. It is the responsibility of publishers and librarians to give full meaning to the freedom to read by providing books that enrich the quality and diversity of thought and expression. By the exercise of this affirmative responsibility, they can demonstrate that the answer to a bad book is a good one, the answer to a bad idea is a good one.

   The freedom to read is of little consequence when expended on the trivial; it is frustrated when the reader cannot obtain matter fit for that reader's purpose. What is needed is not only the absence of restraint, but the positive provision of opportunity for the people to read the best that has been thought and said. Books are the major channel by which the intellectual inheritance is handed down, and the principal means of its testing and growth. The defense of their freedom and integrity, and the enlargement of their service to society, requires of all publishers and librarians the utmost of their faculties, and deserves of all citizens the fullest of their support.

We state these propositions neither lightly nor as easy generalizations. We here stake out a lofty claim for the value of books. We do so because we believe that they are good, possessed of enormous variety and usefulness, worthy of cherishing and keeping free. We realize that the application of these propositions may mean the dissemination of ideas and manners of expression that are repugnant to many persons. We do not state these propositions in the comfortable belief that what people read is unimportant.

We believe rather that what people read is deeply important; that ideas can be dangerous; but that the suppression of ideas is fatal to a democratic society. Freedom itself is a dangerous way of life, but it is ours.

This statement was originally issued in May 1953 by the Westchester Conference of the American Library Association and the American Book Publishers Council, which in 1970 consolidated with the American Educational Publishers Institute to become the Association of American Publishers (AAP).

Adopted June 25, 1953. Revised January 28, 1972 and January 16, 1991, by the ALA Council and the AAP Freedom to Read Committee.

A joint statement by:

American Library Association
Association of American Publishers

Subsequently endorsed by:

American Booksellers Association
American Booksellers Foundation for Free Expression
American Civil Liberties Union
American Federation of Teachers AFL-CIO
Anti-Defamation League of B'nai B'rith
Association of American University Presses
Children's Book Council
Freedom to Read Foundation
International Reading Association
Thomas Jefferson Center for the Protection of Free Expression
National Association of College Stores
National Council of Teachers of English
P.E.N.—American Center
People for the American Way
Periodical and Book Association of America
Sex Information and Education Council of the U.S.
Society of Professional Journalists
Women's National Book Association
YWCA of the U.S.A.

Permission to adapt and reproduce granted by Mary Ghikas, Associate Executive Director, ALA.

4 CONDUCTING A COMMUNITY NEEDS ASSESSMENT

> *Conducting a community needs assessment serves as notice to the general community that your library is serious about developing or strengthening ties between the library and the Latino community. The needs analysis itself can often serve as a method of marketing your existing library services.*

In this chapter, we provide some tips on how to analyze the specific information needs of your local Latino residents. Analyzing a community and its information needs is certainly nothing new. Fortunately, there is a well-established, comprehensive, and easily accessible body of literature on the subject. Salvador Güereña has compiled a very useful bibliography that will be of assistance to those who are responsible for doing community analysis and needs assessment of Latino communities. (Güereña, 1990)

PLANNING THE NEEDS ASSESSMENT

Conducting a needs assessment offers your library numerous benefits. By interacting with and obtaining data about the Latino community, you will gain valuable information about the perceived quality or extent of your existing services, programs, and collections. As such, you will be better able to determine how well or poorly your library is currently meeting the needs of Latinos. You will be able to use this information to help you make decisions about how your library can improve. Identifying the information needs and wants of Latinos in your community will enable you to develop new programs, services, and collections that meet Latino customer needs. Finding out what Latinos in your community currently think of your services and collections will help you develop a plan to meet their current and future information needs.

Why would this information be relevant to you, since you obviously don't have any services for the Latino community, or if you already have a person on staff knowledgeable and experienced in Latino community outreach? Most libraries that have been successful in developing library services for Latinos systematically collected primary data about the Latino community and used the data to guide the development of services, programs, and collections. In East Austin, Texas, during the late 1990s, a community needs assessment was done in conjunction with Sanchez Elementary School and the Henry S. Terrazas Branch Library. The objective behind the surveys that were sent home to the parents of the 478 students was to determine the reason why families in the predominantly Latino neighborhood were not visiting the library. As a result of the survey, the school and the library were better informed about non-users in the community. The number one reason that parents were not letting their children use the Terrazas Branch Library was that they could not afford to pay overdue fines or replacement material costs for lost books. The barrier was an economic one and something that branch manager Elva Garza was able to address with the permission of the Austin City Council. (Margolis, 2001) In this situation, the partners involved could have pointed to a number of factors that prevented the full engagement of the Latino community; but to obtain the best information they went directly to the target audience and by doing so were armed with information that allowed library staff to work on one of the many issues that arose. The restructuring of fines that took place had little to do with Latino services per se but could be resolved fairly quickly and without exhausting resources that were needed to address remaining issues. This is just one example in which needs assessment was considered to be an essential element in planning services for Latinos.

If we lived in an ideal world with unlimited library resources, we would not have to be so concerned with such assessments. The real world of financial constraints, with citizens and politicians calling for smaller government and larger accountability, requires us to use our limited resources wisely. The needs assessment will help you decide where best to put your limited human and financial resources in order to maximize results.

You may be faced with staff, managers, boards of trustees, or vocal users who are reluctant to change the status quo. The information you obtain may help you to convince major constituencies that significant changes in library services or operations are needed and will serve as ammunition when you are challenged for advocating significant changes.

A fair amount of interaction between the library and the Latino community will be required in conducting a needs assessment. It is a major library initiative that involves significant outside contact with the public as well as a commitment of resources. Gaining board approval for this project will help ensure your success.

We will detail three very general techniques for conducting a needs analysis of the Latino community in your service area—focus groups, questionnaires, and informal surveys. For each, we will provide a brief overview of the methodology, discuss the advantages and disadvantages, and address the major challenges that await the library planner who is responsible for conducting such analyses with the Latino community. Although you will be required to devote human and financial resources to this process, we promise that the rewards greatly outweigh the costs.

Since many variables are involved (such as history and background of your library, history of the relationship between your library and the Latino community, financial and human resources available to conduct such analyses), you are in a better position to decide which technique, or combination of techniques, is best for your local situation. There is no hard-and-fast rule for which of these three assessment techniques you should select. In fact, you may find it useful in your Latino needs assessment to use more than one of these techniques. Finally, remember that you can write a grant proposal to obtain external funds to do a Latino community needs assessment.

> Explore external funding to underwrite your community needs assessment.

It is impossible to address each and every issue involved in needs assessment, especially since this is not a library science research methods text. We offer this introduction and urge you to learn more about needs assessment techniques—which you will need to have in your tool kit because of the dramatically changing demographics of our nation.

CREATING A FOCUS GROUP

Our first type of assessment will be focus groups. Focus group sessions are essentially group interviews during which a group moderator asks a series of open-ended questions designed to encourage participants to interact with the moderator and, most important, with each other. These sessions have been popular among librarians, and the technique has been used successfully in libraries in many states around the country. Perhaps one reason they work so well is that sometimes people need to hear and acknowledge a variety of viewpoints on certain issues before they form their own personal opinions. In a focus group session, participants can:

- listen and react to responses of the other members of the group;
- change their minds as many times as they want, based on information they obtain from their co-participants;
- attempt to influence the opinions of others;
- learn directly from their co-participants about the wide range of opinions on certain issues.

COMPONENTS OF A FOCUS GROUP

Focus group interviews conducted by you and your staff will not require you to spend a great deal of money, but if your system is able to absorb the costs, you may prefer to hire experienced consultants to manage the assessment and deliver results. Successful focus group projects include three key components:

1. focus group members
2. a focus group moderator
3. focus group questions

Each of these components is discussed below.

Members

Many kinds of Latino focus groups are possible and may be useful in conducting your needs assessment. For example, you can conduct Latino focus groups with young adults, business owners, ESL (English as a Second Language) or ESOL (English for Speakers of Other Languages) class members, college students, Latino leaders, or (with skill, patience, and creativity) even children, to name just a few of the possibilities.

It is impossible to recommend a specific number of groups to convene. You will not be able to rely solely on the input of just one focus group to gather all the information you need, since no one focus group has all the answers. Therefore, you will want to set up a variety of groups, each with participants sharing some demographic characteristic, in order to get a cross-section of opinion. The proper number is reached when you feel you have a good cross-section of Latinos represented in your focus groups. This involves determining the point at which the many costs involved with conducting more focus groups is no longer worth the added effort and expense. You can use your demographic data to help determine the optimum type and number of focus groups.

For the purposes of the following discussion, let us assume that you want to conduct a focus group session with the formal leaders of the Latino community. Your first step is to identify Latino leaders from a variety of organizations (such as K–12 and higher education, churches, professional groups, social agencies, and civic groups) who might be interested in participating.

The next step is to inform them of the library's intent to improve services and collections for Latinos. Describe the focus group process and invite them to participate. Since they are highly committed to Latino causes, you will probably have no trouble getting a number of Latino leaders to accept your invitation. Indicate that if needed, a bilingual translator will be available during the session, and ask each participant if this service is needed. When you get at least six willing participants from a variety of organizations, you have successfully completed the first step.

> Hold one or more focus groups, each composed of six to ten individuals who share a demographic characteristic.

Moderator

If your moderator has formal and specialized training in conducting focus groups, this will help ensure the success of the project. Certainly, if you have such a resource, make use of it. If you have the financial resources to hire a focus group consultant, there are companies that specialize in conducting Latino focus groups for literacy and library communities. Since most small and medium-size libraries do not have the resources to hire someone to do this, you will probably rely primarily on in-house resources. Your library may be lacking in specialized focus group expertise, but you can easily make up for this with commitment and resourcefulness!

The most important qualifications for a moderator include:

- interest in conducting focus groups
- skill and experience in leading group discussions
- familiarity with library operations

You can probably readily identify a number of individuals among your staff, including yourself, with these skills and attitudes, whom you could recruit to take part in such a project. In addition to a moderator, one or two individuals or transcribers, who can assist by noting the significant points of the group's discussion on flip charts, could be provided.

Getting back to our example, since it is possible that one or more of the Latino leaders will be monolingual in Spanish, ideally your focus group moderator and transcriber should be bilingual/bicultural library employees. Realizing that this may not be a possibility right now, the next best option is for the focus group to be moderated by a library employee with assistance from a bilingual community volunteer.

> Use a focus group moderator to guide the group discussion.

Questions

Public libraries commonly conduct focus group sessions to analyze the information needs of Latinos in their communities. Appendix 4A (Spanish) and 4B (English) are copies of the questions used in just such a session in the state of Arizona. The focus group was conducted in Spanish, and a Library Services Response Form (Appendix 4C-Spanish, and 4D-English) were distributed along with instructions (Appendix 4E-Spanish, and 4F-English), which allowed participants to anonymously provide feedback on the library's services. On another occasion, a company with a business plan to create a magazine devoted to Latino youth from 13 to 18 years of age needed data from three specific cross-sections of Latinos—educators/librarians, parents, and youth. The focus groups were conducted in San Diego, California. Appendix 4G, the Focus Group Script, includes the time schedule, questions, and guidelines for the facilitators that was used for the youth group. As with other materials in this manual, these questions can be used as a starting point and modified to meet your unique local needs.

> Provide the focus group moderator with a list of open-ended and broad-based focus group questions that can be used to lead the discussion.

Once you have your three key components—focus group members, a focus group moderator, and focus group questions—you are ready to begin the assessment. The following are step-by-step suggestions for conducting a focus group:

STEP 1: SELECT AND EQUIP A SUITABLE SITE

Select a suitably comfortable conference room in the library where the focus group can be conducted. Another possible location for your focus group is at a site in the Latino community itself. Many Latino organizations will gladly offer their meeting facilities for this purpose.

Before the participants arrive, make sure that the conference room is set up to facilitate interaction among all the participants. If possible, use a round table large enough to accommodate comfortably the moderator, all the participants, and, if necessary, the interpreter. Providing light refreshments will add to the comfort level. Provide easels and flip charts with large-size paper so that the moderator or transcriber can take notes that will be affixed to the wall for everyone to see.

STEP 2: PREPARE THE PARTICIPANTS

If you have both English-monolingual and Spanish-monolingual individuals, you will need the services of an interpreter. Translating from one language to the other will slow down the process; however, the benefit of providing this service is a signal that you respect each participant's language abilities, and it is well worth the time and effort.

When all the participants have arrived, the moderator should introduce everyone involved in the focus group (or encourage self-introductions), provide a brief introduction to the focus group method, and present a brief overview of why the research is being conducted. If needed, the bilingual interpreter translates during the session.

Here are some possible rules:

- Each individual has an opportunity to speak without interruption.
- Each individual has the right to an opinion and the right to express that opinion.
- Everyone has the right to agree or disagree with an expressed opinion.
- No one has the right to ridicule an individual's ideas or opinions.
- The moderator's role is simply to facilitate group discussion, not to take sides or settle any disputes that occur.
- Each individual has the right to change his or her own opinions at any time during the course of the session.
- To encourage full participation, each individual agrees that all personal opinions expressed during the session are to be considered confidential.
- Each participant agrees that there should be documentation of the significant points made during the session; the note taker is responsible for this activity by making notations on the flip-chart for all participants to see, but maintains strict confidentiality by not linking specific comments to a specific individual.
- Participants agree to a maximum time limit of 90 minutes for the session; if time constraints require the moderator to call for an end of discussion to a particular item, each agrees to move on to the next question.

These are only suggested ground rules. The moderator can make modifications to suit personal style.

> The moderator should provide the ground rules on how the focus group session will be conducted

STEP 3: CONDUCT THE SESSION

After setting the ground rules, the moderator asks the first question, encourages interaction among the participants, and then asks any appropriate sub-questions or follow-up questions. The visual aid for these verbal questions may be a copy of the question projected on a screen or written on the flip chart. It is important for the moderator, or in the best-case scenario the transcribers, to make notations on the flip charts and to provide a written record of the group's significant points.

When it appears to the moderator that the question has been fully discussed, the moderator should verbally summarize the main points brought up during the discussion and make certain that these key points appear on the flip chart. This process is continued until all questions have been asked and fully explored within the 90-minute framework.

The moderator concludes the focus group session by thanking the participants for their time and effort and assuring them that their important ideas will be taken into consideration in planning programs, services, and collections for Latinos. After the session is concluded, the moderator gathers up the flip charts with the written notations and provides the material to the person responsible for preparing the overall assessment.

STEP 4: SYNTHESIZE AND SUMMARIZE THE RESULTS

It is important to synthesize the results of your focus group research. Since there is a written record of each focus group that summarizes the key points for each question, this task is relatively easy.

It will be helpful to summarize key points by developing a series of Latino needs/wants statements and to provide them, translated into Spanish, for the benefit of interested Spanish-monolingual individuals in the community. The Latinos in your community may express concerns in very general terms; they may be quite specific about others. One effective way to summarize these concerns in your report is to develop a series of "Latino needs/wants statements." Figure 4-1 on page 59 provides a few examples of needs/wants statements.

These needs/wants statements give life to your report. They are easy to read and understand, and they can provide very useful information to staff who use the results to develop programs, services, and collections for Latinos.

STEP 5: PUBLICIZE THE RESULTS

Conducting your needs assessment is sure to generate widespread interest in your findings. By all means, publicize your findings both internally and externally, and especially to the Latino community. Try to reach the Latino

```
1. Specific need/want example:
   Need/Want Statement:        Latino young adults in our community want Spanish-
                               language magazines.
   Collection Strategy 1:      Library will purchase ten Spanish-language magazines,
                               graphic novels, and comic books for Latino YA males.
   Budget Allocation:          Ten Spanish-language magazines at $40/each = $400.
   Collection Strategy 2:      Library will purchase ten Spanish-language magazines,
                               graphic novels, and comic books for Latino YA females.
   Budget Allocation:          Ten Spanish-language magazines at $40/each = $400.
   Total Budget:               $800
2. General need/want example:
   Need/Want Statement:        Latinos in our community want their elementary school
                               children to read and have an appreciation for both
                               English and Spanish.
   Collection Strategy:        Library will purchase bilingual recreational books for
                               elementary school children.
   Budget Allocation:          100 books at $30/each = $3,000.
   Collection Strategy:        Library will purchase bilingual language instructional
                               DVDs for children and their families.
   Budget Allocation:          50 DVDs at $25/each = $1,250.
   Total Budget:               $4,250
```

Figure 4-1. Sample Needs/Wants, Collection Strategies, and Budget Allocations

community through your local Spanish-language media, if this is available, to show your genuine interest in serving Latinos in your community and indicate that you are reviewing the results and are serious about making changes to benefit Latinos.

If access to the media is limited or nonexistent, use the flyer distribution method to share the information. Usually, the key points/results from your survey can be covered in a double-sided, one-page flyer. Be sure to have the analysis available in both English and Spanish.

ADMINISTERING A SURVEY

A second method for assessment is the questionnaire. You should be very convinced that this is the best tool for your needs, because questionnaires carry with them significant practical and methodological challenges. We will take you step-by-step through each major phase involved in surveying Latinos in your community, with particular emphasis on the challenges you face if you choose this method.

STEP 1: DEVELOP THE QUESTIONNAIRE

Librarians are familiar with questionnaires; they are often used in library research. If you decide to use this type of assessment, one of the major challenges that awaits you is the development of the questionnaire.

We believe that it is easy to construct a questionnaire; it is relatively difficult to construct an effective questionnaire that obtains the right information. The questionnaire you develop should ask Latino respondents about their information needs and wants and their perceptions of library services and collections. It should also include questions to elicit demographic characteristics about the respondent. This information will enable you to link responses to any pertinent characteristics. Including such questions in your survey enables you to make a statement such as, "Most Latino young adult respondents say they would go to the library if they were invited to make recommendations on what music compact discs and DVDs to buy in Spanish for users of the library."

Another major challenge is the Latino population's heterogeneous language usage. For example, in any Latino community, you are likely to find English-Spanish bilingual individuals as well as English-monolingual and Spanish-monolingual individuals. Therefore, your questionnaire should be bilingual. Since each Latino community is unique, it is impossible for us to provide a questionnaire that can be used in all circumstances.

> Pre-test your questionnaire.

We highly recommend that your questionnaire be reviewed by a bilingual person from your area; he or she may recommend modifications that will take into account the subtle language variations that can occur from one place to another. Appendix 4H at the end of this chapter provides a questionnaire from the McMinnville Public Library (Oregon) that can be modified to meet the needs of your own local assessment. For example, you may add different categories to the first question to cover the Latino subgroups in your community. Additionally, before embarking on your community analysis, pre-test your questionnaire with a smaller group to find out if you need to make further modifications.

As you know, one of the major problems with questionnaires in general is the low return rate. Generally speaking, you will get a higher return if your questionnaire is short. It is very possible that a high rate of return could be tied directly to an incentive received for completion, or to administering it to a "captive" audience. Your questionnaire need not be long in order to be effective; you only need to ask the right questions.

> A bilingual person from your local town or neighborhood should review your questionnaire.

STEP 2: IDENTIFY A LATINO SAMPLE TO STUDY

The second step is to identify Latino respondents to whom your questionnaire can be distributed. Let us say for discussion purposes that your universe is all the Latino households in your service area. For your results to have scientific validity, your questionnaire ideally would be distributed to a random sample of households generated from the entire universe of Latino households.

At first this sounds like an easy enough matter. What makes your task particularly difficult, however, is that there is no such thing as a database of all Latino households in your service area. Lists that are traditionally used in social science research (voter registration lists, property ownership records, telephone directories, criss-cross directories, and the like) all have their obvious biases and shortcomings.

In short, since it is not feasible to identify all of the Latino households in your service area, it is impossible to generate a truly random sample from the universe of Latino households. To deal with sampling problems such as these, social scientists use specialized sampling techniques (for example, cluster sampling and stratified sampling), but these techniques are very expensive, and most public libraries do not have the personnel or financial resources necessary to perform these sophisticated samples. Fortunately, your goal is not to be statistically impeccable. Instead, your goal is to obtain valuable information that your library will use to its advantage in developing services and collections for Latinos in your service area—and to do this without spending a fortune! You can accomplish this by interacting as much as possible with a cross-section of Latinos in your community.

Many communities have distinct and recognizable Latino neighborhoods. You may already be familiar with the locations of such neighborhoods in your service area. Interacting with formal and informal Latino leaders or with social service providers in the community will also give you some useful information about where Latinos live.

Another useful source is the 2000 census. You may want to consult the Fact Sheet available for your city/town by using Fact Finder at www.census.gov.

Let us assume in this discussion that you have already identified a Latino neighborhood in your community. Since it may not be practical to distribute a questionnaire to each household, you need to identify a representative sample. One possibility for identifying a sample is to divide the neighborhood into neighborhood blocks, and then use one or more blocks to serve as your target area. Your sample would include each household in the selected block or blocks.

Another strategy is to select a reasonable number of households in the neighborhood to be included in the sample. Let us assume that this particular Latino neighborhood has 200 households. If you want to reach 20 percent of the households, you need to distribute your questionnaire to 40 households. You could choose every fifth household in the neighborhood to be in your sample.

A third strategy is to obtain addresses from a variety of lists, and then generate a sample from this merged list. Vivian Pisano and Margaret Skidmore used this approach when they conducted a community analysis of Richmond, Virginia, in 1978. (Pisano and Skidmore, 1978) Their suggestions are still applicable to anyone doing such research today. In addition to using reverse telephone directories, they suggest that you obtain information from such community groups as schools, police-community liaison groups, community centers, ESL classes, public health agencies, neighborhood groups, social agencies, and churches. Creating a merged list from all these various sources and then generating a sample from this merged list is not perfect statistically, but it may be the most feasible approach.

> Your sample, as much as possible, should reflect the full range of Latinos in your community.

The full spectrum of Latinos in your community should be represented in whichever sampling technique you use. If, for example, Latinos in your community have generally low levels of educational attainment, your sample should reflect this; therefore, you would not want your sample to be made up primarily of Latino college students.

STEP 3: DISTRIBUTE THE QUESTIONNAIRES

Once a sample is selected, questionnaires are then distributed using one or more of the following methods:

- through the mail
- by hand delivery
- by personal interview
- by interview over the telephone

Usually surveys are conducted through the mail. Respondents answer the questions at their convenience and deposit the response in the mail. If you take this approach, you will get a higher return rate if you include a self-addressed, stamped envelope. You might consider including some other small benefit that encourages a response. You have probably received mailings from professional marketing firms that include a one-dollar bill as a small incentive to answering a questionnaire. You can do something similar, but with a library twist. For example, you can consider including a coupon for a free DVD rental next time materials are borrowed, or a seat in the reserved row of any library-sponsored program during the Latino

Heritage Celebrations in September. Small things like this can make a big difference.

Your survey can also be conducted in a one-on-one interview in person or by telephone. An obvious factor to consider when using this interview approach is the language skill of the interviewers. If you decide to use this interview approach, you will need bilingual interviewers.

Assuming your library does not have enough bilingual interviewers to conduct this assessment, you will have to get outside assistance. Refer to Chapter 5 to identify potential partners to help you in this task. Local higher education institutions can provide the assistance you might need. Individuals with expertise in research methodology and/or with Spanish-language fluency are typically found there, and they are often willing to serve as consultants because of the service mission of the institution.

Another distribution method that libraries sometimes use in conducting a needs assessment is to distribute the questionnaire to Latino users as they enter the library. Distributing the needs assessment tool in the library is an inexpensive method that may work for libraries or branches in neighborhoods with very high concentrations of Latinos. In general, this approach has limitations concerning non-users and works only if your sole intent is to study the information needs of current Latino library users. If you are interested in attracting new Latino users to the library, it is essential to go out into the Latino community to conduct your analysis.

STEP 4: COLLECT THE INFORMATION AND SYNTHESIZE THE RESULTS

Because most libraries have access to someone familiar with collecting and synthesizing data, we will not discuss this topic at length. It is critical, however, that you devote time and effort to distilling the collected information into a brief report. The report should specify the purpose of the study, the methodology used, and the results. The results section should itemize the concerns that Latinos have expressed in the survey. It might also be helpful to have a list of these needs/wants statements translated into Spanish for the benefit of interested Spanish-monolingual individuals in the community. See Figure 4-1 for examples of wants/needs statements.

STEP 5: PUBLICIZE THE RESULTS

Conducting your needs assessment is sure to generate widespread interest in your findings. By all means, publicize your findings both internally and externally, and especially to the Latino community. Try to reach the Latino community through your local Spanish-language media, if this is available, to show your genuine interest in serving Latinos in your community and to indicate that you are reviewing the results and are serious about making changes to benefit Latinos.

If access to the media is limited or nonexistent, use the flyer distribution method to share the information. Usually, the key points/results from your survey can be covered in a double-sided, one-page flyer.

Those who conduct surveys face three major limitations:

- They are costly
- They are labor intensive
- They are time-consuming

Nonetheless, if this is the methodology you choose, you can enlist volunteers to help and/or secure external funding to accomplish this task.

HOLDING INFORMAL INTERVIEWS

In this last method, your focus is on obtaining qualitative information by conducting one-on-one interviews. Because questionnaires present significant methodological and practical problems, you may want to try informal interviews, which will allow you to concentrate your efforts on interacting with Latino and non-Latino leaders and with Latinos in the community from different socioeconomic backgrounds. One major benefit of this approach is that your sincere interactions with a large number of Latinos is a strong and clear message that your library is serious about providing services and collections to this segment of the community. These interviews can be conducted in a variety of settings outside the library.

STEP 1: DEVELOP THE INTERVIEW QUESTIONS

Develop interview questions that address issues such as the information needs of the Latino community, the perceptions of the library among Latinos, perception of barriers to providing services and collections, and suggestions from the Latino community on improving library services and collections.

The model focus group questions, model focus group scripts, and McMinnville Public Library questionnaire in Appendix H in this chapter provide some good ideas as to the kinds of questions you will need to ask. This technique presents the advantage of allowing open-ended and follow-up questions.

to show your genuine interest in serving Latinos in your community and to indicate that you are reviewing the results and are serious about making changes to benefit Latinos.

If access to the media is limited or nonexistent, use the flyer distribution method to share the information. Usually, the key points/results from your survey can be covered in a double-sided, one-page flyer.

Those who conduct surveys face three major limitations:

- They are costly
- They are labor intensive
- They are time-consuming

Nonetheless, if this is the methodology you choose, you can enlist volunteers to help and/or secure external funding to accomplish this task.

HOLDING INFORMAL INTERVIEWS

In this last method, your focus is on obtaining qualitative information by conducting one-on-one interviews. Because questionnaires present significant methodological and practical problems, you may want to try informal interviews, which will allow you to concentrate your efforts on interacting with Latino and non-Latino leaders and with Latinos in the community from different socioeconomic backgrounds. One major benefit of this approach is that your sincere interactions with a large number of Latinos is a strong and clear message that your library is serious about providing services and collections to this segment of the community. These interviews can be conducted in a variety of settings outside the library.

STEP 1: DEVELOP THE INTERVIEW QUESTIONS

Develop interview questions that address issues such as the information needs of the Latino community, the perceptions of the library among Latinos, perception of barriers to providing services and collections, and suggestions from the Latino community on improving library services and collections.

The model focus group questions, model focus group scripts, and McMinnville Public Library questionnaire in Appendix H in this chapter provide some good ideas as to the kinds of questions you will need to ask. This technique presents the advantage of allowing open-ended and follow-up questions.

STEP 2: IDENTIFY LEADERS IN THE LATINO COMMUNITY

> Latino leaders will be able to provide valuable information on their perceptions of Latino information needs.

We recommend that the recognized formal leaders in areas of business, political, civic, and social organizations within the Latino community be identified and interviewed. Latino leaders will be able to provide valuable information on their perceptions of Latino needs. They will also be able to provide the names of other important Latino contacts, including both formal and informal leaders, for your assessment.

An excellent source of respondents is the local Spanish-language media (print, radio, and television), if available. Leaders in this industry are usually well-connected with the Latino community and can therefore provide useful information for your assessment as well as further contacts. A side benefit of contacting the media is that you may get some free advertising. If there are no Spanish-language media in your community, Latino columnists or Latino journalists employed by the local media can be very helpful contacts.

STEP 3: DEVELOP A LIST OF COMMUNITY RESOURCES

Develop a list of agencies, organizations, and businesses in your community where you are likely to find willing respondents who can provide useful information about Latinos and their information needs.

> It is critical that your assessment includes the viewpoints of Latinos from *all walks of life*.

Since religion is very important in Latino culture, many Latinos are likely to be church members. Consequently, you can get valuable information by interviewing religious and lay leaders in churches that have significant numbers of Latinos. Most will be very supportive of your efforts to reach out to the Latino community.

Also at the top of your list of possible interviewees should be K–12 and higher education administrators. Not only can these administrators be good sources of information themselves, they can also put you in touch with interested Latino faculty and students in their institutions.

If your community has businesses that employ a large number of Latinos, the human resources professionals in these companies may be a valuable source of employment information about Latinos in your community. Specifically, they are in a good position to tell you about particular occupations or skills that their companies need now or will need in the near future. You can use this information to guide the development of a self-help or job-skills collection for Latino adults.

In this and the two previous steps, you will have identified important contacts (both Latino and from the larger community) who are knowledgeable about and can comment on the information needs of the Latino community. Interviewing these individuals can give you valuable insight, but bear in mind that these individuals, by definition, are elite members of the community. Such interviews may yield incomplete or, worse yet, erroneous information. Therefore, it is critical that your assessment includes the viewpoints of Latinos from *all walks of life*.

STEP 4: COMPILE A LIST OF EVENTS OR PLACES THAT ATTRACT LATINOS

There are numerous celebrations and festivals in communities around the country that attract Latinos. Especially important are the festivals organized by the Latino community itself. *16 de septiembre*, or Mexican Independence Day, is a good example of a Mexican holiday celebrated by Latinos of Mexican descent. See Appendix 5A for a list of other holidays that may be celebrated in your community. Consider contacting your local festival organizers to set up a library booth where you can display examples of Spanish-language materials and promotional literature about your library. You can distribute brief questionnaires, interview passersby who take an active interest, and sign people up for library cards. A needs assessment does not have to be drudgery. Whenever possible, make it fun and enjoyable for everyone by conducting it in an informal, relaxed atmosphere.

Consider setting up a library booth at other places where Latinos congregate. For example, visit with local church leaders to ask permission to distribute questionnaires or conduct interviews at church after Sunday services. Also, many churches have annual festivals or bazaars that offer great opportunities to interact with the Latino community in a more relaxed, fun atmosphere.

Another place to set up a booth and interviewing area is the local supermarket. Check with the managers of supermarkets in Latino neighborhoods to ask if you can set up a booth on payday. Similarly, you can set up a booth at the local mall or shopping center, or even the local flea market or swap meet.

STEP 5: INCLUDE ALL SOCIOECONOMIC GROUPS

Your most difficult challenge will be to obtain information from the poor and the working poor. One of the more effective ways of accomplishing this is to compile a list of the directors of the various community agencies that assist those in need of financial assistance and/or other support services. Try to convince the directors of these agencies to provide you, temporarily, with a small area in the agency's waiting area for interviewing purposes. Remember that your library and these agencies are possible partners, and you may have something to offer them in exchange for making this temporary arrangement.

STEP 6: START CONDUCTING THE ASSESSMENT

You can start by developing a schedule to interview the various contacts you have identified in the previous steps. If at all possible, we recommend interviewing the formal and informal Latino leaders first, thus signaling to Latinos and others that you consider the information needs of Latinos to be of vital importance. This approach will go a long way toward ensuring the success of your needs assessment and will facilitate your library's future interactions with the Latino community in general. After interviewing the Latino leadership, you can proceed to interview respondents that were identified in steps 3–5 above.

One of the major challenges in using this informal interview technique is that you must have enough bilingual interviewers to accomplish the task. When you go out into the community to conduct your assessment, you will encounter Spanish-monolingual, English-monolingual, and bilingual individuals, so you will need to recruit and train bilingual individuals for this assessment project.

The ideal is to have bilingual library personnel conducting the various interviews. However, this resource is often not available to you. The next best option is to conduct interviews using a two-person team that includes a library employee and a bilingual individual from the community. Include this community person in the development of your questions or as a pilot interviewee so that your final assessment tool is tested.

> Take good notes during the open-ended interview and write a summary paragraph after it is concluded.

Another challenge for your interviewers is dealing with open-ended questions. Some of the questions asked during the interview will be multiple-choice items, which do not present much of a problem. The interviewer simply checks off the appropriate answer from the menu of choices. Other questions are much more open-ended. The best advice for interviewers is to take good notes during the interview and to write, while the feedback is still on your mind, a summary paragraph after it is concluded.

STEP 7: COMPILE THE INFORMATION AND ANALYZE THE RESULTS

This step is a bit more difficult than the corresponding step in the questionnaire method, primarily because of the nature of interview data. In a questionnaire, the respondent typically selects an answer from a menu of choices, which makes tabulating results a relatively easy process; however, in an informal interview, there may be lengthy responses to open-ended questions. You will need to keep track of these responses because these will give you valuable insights into Latino needs/wants. Finally, plan to develop Latino needs/wants statements, as suggested in Step 4 of the focus group method.

STEP 8: PUBLICIZE THE MAJOR FINDINGS

See Step 5 in the focus group section to review advice on this step.

APPENDIX 4A: FOCUS GROUP QUESTIONS (SPANISH)

Biblioteca Pública
Preguntas de Discusión para el Grupo de Enfoque
(Translated from the English by Nancy Herrera)

1. Por favor preséntese; ¿Díganos que hace, y como usted, su familia o negocio, utiliza la Biblioteca Pública?

2. ¿Que cree usted que es en particular lo mejor de la Biblioteca?

3. ¿Que es lo que a usted no le gusta? ¿Cuales son las debilidades de la Biblioteca Pública?

4. Los cambios más importantes que la biblioteca ha introducido en los últimos años han sido los servicios electrónicos, por ejemplo; el Internet, el correo electrónico, etc. ¿Cómo ha cambiado su uso de la biblioteca con introducción del Internet y recursos en línea? ¿Ha parado usted utilizando la biblioteca para ciertas cosas? ¿Si eso es el caso qué? ¿Ha encontrado usted nuevos recursos en la biblioteca que usted ahora utiliza? ¿Si eso es el caso, qué es ellos?

5. ¿A donde más acude usted para obtener información, ó de donde obtiene usted la información que necesita? ¿Én su opinión, que es lo que usted considera es la competencia de la Biblioteca?

6. No todas las personas utilizan las bibliotecas. ¿Que razones tendria usted ú otras personas para no utilizar la Biblioteca?

7. ¿Que mejoras ó cambios le gustaria ver en los servicios que ofrece la Biblioteca, por ejemplo; más horas de servicio, una ó mas bibliotecas sucursales, una nueva biblioteca central, un sitio oficial en el Internet de la biblioteca, mejor variedad y surtido en el material de libros, más servicios para niños y adolescentes? (NO MENCIONAREMOS LA LISTA A MENOS QUE EXISTA INDESICION POR PARTE DE LOS PARTICIPANTES A RESPONDER)

8. Folleto de evaluación y respuestas de servicios de la biblioteca. (DISTRIBUYA EL FOLLETO, DEPUES EXPLIQUE QUE ES Y COMO LLENARLO, NO SE TOME MAS DE 10–12 MINUTOS PARA ESTO)

9. Hasta ahora, la discusión ha seguido mi dirección. ¿Existen otras áreas que debemos explorar al planear el futuro de la Biblioteca Pública? ¿Algún otro punto importante para ustedes que no hayamos mencionado y que debamos considerar?

APPENDIX 4B: FOCUS GROUP QUESTIONS (ENGLISH)

Focus Group Discussion Questions

- Please introduce yourself; tell us what you do, and how you (or your family) or business—(for the business group)—use the library and what other libraries you use.

    Probes/follow-ups:
    - What services, programs, or materials in particular?
    - Is your primary use related to personal interests or your job or work?
    - Do you access library services remotely?

- What do you think is particularly good about the Library?

    Probes/follow-ups:
    - Is there anything in particular that seems especially good or noteworthy about your library?
    - What about particular services, programs, or materials? Which ones are best?
    - Are you usually able to find what you're looking for?

- What seems not so good? What do you see as the weaknesses of the Library?

    Probes/follow-ups:
    - What is your biggest complaint? How could we fix that?
    - What problems does lack of space cause? How could we address those problems? How would you use more space?
    - Is there anything in particular that seems to be missing that you think ought to be in the library?
    - Which services, programs, or materials have disappointed you?
    - What would you improve?

- One of the major changes in library services over the past years has been the introduction of electronic services, such as the Internet, e-mail, databases, etc. How has your use of the library changed with introduction of Internet and online resources? Have you stopped using the library for certain things? If so, what? Have you found new resources at the library that you now use? If so, what are they?

    Probes/follow-ups:
    - Are you satisfied with the available technology at the Library?
    - What changes/improvements in the area of technology would you like to see?
    - Do you use the Library's Web site?

- Where else do you go when you need information?

    Probes/follow-ups:
    - Friends? Bookstores? Internet? Other libraries? TV?

- Not everybody uses libraries? What reasons do you think people might have for not using the XXX Library?

    Probes/follow-ups:
    - What are the barriers to using the libraries?
    - Explore physical, cultural, personal obstacles to library use.

- What changes/improvements would you like to see at the library? For instance: open more hours, branch library buildings, more parking, more computers for public use, stronger collections, more services for children and teens, other?

    Probes/follow-ups:
    - If participants are reluctant to speak, then make some suggestions.
    - We want to get their thoughts about renovating/expanding current facility vis-à-vis an all new facility.

- Given electronic access to library services and information, how do you see that influencing future library building projects?

- The discussion has followed my direction thus far. Are there any other areas we should explore in planning for the future of the library? Anything we have missed that is really important to you?

Permission to adapt and reproduce granted by Laura Isenstein, Providence Associates LLC.

APPENDIX 4C: LIBRARY RESPONSE QUESTIONNAIRE (SPANISH)

Forma de Respuesta a los Servicios de la Biblioteca
(Adaptó de la Asociación de Biblioteca pública Nueva Planificación para Resultados, 2001)

___ **La Capacidad de Leer y Escribir básica:** La biblioteca ofrece los servicios que dirigen la necesidad básica saber cómo leer y realizar otras tareas diarias esenciales.

___ **La Información del Negocio y la Carrera:** La biblioteca ofrece el Negocio y los servicios de Información de Carrera que benefician los negocios locales, residentes de ayuda a hacer las elecciones de la carrera, sostienen compañia nueva de negocio e información de oferta para esos empleo que busca.

___ **El Lugar de la Reunión de la Comunidad:** La biblioteca proporciona un invitar y el ambiente acogedor y los espacios para personas para encontrar e interactuar con otros en su comunidad.

___ **La Información de Consumo:** La biblioteca proporciona Información de consumo en respuesta a la necesidad de la comunidad para la informatión para ayudarios hacen las decisiones de consumo informadas.

___ **El Conocimiento Cultural:** La biblioteca ofrece los recursos, las actividades, y los programas que promueven el conocimiento de la comunidad y entendiendo de su propia herencia cultural y la herencia cultural de los otros que residen en la comunidad.

___ **Los Temas Actuales y Titula:** La biblioteca proporciona los Temas y los Titulos Actuales en respuesta a los residentes de la comunidad' el interés en la lectura recreativa popular.

___ **El Recurso Temprano de la Niñez:** La biblioteca ofrece, en la asociación con otras agencias, los recursos, los servicios y los programas para padres y cuidadores de niños muy jóvenes, para sostener el desarrollo de las habilidades tempranas de la capacidad de leer y escribir que ayuda a padres ayuda a niños para ser "se prepara para aprender."

___ **El Apoyo Formal que Aprende:** La biblioteca proporciona las colecciones, los centros de recursos y deberes que ayudan a estudiantes (gradúa K por 12) y en casa schoolers a alcanzar sus metas educativas.

___ **La Zona del Joven:** La Biblioteca crea a joven los grupos consultores comprendieron de voluntarios de joven para participar en el diseño y proporcionando del espacio dedicado para acomodar las colecciones, la música y la tecnología que llegarán a ser un lugar del "destino" para jóvenes en la comunidad.

___ **La Información General:** Las ofertas de la biblioteca Información General, en una variedad de formatos, eso encuentra la necesidad de la comunidad para la información y repuestas a preguntas que cubren una serie ancha de temas.

___ **La Capacidad de la Tecnología:** La biblioteca ayuda con habilidades individuales fortificantes para encontrar, para evaluar, y para utilizar información, información especialmente electrónica, efectivamente.

___ **Aprender de Toda la Vida:** La biblioteca proporciona información y recursos que sostienen las oportunidades personales, liberta-selectos y auto dirigidas del crecimiento y el desarrollo.

___ **La Historia y la Genealogía Locales:** La biblioteca ofrece las colecciones Locales de la Historia y la Genealogía que permiten a residentes de comunidad para aprender acerca de y entender mejor personal o la herencia de la comunidad.

APPENDIX 4D: LIBRARY RESPONSE QUESTIONNAIRE (ENGLISH)

Library Services Response Form
(Adapted from the Public Library Association's *New Planning for Results*, 2001)

___ Basic Literacy: Library offers services addressing the basic need to know how to read and to perform other essential tasks.

___ Business and Career Information: Library offers Business and Career Information services that benefit local businesses, help residents in making career choices, support business start-ups and offer information for those seeking employment.

___ Community Gathering Place: Library provides an inviting and welcoming environment and the spaces for people to meet and interact with others in their community.

___ Consumer Information: Library provides Consumer Information in response to the community's need for information to help them make informed consumer decisions.

___ Cultural Awareness: Library offers resources, activities, and programs that promote the community's awareness and understanding of their own cultural heritage and the cultural heritage of others residing in the community.

___ Current Topics and Titles: Library provides Current Topics and Titles in response to the community residents' interest in popular recreational reading.

___ Early Childhood Resource: Library offers, in partnership with other agencies, resources, services, and programs for parents and caregivers of very young children, to support the development of early literacy skills helping parents help children to be "ready to learn."

___ Formal Learning Support: Library provides collections, resources, and homework centers that assist students (grades K through 12) and home schoolers in attaining their educational goals.

___ Teen Zone: The Library creates teen advisory groups comprised of teen volunteers to assist in the design and furnishing of dedicated space to accommodate collections, music, and technology that will become a "destination" place for teens in the community.

___ General Information: Library offers General Information, in a variety of formats, that meet the community's need for information and answers to questions covering a broad array of topics.

___ Technological Literacy: Library assists with strengthening individual skills for finding, evaluating, and using information, especially electronic information, effectively.

___ Lifelong Learning: Library provides information and resources that support self-directed, free-choice personal growth, and development opportunities.

___ Local History and Geneaology: Library offers Local History and Genealogy collections enabling community residents to learn about and better understand personal or community heritage.

Permission to adapt and reproduce granted by Laura Isenstein, Providence Associates LLC.

APPENDIX 4E: LIBRARY RESPONSE QUESTIONNAIRE INSTRUCTIONS (SPANISH)

Folleto de Evaluacion de Servicios de la Biblioteca

En la lista de abajo hay algunos servicios que una biblioteca pública podria proveer. No todas las bibliotecas pueden hacer el mismo trabajo al proveer todos los servicios posibles. Cada comunidad necesita una mezcla diferente de servicios, estos dependen particularmente de las caracteristicas y composiciones de la comunidad, y de otros recursos disponibles. Por favor indique la importancia de cada servicio siguiendo las instrucciones siguientes:

En la columna de la izquierda coloque el número 1 al lado del servicio que usted considere de mayor importancia para la biblioteca. Después, también en la columna de la izquierda, coloque el número 2 al lado del servicio que usted considere de segunda importancia. Continúe así hasta que haya marcado 5 de los 13 servicios, de manera que tendremos un #1, un #2, un #3, un #4, y un #5.

Después, indique con una X, en la columna de la izquierda dos servicios. Una al lado del servicio que usted crea que es de menor importancia para la biblioteca, y otra al lado del servicio que usted cree no debe ser considerado.

De manera que, de los trece servicios, usted habrá elegido 5 que considera más importantes y 2 que considera de menor importancia para la biblioteca.

No hay necesidad de firmar su nombre, únicamente doble la hoja y entréguela al encargado del grupo cuando este completa. Cracias.

Permission to adapt and reproduce granted by Laura Isenstein, Providence Associates LLC.

APPENDIX 4F: LIBRARY RESPONSE QUESTIONNAIRE INSTRUCTIONS (ENGLISH)

Listed below are some of the services a public library might provide. No library can do an equally good job of providing all of the services possible. Each community needs a different mix of services, depending on its particular characteristics and composition, and on what other resources are available. Please indicate the importance of the services listed below for the Library as follows:

In the left-hand column place a 1 beside the service you believe is most important for the Library to pursue. Then, also in the left-hand column, place a number 2 beside the service you believe to be second most important. Continue until you have marked five of the 13 services, so that there is one #1, one #2, one #3, one #4, and one #5.

Then, please assign an X, also in the left-hand column, beside the two services you believe to be of *least* importance for the Library or services you think should not be considered at all.

Please do not sign your name. Fold and return the sheet to the Group facilitator when completed.

Thank you.

Permission to adapt and reproduce granted by Laura Isenstein, Providence Associates LLC.

APPENDIX 4G: FOCUS GROUP SCRIPT

ChispaKids Magazine Focus Group Script (Children Version)
Prepared by Ron Baza & Associates, Inc.
(April 2001)

OPENING (5 minutes)

1. Facilitator welcomes the group and thanks them for coming, then introduces himself or herself and the project and explains the purpose of the focus group (See Invitation Letter).

2. Participants introduce themselves to the rest of the group.

3. Facilitator presents the agenda for the session.

   Script: *Welcome to the group, and thank you for joining us. This is one of several focus groups that are being conducted to gather information for ChispaKids Magazine. ChispaKids Magazine staff members hope that by understanding your thoughts about our magazine, they can produce an exciting magazine that you will really enjoy. A gocus group brings people together in one place to share their opinions on a topic or a product. Each of you will be sharing your very own opinion and no one else's opinions; you do not need to view your comments as representative of an organization or group of people. Please be as honest and as open as possible in your answers to our questions. No one outside of this group here today will know who said what. The results of the focus group will help the ChispaKids staff develop an exciting magazine for the future. We will move quickly through several questions and should be done in about an hour or maybe less. Let's start by introducing ourselves.*

WARM-UP (5 minutes)

4. Facilitator plays a CD-ROM (or reads aloud) vignette entitled **The House Guest**. Facilitator takes a quick group survey (shows of hands) of how many participants can relate to the vignette. Facilitator will ask the participants for a couple of reactions to the vignette.

Questions

12 minutes

5. Facilitator poses Question 1. Participants should first record throughs by themselves on a piece of paper. The co-facilitator writes comments on a flip chart, taking one comment per person until everyone has had a chance. Continue around the room until all comments are exhausted. Note: Facilitator will head off destructive exchanges of opinions.

   Script: *Do you like the (ChispaKids) magazine? If yes, what do you like about it? If no, why didn't you like it?*

12 minutes

6. Facilitator poses Question 2. Participants should first record thoughts by themselves on a piece of paper. The co-facilitator writes comments on a flip chart, taking one comment per person until everyone has had

a chance. Continue around the room until all comments are exhausted. Number each comment as it is written on the flip chart. Note: Facilitator will head off destructive exchanges of opinions.

Script: *Would you share the magazine with others? Who would you share it with?*

12 minutes

7. Facilitator poses Question 3. Participants should first record thoughts by themselves on a piece of paper. The co-facilitator writes comments on a flip chart, taking one comment per person until everyone has had a chance. Continue around the room until all comments are exhausted. Number each comment as it is written on the flip chart. Note: Facilitator will head off destructive exchanges of opinions. Clarify any comments for yourself or other participants. Combine comments when the entire group agrees that they should be combined.

Script: *Would you ask your parent or teacher to get it for you?*

12 minutes

8. Facilitator poses Question 4. Participants should first record thoughts by themselves on a piece of paper. The co-facilitator writes comments on a flip chart, taking one comment per person until everyone has had a chance. Continue around the room until all comments are exhausted. Number each comment as it is written on the flip chart. Note: Facilitator will head off destructive exchanges of opinions. Clarify any comments for yourself or other participants. Combine comments when the entire group agrees that they should be combined.

Script: *Do you see yourself in the magazine (i.e., do you relate to the people in the magazine?)? If no, what magazine do you see yourself in?*

12 minutes

9. Facilitator poses Question 5. Participants should first record thoughts by themselves on a piece of paper. The co-facilitator writes comments on a flip chart, taking one comment per person until everyone has had a chance. Continue around the room until all comments are exhausted. Number each comment as it is written on the flip shart. Note: Facilitator will head off destructive exchanges of opinions. Combine comments when the entire group agrees that they should be combined.

Script: *How would you describe the (ChispaKids) magazine?*

CLOSING (8 minutes)

10. Facilitator invites the group to note any last thoughts. Facilitator adjourns the session by thanking everyone for their participation and reminds them how the data will be used.

Script: *Do you have any last thoughts, comments, or things you wish to emphasize for the ChispaKids Magazine staff? Thank you again very much for your participation. All of the information from this and other focus groups will be reviewed next month and summarized for the ChispaKids staff by the end of next month. ChispaKids Magazine staff hopes to have its first edition out by January 2007.*

Permission to adapt and reproduce granted by Ron Baza, Ron Baza and Associates, Inc.

APPENDIX 4H: MODIFIABLE QUESTIONNAIRE

McMinnville Public Library
Customer Satisfaction Survey 2004

We are interested in YOUR opinion about the services we provide as we plan for the future of your library. Please take a moment to let us know how we are doing. Feel free to use the back of this survey for further comments.

1. **How often do you use McMinnville Public Library?**
   (Including website, telephone or email access)

   ☐ At least once a week   ☐ Once every six months
   ☐ Once every three weeks   ☐ Once a year
   ☐ Once a month   ☐ Never been here before

2. **What are your main reasons for using the library today?**
   Check all that apply.

   ☐ Borrow new books   ☐ Pay my library fines
   ☐ Borrow adult books   ☐ Renew my books
   ☐ Borrow teen books   ☐ Pick up a book on hold
   ☐ Borrow children's books   ☐ Use the children's room
   ☐ Borrow large print books   ☐ Go to a story hour or children's program
   ☐ Borrow videos or DVDs   ☐ Work on a school project/report
   ☐ Borrow books on CD or cassette   ☐ For information/reference help
   ☐ Borrow books in Spanish   ☐ Find income tax forms
   ☐ Borrow videos in Spanish   ☐ Use the copy machine
   ☐ Borrow audio cassettes or CDs in Spanish ☐ Use car repair manuals
   ☐ Use the Internet computers   ☐ Quiet reading/study space
   ☐ Use the word processing computers   ☐ Read magazines or newspapers

   Other (please specify)_____

3. **Did you find what you were looking for today?**

   ☐ Yes   ☐ No   ☐ Partly

   If your answer is "yes", skip to question #4

If your answer is "no" or "partly," please explain

☐ Item was checked out   ☐ I could not find the item

☐ Library had no information on the subject   ☐ Staff requested the item from another library
What subject_____

☐ I did not know how to use the computer   ☐ I placed a hold on the item myself
catalog

☐ Librarian was too busy to help   ☐ Other:_____

4. Please rate our services:

	Excellent	Good	Fair	Poor	Don't Know
Parking					
Comfort/cleanliness					
Seating availability					
Helpfulness of signs					
Easy to reach us by phone					
Places for quiet study					
Easy to use the computer catalog					
Easy to find library materials					
Easy to borrow from other libraries					
Easy to check out library materials					
Length of check out lines					
Internet computer access					
Word processing computer access					
Computer classes					
Telephone reference service					
Reference services					
Children's programs					
Adult programs					
Homebound services					
Bookmobile services					

5. What would you like to see added or increased?

- ☐ Best sellers
- ☐ Adult books
- ☐ Children's books
- ☐ Teen books
- ☐ Large print books
- ☐ Books on audio cassette
- ☐ Books on CD

- ☐ Video cassettes
- ☐ DVDs
- ☐ Music on CD
- ☐ Spanish videos
- ☐ Spanish DVDS
- ☐ Adult books in Spanish
- ☐ Children's books in Spanish

- ☐ Spanish books on audio cassette
- ☐ Spanish books on CD
- ☐ Internet access computers
- ☐ Word processing computers
- ☐ Newspapers
- ☐ Magazines
- ☐ More hours open

Anything else?_____

6. What time of day do you usually come to the library?

☐ Weekday mornings   ☐ Weekday afternoons   ☐ Weekday evenings   ☐ Weekends

7. How were you treated by our staff today?

	Excellent	Good	Fair	Poor	Don't Know
Were we available to help?					
Were you treated courteously?					
Were we efficient/ knowledgeable?					

8. In general, how would you rate your experience at the library today?

☐ Excellent   ☐ Good   ☐ Fair   ☐ Poor

Comments:

9. About you

☐ Male   ☐ Under 11 years   ☐ 18-29 years old   ☐ 40-49 years old   ☐ Over 60
☐ Female   ☐ 12-17 years old   ☐ 30-39 years old   ☐ 50-59 years old

10. Is there anything else you would suggest to help us plan for the future of your library?

Thank you for helping us with ideas to improve your library.

5 STARTING OUT: PROGRAMS, SERVICES, AND PARTNERSHIPS

> *Acknowledge the fact that there is a language barrier and move past this to solutions for providing effective service to your Latino community.*

In providing library and literacy services, one can become overwhelmed by what needs to be done. The needs assessment methods described in Chapter 4 will uncover the issues and concerns of your Latino participants. Contacting other libraries that already serve their Latino communities is another way to obtain more ideas for programming, serving, and partnering in your own community. This is the "ideas" chapter. We provide here a list of the types of groups with which you can establish partnerships and we offer real-life examples of successful library partnerships from across the nation. We also recommend that you use the REFORMAnet discussion list to find out who might be doing a certain type of program or service. People on this listserv are very receptive to helping each other and to providing suggestions. You will have to have a REFORMA membership (individual, or a library/institutional) to participate in the listserv. No matter where you are in the planning process, there are plenty of ideas from which to choose, with your individual circumstances guiding your choices.

One of the predominant themes we found in researching various libraries throughout the country was the strong partnerships the libraries had established with other groups in the community. They all had one goal in mind—meeting the needs of Latinos in their community.

The program, service, and partnership ideas presented in this chapter are by no means exhaustive. Many of these suggestions are based on successful projects from all across the country, and some are just ideas. Almost every person we interviewed presented a brand-new idea or unique twist on partnering, for example. We encourage you to be creative. The important point in this chapter is to begin designing programs and services and engaging in partnerships to fit your particular Latino community's needs. If at all possible, arrange for the programs to be bilingual or in Spanish. Acknowledge the fact that there is a language barrier and move past this to solutions for providing effective service to your Latino community. When you are ready, make sure that all your program flyers and publicity materials are bilingual.

Funding, staffing, and materials are critical and can often be challenges to successful programming. The program, service, and partnership ideas presented in this chapter are not the only topics critical to the success of programs and services to Latinos. We realize that each idea has many implications, which we deal with in other chapters.

EXPANDING BASIC SERVICES

Basic services are the place to start when planning for your Latino community. Working hand in hand with basic services planning is knowing your Latino community (see Chapter 4). Because it is so key, planning is emphasized in this chapter, as well as throughout the book. We suggest the following steps to help get you started:

STEP 1: IDENTIFY EXISTING BASIC SERVICES

You and your staff are in the best position to evaluate and identify the basic programs and services that are already available to Latino residents.

By basic services, we mean those services that can be provided at no extra cost because they are already covered in your current budget. For example, many services, such as circulation, general reference, readers' advisory, meeting rooms, or programming for different audiences, such as children, teens, and adults, are available to those Latinos who are either monolingual in English or bilingual.

STEP 2: MODIFY THOSE BASIC SERVICES

After you have identified those existing basic services and programs, you need to modify them to ensure that Latino residents in your community can benefit from them.

Consider children's programming, for example. If you are planning children's programming for the month of April, you may want to include activities for all children (non-Latino and Latino) around El Día de los niños/El Día de los libros, which is traditionally celebrated on April 30. Activities could include a story hour planned around a children's book with multiethnic characters, and a performance by a children's dance troupe that would depict the Latino subgroup or subgroups in your community.

STEP 3: ASSESS THE MARKETABILITY OF BASIC SERVICES

You will need to determine which basic services can realistically be marketed to Latinos. First highlight and market those basic services that you learned were important from the results of your Latino community analysis. As we mentioned earlier, almost all general services can be marketed to bilingual and English-speaking Latinos.

STEP 4: CONDUCT TARGETED PROGRAMMING

Programming around holidays is also a good way to attract Latinos of any age. Christmas, Easter, and Thanksgiving are major U.S. holidays, but also consider, for example, a popular celebration in Latin America, *El Día de las madres* (Mother's Day), which in Mexico is celebrated every May 10th. The tradition of honoring mothers, grandmothers, and godmothers during *Día de las madres* can provide a good theme for Latino programming incorporating crafts, literature, and oral tradition or storytelling.

STEP 5: SET UP LIBRARY DISPLAYS

Another easy way to get started is to set up displays based on a theme or subject and organized in such a way that visitors to the library can read and appreciate their content. Most public libraries develop periodic displays, exhibits, and art shows. Think about developing a display or exhibit to highlight the Latino culture; it is a great ice-breaker. Ask your formal and informal Latino community leaders to help you with ideas and materials. If there are Latino artists in the community, including young adults, invite them to display their artwork in the library. This is one of the best ways to introduce the library to the Latino community and to attract the Latino community to the library.

Your Latino community might have a variety of subgroups, so if you have books about the various countries that they come from, a display is a great way to highlight your collection. A national holidays display is very effective in attracting Latino adults to the library. Almost all countries have an embassy or a visitors' bureau in Washington, D.C. If you can write and tell them what you would like to do, they may send you posters, maps, small flags, and other materials to use in your displays. Appendix 5A at the end of this chapter lists and briefly describes some national Latino holidays for the various Latin American and Caribbean countries.

STEP 6: IMPLEMENT SIGNAGE IN SPANISH

If your library really wants the Latino community to feel welcome, there is no better way to do so than by using Spanish signage in the library. Signage is a very basic service that can be done at minimal cost. With bilingual signage, you tell Latinos that you recognize and accept their cultural differences and want to serve them, and that they are welcome in your library. Figure 5-1 provides a Spanish translation for the Dewey Decimal Classification (DDC) system signage. Figure 5-1a lists DDC revisions.

SOL search

SOL's Sister Site

Home

What's New

Patron Services
Forms and documents in Spanish

Outreach and Media
Press releases and programming ideas

DDC
Dewey in Spanish

About the Language
Linguistic guidance, library glossary, translators

Print & Post
Spanish signage for the multilingual library

Library Links
Whassup on the Web

Dance Floor
Music reviews

Un Poco de Todo
Items that defy classification

Help

Contact Us

Suggestions

This Spanish version of the Dewey Decimal Classification System is based on the 18th edition of DDC; its gaps are reflected here. Click hotlinks to bring up the 1,000 sections, presented on 10 separate pages Also see *emendations and additions* suggested by working librarians

THE 100 DIVISIONS

000 Generalidades
010 Bibliografía
020 Bibliotecología e informática
030 Enciclopedias generales
040
050 Publicaciones en serie
060 Organizaciones y museografía
070 Periodismo, editoriales, diarios
080 Colecciones generales
090 Manuscritos y libros raros

100 Filosofía y disciplinas afines
110 Metafísica
120 Conocimiento, causa, fin, hombre
130 Parapsicología, ocultismo
140 Puntos de vista filosóficos
150 Psicología
160 Lógica
170 Ética (Filosofía moral)
180 Filosofía antigua, medieval, oriental
190 Filosofía moderna occidental

200 Religión
210 Religión natural
220 Biblia
230 Teología cristiana
240 Moral y práctica cristianas
250 Iglesia local y órdenes religiosas
260 Teología social y eclesiología
270 Historia y geografía de la iglesia
280 Credos de la iglesia cristiana
290 Otras religiones

300 Ciencias sociales
310 Estadística
320 Ciencia política
330 Economía
340 Derecho
350 Administración pública
360 Patología y servicio sociales
370 Educación
380 Comercio
390 Costumbres y folklore

400 Lenguas
410 Lingüística
420 Inglés y anglosajón
430 Lenguas germánicas; alemán
440 Lenguas romances; francés
450 Italiano, rumano, rético
460 Español y portugués
470 Lenguas itálicas; latín
480 Lenguas helénicas; griego clásico
490 Otras lenguas

500 Ciencias puras
510 Matemáticas
520 Astronomía y ciencias afines
530 Física
540 Química y ciencias afines
550 Geociencias
560 Paleontología
570 Ciencias biológicas
580 Ciencias botánicas
590 Ciencias zoológicas

600 Tecnología (Ciencias aplicadas)
610 Ciencias médicas
620 Ingeniería y operaciones afines
630 Agricultura y tecnologías afines
640 Economía doméstica
650 Servicios admin. empresariales
660 Química industrial
670 Manufacturas
680 Manufacturas varias
690 Construcciones

700 Bellas artes
710 Urbanismo y arquitectura del paisaje
720 Arquitectura
730 Artes plásticas; escultura
740 Dibujo, artes decorativas y menores
750 Pintura y pinturas
760 Artes gráficas; grabados
770 Fotografía y fotografías
780 Música
790 Entretenimientos

800 Literatura
810 Literatura americana en inglés
820 Literatura inglesa y angiosajona
830 Literaturas germánicas
840 Literaturas de las lenguas romances
850 Literaturas italiana, rumana, rética
860 Literaturas española y portuguesa
870 Literaturas de las lenguas itálicas
880 Literaturas de las lenguas helénicas
890 Literaturas de otras lenguas

900 Geografía e historia
910 Geografía; viajes
920 Biografía y genealogía
930 Historia del mundo antiguo
940 Historia de Europa
950 Historia de Asia
960 Historia de Africa
970 Historia de América del Norte
980 Historia de América del Sur
990 Historia de otras regiones

Previous Page

Figure 5-1. Index of Dewey Decimal Classification in Spanish (Spanish in Our Libraries)

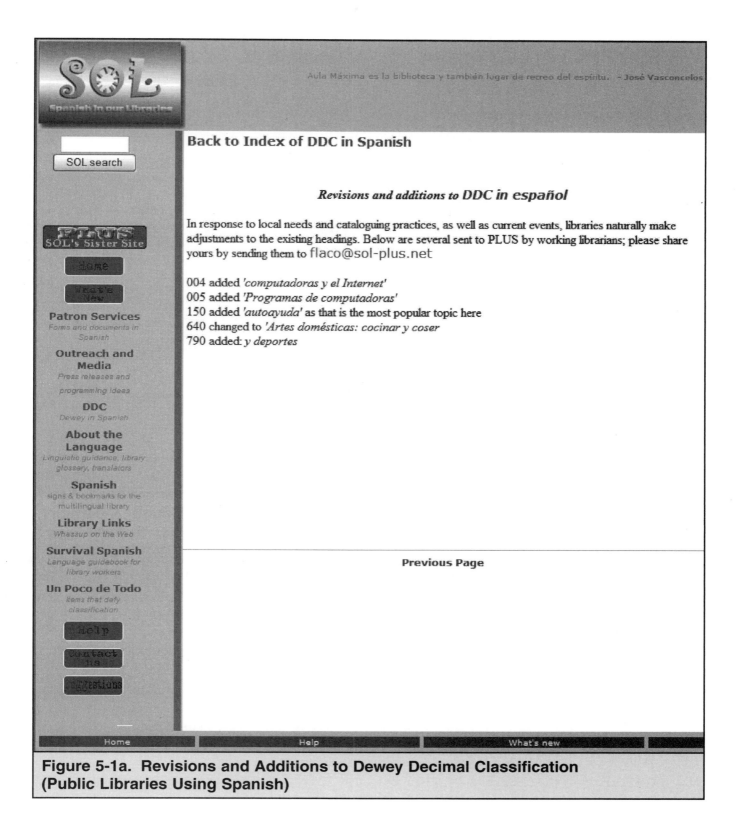

Figure 5-1a. Revisions and Additions to Dewey Decimal Classification (Public Libraries Using Spanish)

STEP 7: EXPORT LIBRARY CARD SIGN-UP

Another basic service for Latinos that takes little, if any, additional funds is the library card application process. You can choose to design one bilingual form or two separate forms—one in English and one in Spanish. Whichever you choose, merely providing the application in both languages leaves a favorable impression in the community.

The process of signing up Latinos does not have to be conducted in the library. The county of Arlington, Virginia, for example, held a library card sign-up in conjunction with a bilingual Reading Readiness program at Hecht's Department Store. Library card sign-ups are also held at cultural celebrations throughout the county and annually at the Arlington County Fair. (T. Bissessar personal communication, October 28, 2006)

Export your library card sign-up with volunteers and a table set up at the grocery store, schools, post office, outside social services offices, after church, or at Latino festivals. Figures 5-2 and 5-3 provide you an example of San Diego County (California) Library's English/Spanish double-sided library card application form, and Figure 5-4 is a copy of Beaufort County (South Carolina) Library's bilingual card application form.

STEP 8: CONDUCT OPEN HOUSES AND TOURS

You can work with a partner in the Latino community to organize another no-cost or low-cost service in the form of library open houses and tours designed specifically for the community. If possible, distribute library card applications in advance and with the help of your partnering organization have them completed and returned to you in time to have the processed cards ready for distribution at the event. These programs should be offered at times when the entire Latino family is available. Your focus groups, surveys, or interviews can help you determine the best time. Be creative to keep the costs down. We suggest you get a local food business to donate some food for coffee hour or an informal reception after the tours.

STEP 9: CONSIDER HIRING A TRANSLATOR

An intermediary translator could work in the library for three hours once a week (for example, Thursday evenings from 5 to 8 p.m.). If you can find the funds, pay a bilingual resident to serve as translator (between Spanish-speaking user and English-speaking library staff). Even at a $10 hourly rate, that is only $1,560 per year. If that is still impossible, try to get some bilingual community residents to volunteer several hours a week. Teens could serve in this capacity and can either work on behalf of your library's Teen Advisory Group (or TAG) or perform the hours of volunteer work in

San Diego County Library

Library Card Application

Please Print Clearly

(La solicitud en español está al dorso)

www.sdcl.org

First Name (Full Legal Name)	Middle Name (Required)	Last Name

Mailing Address (Duty Station if Military)	Apt/Space/Unit No.

City	State	Zip Code

Telephone:
Home: (   )   -   Work:(   )   -

E-Mail Address:	Birth Date: Month/Day/Year (Required if under 18) / /

Parent or Guardian of Applicant under Age 18

First Name	Middle Name (Required)	Last Name

Address (If different from applicant)	Apt/Space/Unit No.

City	State	Zip Code

Children under the age of 18 must have parental permission to use the Internet when their parent/guardian is not with them. Would you like to complete an Internet Parental Consent Form? ☐Yes ☐No

Residential Address If Different from Above

Residential Address	Apt/Space/Unit No.

City	State	Zip Code

Acceptance of Responsibility

- **I will be financially responsible for all materials borrowed and any fines accrued on this card.**
- **I will report a lost card or any change in address immediately.**
- **Parents are solely responsible for their child's use of library materials.**

I would like to receive information concerning Library services from library support organizations. ☐Yes ☐No

Signature of APPLICANT:

Signature of PARENT/GUARDIAN:

STAFF USE ONLY

Home Branch:	Barcode	Address Verified? ف Yes ف No
		Picture ID Verified? ف Yes ف No
		Parent's Account Checked for Customer in good standing? ف Yes
Patron Code: ف AD ف JV ف NA ف NJ ف HB ف IN ف TR ف JI ف ML		Juvenile to Adult ف
Application Taken By: Date:	Registration Input By: Date:	Final Check By: Date:

LIB 10-03 (Rev. 03-22-2004)

Figure 5-2. San Diego County (California) Library's English Library Card Application Form

(Permission to adapt and reproduce by the San Diego County Library System.)

San Diego County Library Favor de deletrear claramente	**SOLICITUD PARA TARJETA DE LA BIBLIOTECA** (The English form is on the reverse)	www.sdcl.org

Primer Nombre (Nombre Legal)	Segundo Nombre (Requerido)	Apellido
Dirección Postal (Nombre de la base si es Militar)		Número de apt/unidad/local
Ciudad	Estado	Zona Postal
Teléfono Casa: ( ) -	Trabajo: ( ) -	
Correo Electrónico:		Fecha de Nacimiento: Mes/Día/Año (Requerido para menore de 18) / /

Información de los padres o guardianes legales de los menores de 18 años de edad

Primer Nombre	Segundo Nombre (Requerido)	Apellido
Su dirección si es distinta a la del menor		Numero de apt/unidad/local
Ciudad	Estado	Zona Postal

Los menores de 18 años de edad tienen que tener permiso por escrito para poder usar el Internet sin que sus padres esten presentes. ¿Gustaría firmar el permiso? ☐Sí ☐ No

Su Domicilio si es distinto a su dirección postal

Domicilio	Número de apt/unidad/local
Ciudad	Estado	Zona Postal

Sus Responsabilidades

- **Seré responsable por el costo de los materiales prestados con esta tarjeta y cualquier multa acumulada.**
- **Notificaré a la biblioteca inmediatamente si se pierde la tarjeta o si hay cambio de domicilio.**
- **Los padres son responsables por los materials de la biblioteca que sus hijos usen.**

Me gustaría recibir información tocante a organizaciones que apoyen a la biblioteca. Sí ☐ ☐No

Firma del SOLICITANTE:

Firma de PADRES/GUARDIANES:

PARA USO DEL PERSONAL SOLAMENTE

Home Branch:	Barcode	Address Verified? ﺏ Yes ﺏ No
		Picture ID Verified? ﺏ Yes ﺏ No
		Parent's Account Checked for Customer in good standing? ﺏ Yes
Patron Code: ﺏ AD ﺏJV ﺏNA ﺏNJ ﺏHB ﺏ IN ﺏTR ﺏ JI ﺏ ML		Juvenile to Adult ﺏ
Application Taken By: Date:	Registration Input By: Date:	Final Check By: Date:

LIB 10-03 (Rev. 03-22-2004)

Figure 5-3. San Diego County (California) Library's Spanish Library Card Application Form

(Permission to adapt and reproduce by the San Diego County Library System.)

County Library System   Library Card Application
To register for a library card, you will need to complete this form and provide current identification for proof of address. The information on this form is solicited in order to maintain a complete list of library patrons, and will be used to record the location of library materials. This information is kept confidential by South Carolina State Law Title 60-4-10.

Solicitud de tarjeta de la Biblioteca del Condado de Beaufort
Para obtener una tarjeta de la Biblioteca del Condado de Beaufort, hay que completar esta solicitud y proveer una identificación que demuestre su dirección actual. Se solicita esta información para mantener una lista actualizada de los usarios de la biblioteca, la cual se usará para registrar la localización de los materiales bibliotecarios. Esta información es confidencial.

First Name, Middle Name, Last Name   Primer nombre, segundo nombre, apellido

Social Security Number (Optional)
Número de Seguro Social (Opcional)

Driver's License Number
Número de licencia de conducir

State
Estado

Home Telephone Number
Número telefónico (Casa)

Work Telephone Number
Número telefónico (Trabajo)

Local Mailing Address   Dirección postal (Local)

City   Ciudad   **State   Estado**   **Zip Code   Código postal**

Parent/Guardian: First Name, Last Name – FOR CHILDREN 5-14
Padre/Madre/ o Guardián: Nombre y Apellido – PARA LOS NIÑOS QUE TIENEN 5-14 AÑOS

Secondary Address   Dirección secundaria

City   Ciudad   **State Estado   Zip Code   Código Postal**

PLEASE DO NOT WRITE BELOW THIS LINE   (NO ESCRIBA DEBAJO DE ESTA LINEA, POR FAVOR)

Barcode Number: 15301	Identification:		Amount Paid:
Registration Qualifier:	Class:	Registration Qualifier: Class:	Staff Initials: _____
Local Adult LA	1	Milit Juv MJ 1	
Local Juv LJ	1	Visitor (paid) P 3	Date: _____
Milit Adult MA	1	Staff/Volun LA 4	

Welcome to the Library!

I agree to be responsible for material borrowed on this card, for all fines incurred and for loss and damage of material charged upon it. I accept responsibility for the selection of materials made by this person. The Beaufort County Library assumes no responsibility for any damage to your equipment while used in conjunction with our audiovisual materials.

Please circle one age category:
5-14   15+

If applicable:
Length of Stay: _____
School: _____ Grade: _____

Signature:
_____

¡Bienvenido a la Biblioteca!

Yo, me hago responsable de los materiales que pido prestados con esta tarjeta, de todas las multas pendientes, como también de la pérdida y del daño de los mismos. Acepto la responsabilidad de la selección de los materiales que hace esta persona. La Biblioteca del Condado de Beaufort no toma ninguna responsabilidad del daño a sus equipos usados en conjunto con nuestros materiales audiovisuales.

Por favor, escriba un círculo alrededor de una de las categorías de edad:
5-14   15+

Si son aplicables:
Duración de la visita: _____
Escuela: _____ Grado: _____

Firma:
_____

Revised Feb. 2007

Figure 5-4. Beaufort County (South Carolina) Library's Bilingual Card Application Form

(Permission to adapt and reproduce granted by the Beaufort County Public Library.)

order to satisfy requirements toward graduation from high school. We suggest that you set a time and day to offer bilingual services.

If you do not have bilingual staff or volunteers available yet, then your staff needs to be prepared to provide basic services to Spanish-speaking Latinos until you can get appropriate staff and/or volunteers. Appendix 5B at the end of this chapter provides some basic Spanish phrases and their phonetic pronunciation.

We encourage use of these steps as a guideline to discuss the programs and services you currently offer with staff and volunteers. It is highly important to be honest about your cultural knowledge and expertise when planning basic services for any underserved ethnic community. If this is an introduction to library services, do not assume that the public library is a common concept for your target market. When planning to enhance basic services for Latinos, be sure to emphasize that libraries in the United States can be used by anyone in the community and that they loan materials free of charge. (Byrd, 2005)

ENHANCING PROGRAMMING

The purpose of this section is to provide program ideas that have worked in public libraries with similar goals, and which you can adapt to fit your community's needs and your library's resources.

CHILDREN'S PROGRAMS

Library personnel involved in providing library programs to Latinos in their community maintain that the best way to get Latino parents into the library is through children's programming, because the Latino community is very family-centered. Here are some ideas for Latino children's programming.

For All Children: *El día de los niños/El día de los libros*

El día is a movement that has now been infused in the public libraries for Latino and all children. *El día de los niños/El día de los libros* (Day of the Children/Day of the Books), the nationwide celebration of children, literacy, books, languages, and cultures, was founded in 1996 by nationally recognized author of children's books Pat Mora.

Ms. Mora formed the idea as an American version of celebrating the Day of the Child, a popular commemoration in Latin America that focuses on the appreciation and well-being of children. She linked literacy to the day by expanding the name of the celebration to include books. The founding partners included organizations such as REFORMA (the National Association to Promote Library and Information Services to Latinos and the Spanish-Speaking), MANA del Norte (a New Mexico chapter of the national Latina organization), NABE (National Association of Bilingual Educators), and the University of Arizona. Coinciding with *El día del niño*, the celebrations are held annually on April 30. Owing to the efforts and influence of REFORMA members, Austin, El Paso (Texas), and Tucson (Arizona) were the first three cities where library systems actually recognized the value of holding these celebrations of cultural heritage and symbolism. (Garza de Cortés, 2006)

In 2000, the Raúl and Estela Mora Award was established to recognize the *Día* celebrations that best promote literacy to families and children. Only *Día* events that are well-documented can compete. A list of the past winners has been provided below and for information on how to apply, please refer to the REFORMA Web site, www.reforma.org.

Raúl and Estela Mora Award Winners

(in reverse chronological order)

- Kenton County Public Library, El Día Committee of Northern Kentucky/Cincinnati (2006)
- REFORMA de Utah (2005)
- Providence (Rhode Island) Public Library (2004)
- Corvallis-Benton (Oregon) Public Library (2003)
- Multnomah County (Oregon) Public Library (2002)
- El Paso (Texas) Public Library (2001)
- Austin (Texas) Public Library (2000)

Partnerships have been integral to the success of *Día* throughout its history. The American Library Association's division for children, the Association for Library Service to Children (ALSC), began serving as home to the *Día* initiative in 2004. The W. K. Kellogg Foundation as well as other partners provided funding to ALSC in furthering the work of the project, and hundreds of programs are now held each April in libraries throughout the country, resulting in some great community connections.

The Yakima Valley Regional Library (Washington) held three events one year to raise awareness of the *Día* movement. Their partners included a local Spanish radio station that provided games and prizes, community businesses donating money and prizes, and 15 high school volunteers. The three programs consisted of puppet shows, readers' theaters, prize drawings, face painting, piñatas, cakes or *pan dulce* (Mexican sweet bread), games, and free books. (E. Pérez, personal communication, May 2006)

Broward County Library (Florida) celebrated with a Saturday program held from 1:00–4:00 p.m. at their Southwest Regional Library, including a puppet show, dances, readings, storytelling, an author presentation and signing, and a book giveaway. Families filled the space to capacity and parents expressed their gratitude to the library. Partners included ASPIRA (the local chapter of the ASPIRA Association, Inc., a national nonprofit organization devoted to the education and leadership development of Puerto Rican and other Latino youth) and Editorial Panamerica, a book distributor. The tip offered by Lucía González, associate director for youth services, is to invite children from the community to actively participate in the festivities. Children and youth who perform (sing, dance, recite) will bring relatives and friends to your event.

Among the memorable *Día* celebrations is one sponsored by the San Diego County Library (California) at Monarch School. The festivity consists of an assembly featuring Los Alacranes, a local Chicano/Mexicano folklore music group that provides an hour-long concert for the entire student body (from elementary school through high school) while refreshments are provided. Each student tours the Mobile Library and receives a free book. What makes this urban celebration, held annually since 2003, so special is that the students learning and growing at Monarch School are homeless. Teachers, the school principal, and county librarians work closely to provide a celebration of the arts, multiculturalism, and literacy even on this closed campus. Past sponsors of this endeavor with the San Diego County Library are the San Diego County Latinos Employee Association, local Spanish book vendor Casa del Libro, and the Chicano Federation of San Diego.

Pat Mora, a Texas native, was present at a January 2006 ceremony held in the San Antonio Public Library to launch a tenth year of *Día* celebrations. "Hooray for the dedicated librarians who daily share book joy with diverse families and then celebrate by linking all children to books, languages, and cultures on April 30th," she exclaimed. (Garza de Cortés, 2006) Appendix 5C provides pertinent Web sites relating to more information about *Día* history and programs for communities and libraries. The Texas State Library and Archives Commission has developed resources that can be used for programming and can be very useful as a starting point, found at www.texasdia.org. Unfortunately, the Web site is no longer being maintained, so for your convenience we are providing updated links (at the time of press) that you can substitute for inactive links.

Día resource links

For the "papel picado art link" use:
www.tsl.state.tx.us/ld/projects/ninos/papel.html.
For the "bookmarks master link" use:
www.tsl.state.tx.us/ld/projects/ninos/bookmarks.html.
For the words and music to the Día song use:
www.tsl.state.tx.us/ld/projects/ninos/song.html.

Infants

One example of a successful infant program comes from the Columbia Pike Branch Library in Virginia, which offered a lapsit storytime to teach teen parents about reading readiness and early literacy concepts so that they could read to their infant children. The parents were attending an alternative high school, the Arlington Public Schools Career Center in Arlington county, Virginia, which partners with the library on a regular basis. Because the Latino culture emphasizes the extended family, this type of program recognizes the reality of working parents and offers practical experience to those studying for early childhood education degrees.

An important factor to be aware of when planning programs for infants is that they should be only 10 to 15 minutes long, owing to the short attention span of the children. Rose Treviño provides suggestions for an effective program. "The attention span for toddlers is very short. Share a story and then recite a nursery rhyme or sing a song." (Immroth, 2000: 25) The attention span does not increase very much for the next age group of children.

Preschool Children

If you do not have a bilingual staff person, bilingual storyhours can still be presented in your library. Invite someone who is bilingual, such as a Latino parent or grandparent, to volunteer to read and do Spanish fingerplays, or to train staff to do them. Appendix D at the end of this chapter includes a few examples.

The North Central Regional Library (Washington) has offered storytimes without bilingual staff in the past. At the Bridgeport Library, a preschool staff member shared the reading responsibility during bilingual storytime for EPIC preschoolers. For the Cashmere Library, the storytime was not completely bilingual. Instead, Linda Finkle invited the translator from Head Start to join her for the storytime, where she incorporated a Spanish-English presentation of one simple book, usually a concept book (colors, numbers, and so on) with very limited text, into her English-language programming. The storytime became interactive, with both adults first pronouncing the words in English and Spanish and the children repeating after them. (Neumiller, 1997)

If you have favorite fingerplays that you use with your monolingual English-speaking children, ask a local Spanish teacher or a Latino to volunteer translating these fingerplays into Spanish. Also, you can get great ideas for bilingual story hour from the REFORMA Web site under the "Children and Young Adult Services Committee," and recommended books from a book written by Tim Wadham, *Programming with Latino Children's Materials*, which provides extensive resources and a wealth of information that will serve anyone in programming for Latino children in public and school libraries. (Wadham, 1999)

The Aurora Public Library (Colorado), which knows that children are very comfortable using computers at an early age, has a project to address the need for toddlers to have good content online. The KidsOnline project is a multilingual feature on the Library's Web site providing activities such as stories for children of all ages. Parents and their toddlers can listen to stories in Spanish that will entertain them as well as improve their literacy goals. (B. Baxendale, personal communication, July 23, 2006)

School Children

The Mary Ann Mongan branch of Kenton County Public Library (Covington, Kentucky) created *De Colores* Bilingual Storytime in fall 2002. The format was a 90-minute Saturday morning storytime held once each month. For the bilingual stories and poems, Sarah P. Howrey, the youth services librarian, enlisted the help of her Spanish-speaking community *compadres* to sing and read in Spanish. The meeting room in the library was always decorated in advance with flags representing the various Latino subgroups in the community, piñatas, fiesta flags, and a large selection of bilingual ALA posters. (Howrey, 2003)

In addition to live music, the distribution of confetti-filled egg shells or *cascarones* (Pavon and Borrego, 2003) and the singing of *De colores* as a tribute to United Farm Workers of America leader Cesar E. Chavez were repeated at each storytime. Involvement of partner or community *compadres* led to the success of the series. (Howrey, 2003)

Summer reading programs are always a great mainstay of children's programming. Bilingual programs and materials will definitely make some Latino children feel more comfortable with the programs and if you can design your regular summer program to include bilingual activities or books, please do so. For those of you in the Summer Reading Program cooperative, Spanish-language materials are provided as regular resources or can be ordered from companies providing supplies and promotional materials to libraries.

We mentioned this in the first edition, but it is a fun program idea and worth mentioning again: Show Disney films for a month. Many of your Latino children will probably be bilingual, and they will enjoy Disney films. If you have DVD equipment, a DVD with language preference will allow you to show the film in Spanish. This was a successful program at South Chula Vista (California) Library. You can introduce reading materials and activities on the theme or characters in each Disney film.

Programs on live animals, all kinds of music programs, bilingual puppeteers and clowns work well for this age group. We realize that these resources may not be available to you right now, but it doesn't hurt to look for them in the Latino community. Work with your local Division of Wildlife for programming ideas and animals available for use in library programming. If there is a local or regional pet store, form a partnership with the owners; they will have all kinds of animals—ferrets, parrots, snakes, fish, and many more!

Any program involving the library and showcasing the talent of Latino children will not only bring the Latino adults and family members into the library but will also instill pride and reinforce self-esteem in the school children. For this you can partner with your parks & recreation department or a city/county museum that might be interested in coordinating an art show for local students.

Some libraries are recruiting and exposing children to the library profession. In Spring Valley (California), elementary students that partake in

"Librarians in Training" learn about providing service to others. They are taught how to use library resources, which is a personal benefit, and how to treat their peers as customers. We loved this program idea! Additionally, the library benefits from the possibility that these bilingual children will become its future volunteers, pages, staff, and librarians. (A. Guerrero, personal communication, November 7, 2006)

TEEN (YOUNG ADULT) PROGRAMS

Although teens are a challenging group to attract, in general, music, animals, sports, and *food* will usually work, and there is a definite need to reach out to them. With information technology developing as it is and with public libraries offering Internet access, technology might also draw Latino young adults to the library.

One program aimed at teens (ages 16–19) who are reluctant readers or new to reading English is called Selections of Arlington Readers or SOAR. It was started in 2000 and is a collaboration between the library and the Arlington (Virginia) Public Schools Career Center, an alternative high school. In order to effectively work with the teens, their reading levels were first assessed and found to be between 2nd- and 4th-grade reading level. The reading specialist at the school works closely with the librarian and they have devised a program that includes visits to the library, a bi-weekly lunch with the librarian where pizza and soda are provided while the students discuss what they are reading, listen to author lectures, and more. The goal of the program is to introduce the concept of reading for pleasure, demonstrate the fundamentals of book discussion and review, and teach the process of how to recommend books to others. The students enrolled in the program have been improving their reading skills and test scores and have embraced the reading environment, making frequent trips to the library on their own. The program is included here because the largest linguistic minority in Arlington County (Columbia Pike area) Virginia are Spanish speakers and at least one of every five Arlington county residents is foreign born. (T. Bissessar, personal communication, October 28, 2006)

The Caribbean Festival, one of many multicultural events held at the Broward County Main Library in Ft. Lauderdale (Florida) was a teen-generated event. Members of the Teen Advisory Board (TAB), many of whom had roots in the Caribbean, planned a program that showcased cultural traditions with teen storytelling, music (calypso provided by Invaders of Steel Band), craft projects for children, a limbo contest, and a food tasting table. Along with their activities, the teens planned a Caribbean Tourist Center that would show continuous videos of the islands and display complementary brochures. With the help of the young adult services librarian, Sylvia R. Wexler, the library staff was informed of the program.

Many of the staff volunteered to prepare traditional dishes, or to assist. This was a unique event for the library—all staff (even those not part of the youth services section) became involved in this program. Of course this created buzz, and the marketing department provided signs and press releases for publicity, which resulted in teens calling the library to volunteer their time and talents! The partners included the Friends of the Library, the International Club at Dillard High School, the Revelacion Troupe, a Haitian teen dance ensemble from Sunrise Middle School, the Puerto Rico Tourist Company, an array of tourist promotion agencies, and a local radio station that advertised the festival in Creole to their non–English speaking listeners. Planning was instrumental in the creation and promotion of this first-time event held in January 2000, to celebrate Caribbean Heritage Month. (Wexler, 2001)

Remember that even if you do not have the expertise to offer bilingual teen programming, your marketing and publicity materials for all teen programs should still be bilingual. Parents who are monolingual in Spanish need to know about teen programs so that their teens can be encouraged to participate.

ADULT PROGRAMS

The results of your Latino community needs assessment can provide useful information on the types of programs that might be popular with adults. We recommend that at all adult programs you display a variety of adult materials, including self-help materials and reading lists for the adults. To promote library card registration, set up a table at the program.

Boulder Public Library in Boulder, Colorado, has been very aggressive in outreach to its Latino community (www.boulder.lib.co.us) and provided the bilingual flyers describing the library's outreach program. (See Figure 5.5) A very visible community program series that they offered is entitled *Caras de la Vida Latino Americana* (Faces of Latin American Life). The beauty of the series is that the library partners with the Boulder ESL program, and the ESL students do most of the presentations in the series. This is a win-win situation. The students' involvement in the series helps them with their English skills and also helps develop their self-esteem and self-confidence, while the library benefits from programming that offers cultural awareness to its community. One such series celebrates *El Día de los muertos*, in which the library invites the whole community to set up *altar* exhibits. Each *altar* display allows the organization to provide information on what their purpose/activities are and what they do in the community. Although this day is intended to promote multicultural experiences, there is a large contingent of Latino community groups that participate. These include groups such as El Centro Amistad, which concentrates on immigration challenges, a local Spanish-language bookstore, and Boulder County Latina Women's League. Other examples of Boulder's programs focus on Latin American food and dance. The library then provides displays of books available for checkout that complement the programs in the series. (G. Elturk, personal communication, October 19, 2006)

Boulder Public Library also partners with the Boulder Community Action Programs and offers citizenship classes. Additionally, they offer Conversations in English, a program for non–English speakers in which the topics are book talks. This program was an award winner at the American Library Association's 1998 Diversity Fair. It was also a semifinalist in the 1999 Innovations in American Government program that is co-sponsored by the Ford Foundation, the John F. Kennedy School of Government at Harvard University, and the Council for Excellence in Government. A bilingual program series entitled *Noches Latinas* (Latin Nights) offers bilingual presentations of various topics that would be of interest to Boulder's Latino community. The library used community volunteers as program presenters. Figure 5-6 illustrates the bilingual Web page flyer for this program.

One of the most successful ongoing programs of Boulder Public Library, and also an excellent example of partnerships, is the annual Boulder Public Library Latino Poetry Festival. This event, centered on poets and poetry readings, also includes performances by musicians, food, books for sale, and other attractions. Figures 5-7a and 5.7b show both the English and Spanish versions for the Latino Poetry Festival flyer for 2006. (G. Elturk, personal communication, October 19, 2006)

You have probably noticed that many of the programs listed are not vastly different from adult programming that you are already offering. Almost all adult programming you currently offer would be of interest to your Latino adults, with two modifications: Your flyers and publicity should be bilingual, and your programs should be bilingual, which is why we have provided you with the examples from Boulder Public Library as a model of attractive and professional library promotional material.

Consult the data from your community analysis as to the programs most in demand by Latino adults in your own community. Most adults, in general, want to improve their lives (socially and economically); Latino adults are no different. Programs on self-help, coping skills, and improving job skills should attract Latino adults. You can consult our "Tips for Planning Adult Programs" at Appendix 5E to make sure your preparation goes smoothly.

In 2006, the Des Plaines Public Library (Illinois) was the only library offering computer classes in Spanish in Cook County. The model was developed during an 18-month pilot program by Webjunction, an online community with a Spanish Language Outreach Program. The classes are one-and-a-half hours in duration and are offered both at the library and at a local high school. Skills such as setting up a free e-mail account and basics about the Internet are taught, as well as tips for searching the Spanish-language media online and instruction in many Microsoft applications. The most popular applications are MS Powerpoint and Photoshop because they can be used to design and make items appropriate for *quinceañeras* and weddings. The attendance at the classes is very diverse—adults aged 18 to 80 years old want to learn and become proficient in computer use. Keys to the success of these classes has been offering them consistently (weekly in this case), making them free, and offering childrens' programming

Figure 5-5. Boulder Public Library Bilingual Community Outreach Flyers

Figure 5-6. Bilingual Web Page Flyer—Latino Nights

(Permission to adapt and reproduce granted by the Boulder Public Library.)

Figure 5-7a. Latino Poetry Festival Flyer—English

Figure 5-7b. Latino Poetry Festival Flyer—Spanish

(storytimes, drawing, etc.) simultaneously so that parents can concentrate on the material in class.

In preparing to launch a literacy program for Latinos, the Des Plaines Public Library was working on assisting librarians to collaborate with community leaders. The staff encountered an early challenge because the Latino community had not identified more than a couple of leaders. The library resolved the dilemma by partnering with the United States Hispanic Leadership Institute, which has an office in Chicago. This organization offers a grassroots program in several states, including Arizona, Tennessee, and Minnesota: their goal here was to prepare Latinos in the Cook County service area to understand and deal more effectively with public agencies, school districts, and government and elected officials. There were 30 persons who signed up for the Institute, 25 of whom actually completed the training and received certificates.

The library was instrumental in providing this opportunity, and as a result the Des Plaines Hispanic Advisory Council was formed and the community now felt a strong connection to the library. Figures 5-8a and 5-8b

---

Our Mission:

The Hispanic Advisory Council of Des Plaines exists to address issues affecting the Hispanic population of Des Plaines Area to foster and coordinate efforts of people and organizations serving the Hispanic community of Des Plaines.

Participants:

Des Plaines Public Library, The Salvation Army, Oakton Community College, St. Mary Church—Heart of Mary, Access/Genesis Center for Health Empowerment, United States Hispanic Leadership Institute, Chamber of Commerce members and others.

LINKS	SUBCOMMITTEES
Membership	Adult Education
Calendar	Children's Education
HGLDP	Substance Abuse

Figure 5-8a. The Des Plaines Hispanic Advisory Council Mission Statement—English

(Permission to adapt and reproduce granted by Alma Read, President, the Des Plaines Hispanic Advisory Council.)

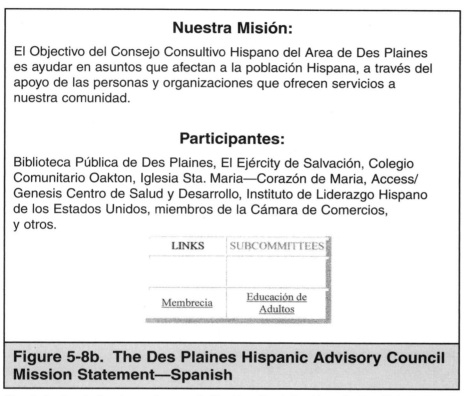

Nuestra Misión:

El Objectivo del Consejo Consultivo Hispano del Area de Des Plaines es ayudar en asuntos que afectan a la población Hispana, a través del apoyo de las personas y organizaciones que ofrecen servicios a nuestra comunidad.

Participantes:

Biblioteca Pública de Des Plaines, El Ejércity de Salvación, Colegio Comunitario Oakton, Iglesia Sta. Maria—Corazón de Maria, Access/ Genesis Centro de Salud y Desarrollo, Instituto de Liderazgo Hispano de los Estados Unidos, miembros de la Cámara de Comercios, y otros.

LINKS	SUBCOMMITTEES
Membrecia	Educación de Adultos

Figure 5-8b. The Des Plaines Hispanic Advisory Council Mission Statement—Spanish

(Permission to adapt and reproduce granted by Alma Read, President, the Des Plaines Hispanic Advisory Council.)

show the bilingual Mission Statements at the Web site for this council. In an effort to partner, the community has been receptive and very supportive of the library, which it values as its center for economic and social development. (H. Marino, personal communication, November 4, 2006)

In many cases, libraries have integrated general programming involving literacy, the General Equivalency Diploma (GED), English for Speakers of Other Languages (ESOL) or English as a Second Language (ESL) classes, and citizenship. An opportunity to partner with the providers of adult education in your community is a great way to catch up with the trend if your system does not or can not offer any of these programs already. In the Tulsa City-County (Oklahoma) Library System, the English classes taught at the Hispanic Resource Center, Martin Regional Library, are done so in partnership with Oral Roberts University and Tulsa Community College. (S. Martínez, personal communication, November 4, 2006)

Boulder Public Library consistently offers programming on citizenship and immigration issues. Figure 5-9 is an excerpt from the library's Web page describing the library's commitment to help Latinos with these issues.

- **Citizenship and Immigration Issues:**

The Outreach Librarian is a member of "Boulder County Immigration Advocacy Coalition." The Library's role is to make current resources (print and nonprint) available for people who are in the process of applying for U.S. Citizenship, and for teachers and organizationas who are involved in teaching and helping the immigrants in this process. Library meeting and conference rooms are also made available for their use. Classes are conducted on a regular basis by two Immigration Lawyers recruited by the Outreach.

Looking at the needs of the Immigrant Community, the Coalition is offering two classes to meet these needs. The first one is ESL, and the second one is U.S. History and Civics. Volunteers are being trained in the library by ESL teachers and by the two immigration lawyers.

The Outreach Program is offering one-on-one help with studying U.S. History and Civics course work that is for the naturalization test. The Outreach Program matches immigrants who are at the last stage of the process with volunteers who will help them study and take practice tests. No legal help is offered through the Outreach Program.

Figure 5-9. Boulder Public Library's Commitment to Latinos

(Excerpt from Web page of Boulder Public Library, Boulder, CO.)

MAXIMIZING PROGRAMMING RESOURCES

When you are ready to develop programs and services specifically for Latinos in your community, you will have at your disposal many good resources to assist you from the library literature. Individuals or organizations play a vital role in helping the library to offer programs. Most organizations or agencies will provide programming for free. Individuals, on the other hand, may not, especially if their program specialty is their livelihood. If that is the case, we suggest you operate by the "four Ifs:"

1. If you do not have funds to pay for programs, ask the individual to consider doing them for free.
2. If you can offer a small honorarium, do so.
3. If the individual does not waive a fee, try to negotiate a lower fee.
4. If you cannot negotiate a lower fee and you really want the individual, then ask an external funding source—for example, the Friends group, a local business, or a civic organization—for funds.

```
Individual/Organization Name _____
_____
Address _____
Telephone _____Fax _____
E-mail_____
Program Services Provided_____
                         _____
                         _____
                         _____
Equipment Necessary
                         _____
Other Special Requirements _____
                         _____
                         _____
                         _____
Fee $ _____    Negotiable:  Yes _____  No_____
Honorarium $ _____
Notes:
_____
_____
```

Figure 5-10. Library Programming Resource Form

If you do not already have one, you need to develop a "Programming Resource File," either in a print or digitized format. This file should contain the names of individuals, organizations, or agencies that have done or are willing to do programs for the library. Figure 5-10 is a sample Programming Resource Form; adapt it as you see fit. Make sure, however, to update it as changes occur.

DEVELOPING PARTNERSHIPS

Partnerships involve a different kind of networking that libraries may or may not be used to. They are absolutely crucial to your success in offering programs and services to your Latino community. Most public libraries already have some external partnerships established to help in some library programs for the general public. The terms *networking* and *collaboration* will all be used interchangeably in the following discussion to connote an extremely important concept.

The importance of partnerships will be discussed and tips on how to establish external partnerships with organizations in and outside the Latino community will be given. We provide a list of the types of groups with which you can establish partnerships and real-life examples of successful library partnerships.

ESTABLISHING A PARTNERSHIP

Partnerships are formed because neither partner has all the resources to meet its challenges on its own. We recognize that going out into the Latino community may be new to some of you, and these specific guidelines about what to do and how to do it are meant to assist you as you accept this challenge of forming new partnerships. Keep reminding yourself that it will be mutually beneficial for the library and your partner. Following are some general suggestions for facing this challenge:

1. Identify the library project that will require an external partner and list the partner possibilities.

2. Obtain the name of the head of the organization and his or her proper title, mailing address, telephone number, and e-mail address for every potential partner on your Latino project list.

3. Perform research on each group or organization you plan to approach so that you are familiar with their missions, vision statements, annual reports, and so on. Some of the organizations you approach may have only Latino clients; others may have Latinos as only part of their client base.

4. Develop a letter to send or e-mail to each group requesting their assistance. Figure 5-11 is a sample of such a letter. You may want to send it as an e-mail attachment, but if you come from a small community, a phone call may suffice. However, you may need to approach organizations at the county level for assistance, in which case a letter would be best. Follow up with an e-mail or telephone call.

5. Create a short survey form to accompany the letter. Figure 5-12 is an example of such a form; feel free to modify it to fit your library/community needs. The results of the survey can be used to develop a community organization/agency database for possible partnerships with the library; to establish a bilingual directory of

February 1, 2008

Mr. Joe Baca
Director
Housing and Urban Development
123 Park Street
Somewhere, Colorado 80000

Dear Mr. Baca:

The Somewhere Public Library recognizes the need to assist all our residents with their information and recreational reading needs. We are in the process of extending our library services to our underserved Latino community. We realize that these services are long past due, and we are aggressively trying to meet those needs.

I understand that HUD has a series of programs that you offer to the community on housing issues such as tenants' rights, home safety, and effective weatherization. I also understand that you have been challenged with finding sites that are open in the evening to offer these programs. The public library could help you with this and offer some additional benefits to your programs. Would your agency be interested in cooperating with the public library in a partnership that would enhance assistance to our Latino community?

I am including a short form that should take no more than ten minutes for you to complete and return. Someone from my administration or I will personally contact you as a follow-up to the survey.

The Somewhere Public Library looks forward to talking with you about a possible partnership to benefit our Latino community.

Sincerely,

Mary Little
Director

Figure 5-11. Sample Letter to Local Organizations

organizations and agencies for the Latino community's use; to send e-mails or mailings announcing library events and programs; and to ask an organization to distribute items such as library program flyers. The form can also easily be adapted and sent to individuals with whom the library might want to establish a partnership.

Update the database information at least annually. This would be a good project for a staff member or volunteer who has certain database software knowledge and skills.

1. Organization/agency name _____
   _____

2. Name of head/contact person _____
   _____

3. Address _____

4. Telephone _____

5. Fax _____

6. E-mail_____

7. Description of organization:

   _____
   _____
   _____
   _____

8. Services and/or programs offered by your organization:

   _____
   _____
   _____
   _____

9. Would your organization be willing to work in a partnership with the public library
   to help meet the information needs of our Latino community? ___Yes ___No
   Comments:

   _____
   _____
   _____
   _____

Figure 5-12. Sample Community Organization/Agency Partnerships Form

6. We suggest that you keep a print form or database of these resources. Figures 5-13 and 5-14 are samples of a form for supporting partners.

COLLABORATING ON PROGRAMS AND SERVICES

Be sincere about the library's commitment to reach out to the Latino community; if you are not sincere, that community will see right through you.

Business				
Address				
Phone Number	Fax Number			
Contact Person				
E-mail				
DATES	LIBRARY EVENT	RESOURCES PROVIDED	RESTRICTIONS	THANK YOU SENT

Figure 5-13. Sample Local Business Resource for Library Events Form

Business	*Martinez Grocery*			
Address	*123 Main Street, Somewhere, CO*			
Phone Number	*462-3511*	Fax Number *462-3512*		
Contact Person	*Rudy Martinez*			
E-mail				
DATES	LIBRARY EVENT	RESOURCES PROVIDED	RESTRICTIONS	THANK YOU SENT
2-15-08	*Latino Community Library Open House*	*Donuts and punch*	*No delivery/must pick up*	*2-25-08*
5-5-08	*Cinco de Mayo Celebration & Program*	*Paper plates, tableware, etc.*	*No delivery*	*5-10-08*

Figure 5-14. Sample Local Business Resource for Library Events Form—Completed

Once you have a database of partners and are ready to proceed further in collaborating on a project, some general guidelines may be useful. To further illustrate our point, we will use a hypothetical scenario in which your library has written a proposal to fund next year's *Día* celebration. Always optimistic, we will assume that you received the necessary funding to hold a series of events leading up to a three-hour Saturday morning program. The local discount store has agreed to be one of the partners in this venture. Here are some general guidelines for you to consider and/or adapt:

1. Set your mutual goals/objectives/activities for the program with your partner (these are probably already listed in the proposal you submitted). Make sure that goals/objectives/activities are agreed upon. In general, the library wants to raise awareness of the celebration

and for the program to be successful in the Latino community; the discount store wants more visibility in the Latino community in the hopes of increasing their customer base and generating interest about job opportunities for any bilingual/bicultural persons who seek employment.

More specifically, the library may set numerical goals that are easily evaluated. For example: *In the first year of operation, the library will sign up 25 Latino students and their families to attend the Día kickoff events to be held in April.*

The discount store's goal could be: *The ABC Mart will supply in-kind refreshments and incentive prizes for the culminating event on the weekend of the Día kickoff celebration.* (Remember, hypothetically, your grant included the funds to help defray the costs of the performers/author honoraria.)

2. The library and its partner need to agree on who is responsible for what activities and the time line for those activities.

3. The library and its partner need to agree on the related costs. Again, these are probably delineated in the proposal. Nonetheless, it is important that the responsibility for expenses and costs be mutually agreed on.

4. To protect both partners, agree to everything in writing. A "Memorandum of Understanding" or an "Agreement" is suggested. Include a paragraph here on what you agree will occur if a cancellation by either partner takes place (such as an agreement that any deposits or down payments will be returned or that a letter will go out from the Library to all the parties notifying of the cancellation). Specifying all of the above will help to prevent any misunderstandings.

5. Some of the partnerships you establish will be with organizations/agencies that are operated by Latinos solely for Latinos. How you approach and work with them can make or break your efforts. Following are some tips for the novice to consider:

   • If you are not familiar with Latino culture and customs, get the advice of someone who is. Identify a Latino you respect in the community; you can probably think of one right this minute. Contact that person to help you with advice on the best ways to approach certain Latino organizations or individuals.

- Be sincere about the library's commitment to reach out to the Latino community; if you are not sincere, that community will see right through you.

- Be assertive, but not pushy. If you don't get a response from the survey form, call the organization and talk to the director or head. The letter serves as a form of introduction; don't be deterred if you don't get an immediate response.

- As a follow-up, visit the local organization, agency, or group. Taking the time to do this demonstrates a real interest and commitment on the library's part. It also enables you to put a face with the name and to communicate with these contacts at other events; it personalizes your efforts.

These general guidelines will get you started in your efforts to form community partnerships in efforts to serve Latinos.

IDENTIFYING POSSIBLE PARTNERS

You will be surprised by the number of organizations and individuals with whom you can collaborate, regardless of the size of your community. Since your aim is to attract and serve Latino residents in your community, arrange for the programs to be bilingual or in Spanish and the partnerships to be with organizations that have an interest in offering services in Spanish as well. We list below some organizations/individuals for you to consider.

Public Education

Public education includes the gamut of K–12 and higher education institutions. It also includes the various organizations within those institutions, such as clubs—including honor societies, Spanish clubs, business clubs, specific Latino student clubs, other service clubs that work on community projects—as well as Parent Teacher Organizations, university faculty spouses clubs, and college fraternities and sororities. The public library serving its Latino community should be considered as a potential partner in the projects of any of these organizations.

If your school district supports a bilingual education program, establishing partnerships with the bilingual education director and teachers is crucial. These individuals can be instrumental in providing Spanish-language assistance. You can hire them, if library funds are available, as translators for programming and for promotional materials. If there are no funds, you can ask them to volunteer. In exchange, the library could provide special story hours for children in the bilingual education classes.

Do not forget about the school administrators or their boards at each level of the public education sector. These are also important groups that could lend support to education/public library partnerships.

Social Services Agencies

Various government agencies (such as the Social Security office, job services office, health and medical clinics, legal aid, welfare office, migrant services, or immigration services) already provide services to the Latino community. These agencies can provide you with formal and informal Latino leaders or information about those leaders, as well as expertise that would be very relevant for programs held in the library. They can also be vehicles for promoting library programs and services to the Latino community by means of newsletters and bulletin boards.

Other Service Organizations

Other service organizations could include ESOL (English for Speakers of Other Languages) or ESL (English as a Second Language) and literacy programs. These services are very popular with Latino immigrants, and if they are not offered by the library, then collaboration with these groups is essential. The library has many support services (materials, programs, access to the Internet, locations) that can be of benefit to Latino clients.

Churches and Religious Organizations

Ascertain which churches have a considerable number of Latinos as parishioners. Introduce yourself to the clergy of the church and establish a professional relationship between the church and the library. The same goes for religious organizations or clubs. With these clubs, you will be working directly with their membership.

Once a relationship is established, churches are great for advertising library programs to the Latino community. Library programs can be listed in the church's newsletter, on church bulletin boards, or linked to the church Web page. If the church has a bazaar, the library can request to set up a booth staffed by Latino library staff or volunteers to talk about library programs and encourage library card applications.

Fine Arts Organizations, Museums, Galleries

The partnerships with these organizations are limitless. Collaboration with any of these groups could include joint art and museum exhibits, multicultural programs and festivals, or fine arts programs for Latino children and adults.

Police and Fire Departments and Societies

Law enforcement agencies offer many possibilities for joint projects that serve all age groups of Latinos. Because these organizations often share a "funding pie" with the public library, their respective boards/commissions welcome collaborative efforts to serve the Latino community.

Professional Associations

Associations such as the local bar association and the medical association can be instrumental in providing library programs on topics that are relevant to the Latino community. Other professional groups might include certified public accountants, realtors, bankers, engineers, dentists, veterinarians, and nurses. Additionally, in larger communities or in surrounding areas that include more than one community, there may be professional associations whose members are primarily from the Latino community. Don't be afraid to approach any of these groups. They usually have similar goals, such as trying to meet the needs of the minority communities, and are very willing to share their expertise with the library.

Community Service Clubs

Clubs such as Kiwanis, Lions, Soroptimist, Rotary, and Sertoma also are involved in service projects to the community. They provide excellent resources, especially human resources, for collaborative programs.

The Friends of the Library

A great partner for our library systems continues to be the Friends of the Library groups. If there is not a Friends or *Amigos de la Biblioteca* group in operation in your community, it is worth the time to cultivate one! These organizations are usually incorporated as 501(c)(3) charitable organizations, which qualifies them for certain types of grant funding. We encourage you to approach your Friends group with creative ideas that the library would normally not be able to accomplish and/or fund alone.

Local Businesses

Fast-food chains (such as McDonald's, Chick-Fil-A, Burger King), as well as grocery stores and other local businesses in small communities, are usually willing to collaborate with the public library on their efforts to reach the Latino community. Because the Latino population in most communities continues to increase in size, these collaborative efforts provide great marketing and advertising for local businesses. They may not be willing to give the library funds, but they are usually more than willing to provide free supplies and food for library programs and events.

Day Care Centers

Day care centers are great partners with which to collaborate on developing programs for preschool children. They are a human resource for bilingual story hours and are also another link to Latino parents. They can assist in marketing all your programs to Latino parents by distributing flyers, hanging posters, and including library program announcements in their newsletters to parents.

Sports Teams/Individual Athletes

With Latinos becoming major players in such sports as baseball, soccer, football, and boxing, these groups might be great partners in library programming efforts. Also, sports training programs and schools (such as martial arts, gymnastics, and tennis) should be approached as potential partners.

MAKING THE PARTNERSHIP A SUCCESS

We mentioned earlier that the libraries we visited had very strong partnerships with groups in their communities. We want to share here some of those successes.

Arlington Public Library

The Arlington Public Library collaborated with the Arlington Virginia Network cable television (AVN 74) to air once a week their "Cuentos y mas" program that promotes reading among children. The bilingual program features stories from all over the Spanish-speaking world and provides an opportunity for viewers to hear the music and learn about the food from the country where the featured stories originate. It is an interactive program that highlights reading and having fun. The host is Mariela Aguilar, a bilingual librarian with the Columbia Pike Branch. She worked in outreach to the community and was responsible for partnerships with the community centers of low-income housing projects prior to focusing on her storytelling ability. The system has offered a lot of support and training to Ms. Aguilar, who, for example, attended the workshops at Centro Barahona para el Estudio del Libros Infantiles y Juveniles en Español (Barahona Center for the Study of Books in Spanish for Children and Adolescents) at California State University–San Marcos. Ms. Aguilar works primarily on the researching and producing of "*Cuentos y mas*," which airs daily before and after school, at 12:30 p.m., and twice on Saturday mornings for her target audience of Latino and all children ages 4–8. Live feeds and archived video clips may be viewed on the library Web site (www. arlingtonva.us/Departments/Libraries/kids/LibrariesKidsCuentos.aspx). Additionally, *"Cuentos y mas"* has been named Outstanding Children's Program by the Virginia Public Library Directors Association and has received the third-place Programming Award from the National Association of Telecommunications Officers & Advisors (NATOA). Nonprofit or community organizations can obtain a videotape or DVD of the program for airing by contacting the library. (T. Bissessar, personal communication, October 28, 2006)

Boulder Public Library

Boulder Public Library and a community organization, the San Juan del Centro Family Learning Center, have formed a partnership as a result of the library's outreach program. The Centro is a pre-school–Kindergarten learning center predominantly for bilingual Latino children. Upon graduation from the Centro, each child receives two free books from the library—one in English and one in Spanish. Boulder Public Library officials attend each graduation to give these gift books to each child. (G. Elturk, personal communication, October 19, 2006)

San Diego County Library

The Solana Beach Branch of the San Diego County Library (California) has connected effectively with their Latino community in Eden Gardens and surrounding areas. The branch operations manager and the branch librarian joined the Education Coalition, a network created by the Solana Beach Elementary School District to assist Latino children in improving their grades and staying in elementary school. The library is a joint-use library built on the grounds of the Earl Warren Middle School in Solana Beach and an example of a very good partnership. The Education Coalition developed a monthly meeting for parents of students called *Noche de padre* with the goal of reinforcing the importance of education to the parents and children attending schools in their district. These meetings are conducted completely in Spanish to provide education geared to parents. Planned originally for only the months that school was in session, the library staff proposed that during the summer months they continue the education of parents and provide activities for their school-age children. Their concept was a six-week series (one night a week) of seminars for parents in Spanish while story hour or entertainment was provided for their children. They called the series *Noche de familia*. Recruiting volunteers from the community, dubbed *embajadores*, the community was surveyed about what topics were needed and whether they would indeed attend programs from 6 p.m. to 8 p.m. at the library. Enlisting Spanish-speaking volunteers and the fact that the parents were familiar with the evening meetings *de la escuela* (school-related) were key factors for the staff, who approached the project with enthusiasm. The partnership includes the Solana Beach Education Coalition, Boys & Girls Club, Head Start, San Diego County Education Migrant Education Project, Casa de Amistad Tutoring, San Dieguito Adult School, University of California San Diego education department, local businesses, churches, and social service agencies. The library, which incidentally hosts three of the *Noche de padre* meetings annually, was a superb backdrop for the series. The seminars have featured parenting classes and computer instruction *en Español*. For the first time last year, parent leaders actively planned the series for themselves and their peers. This program was awarded the Annual Achievement Award by the National Association of County Governments and the FOLUSA/Baker & Taylor Award by the Friends of the Library USA, both in 2005. (J. Gregg, personal communication, October 28, 2006, and M. Rubalcava, personal communication, October 29, 2006)

Toronto Public Library

The Settlement and Education Partnership in Toronto (SEPT) program in Canada is a partnership between the library and immigrant settlement agencies in Toronto, the Toronto District School Board, and Citizenship and Immigration Canada. It provides free, in-person assistance in many languages to help newcomers find information on job searches, English classes, legal advice, citizenship, immigration, and schools. Workers also introduce library services to adults and children. (Mylopoulos 2004) The purpose of the partnership is to allow the settlement services workers (SSWs) to use the public library as a base to meet families during the summer when school is not in session, as many immigrants arrive in the city near the end of the school year. There is information listed on the "Multicultural Connections" section of the Toronto Public Library Web page and can be accessed at www.tpl.toronto.on.ca/mul_ser_settlement.jsp.

APPENDIX 5A: NATIONAL LATINO HOLIDAYS

Argentina

May 25   National Holiday (Revolución de Mayo)—commemorates the revolution of 1810, which initiated the move toward independence, finally achieved on July 9, 1816.

July 9   Independence Day—commemorates Argentina's declaration of independence from Spain in 1816.

Bolivia

Aug. 6   Independence Day—commemorates Bolivia's achievement of independence from Spain in 1825.

Colombia

July 20   Independence Day—Colombia defies Spanish authority and declares its independence.

Costa Rica

Sept. 15   Independence Day—commemorates the achievement of independence from Spain in 1821.

Cuba

Oct. 10   Beginning of the War of Independence—commemorates the commencement of Cuba's war for independence from Spain.

Chile

Sept. 18   Independence Day—commemorates the end of Chile's allegiance to Spain in 1810 and independence in 1818.

Dominican Republic

Feb. 27   Independence Day—commemorates the 1814 revolt against Haiti, in which independence was regained and the Republic established under Pedro Santana.

Ecuador

Aug. 10   Independence Day—celebrates Ecuador's achievement of independence from Spain in 1822.

Guatemala

Sept. 15   Independence Day—commemorates the achievement of independence from Spain in 1821.

Honduras

Sept. 15   Independence Day—commemorates the achievement of independence from Spain in 1821.

Mexico

May 5   Puebla Battle Day, or Cinco de Mayo—commemorates defeat of Napoleon III's forces in 1867.

Sept. 16	Independence Day—Mexico claims independence from Spain in 1810 (the Republic was established on December 6, 1822).
Nov. 20	Mexican Revolution Anniversary—anniversary of the overthrow of the dictatorship of Porfirio Díaz in 1910.

Nicaragua

Sept. 15	Independence Day—commemorates the achievement of independence from Spain in 1821.

Panama

Nov. 3	Independence Day—celebrates Panama's independence from Colombia in 1903.
Nov. 28	Independence from Spain—celebrates Panama's independence from Spain in 1821.
Dec. 8	Mother's Day—consistent with the celebration of the Immaculate Conception, during which the people of Panama honor all mothers.

Paraguay

May 14	National Flag Day—beginning of a two-day celebration marking the achievement of independence from Spain in 1811.
May 15	Independence Day—celebrates the achievement of independence from Spain in 1811 (the second day of a two-day celebration).

Peru

July 28	Independence Day—celebrates independence from Spain in 1821 (two-day celebration).

Puerto Rico

Jan. 11	De Hostos's Birthday—celebrates the birth of the philosopher and patriot Eugenio María de Hostos (1839).
March 22	Emancipation Day or Abolition Day—commemorates the abolition of slavery on the island in 1873.

El Salvador

Sept. 15	Independence Day—commemorates the achievement of independence from Spain in 1821.

Spain

June 24	King Juan Carlos's Saint's Day

Uruguay

June 19	Artigas Day—commemorates the birthday of General José Gervasio Artigas (1764).
Aug. 25	Independence Day—celebrates independence from Brazil in 1825.

Venezuela

July 5	Independence Day—celebrates Venezuelan declaration of independence from Spain in 1811.
July 24	Bolívar's Birthday—commemorates the birth of Simón Bolívar (1783), the "George Washington" of South America.

APPENDIX 5B: SPANISH WORDS AND PHRASES FOR LIBRARY USE

PRONUNCIATION TIPS

There are many Spanish dialects, each with subtle differences in pronunciation. One example is the differences in pronunciation of the Spanish letter *v*. Some Spanish speakers pronounce the *v* like an English *b*, others pronounce it more like the English *v*, and still others use a pronunciation that falls somewhere in between. Using these pronunciation tips, however, will enable you to be understood by most Spanish speakers.

Spanish Letter = Pronunciation:

a = ah (as in walk)
e = eh (as in leg)
i = ee (as in bee)
o = oh (as in bold)
u = oo (as in hoot)
ge = heh
gi = hee
ga, go, gu = gah, goh, gooh (hard g as in goat)
j = h
ll = y (as in yes)
r = (trill tongue slightly)
rr = (trill tongue heavily)
v = b
y = ee
z = s

BASIC WORDS

English	Spanish	Phonetic (Accent in CAPS)
one	*uno*	OO noh (OO as in hoot)
two	*dos*	dohs
three	*tres*	trehs
four	*cuatro*	KWAH troh
five	*cinco*	SEENK oh
six	*seis*	sais (rhymes with race)
seven	*siete*	see EH teh
eight	*ocho*	OH choh
nine	*nueve*	noo EH beh (oo as in hoot)

ten	*diez*	dee EHS
Sunday	*domingo*	doh MEEN goh
Monday	*lunes*	LOO nehs (oo as in hoot)
Tuesday	*martes*	MAHR tehs
Wednesday	*miércoles*	mee EHR coh lehs
Thursday	*jueves*	WEH behs
Friday	*viernes*	bee EHR nehs
Saturday	*sábado*	SAH bah doh
January	*enero*	eh NEH roh
February	*febrero*	feh BREH roh
March	*marzo*	MAHR soh
April	*abril*	ah BREEL
May	*mayo*	MAH yoh
June	*junio*	HOO nee oh
July	*julio*	HOO lee oh
August	*agosto*	ah GOHS toh
September	*septiembre*	sehp tee EHM breh
October	*octubre*	ok TOO breh
November	*noviembre*	noh vee EHM breh
December	*diciembre*	dee see EHM breh
no	*no*	noh
yes	*sí*	see
hello	*hola*	OH lah
good-bye	*adiós*	ah dee OHS
thank you	*gracias*	GRAH see ahs
you're welcome	*de nada*	deh/ NAH dah

LIBRARY-RELATED WORDS

your address	*su dirección*	soo/ dee rek see OHN
author (male)	*el escritor*	ehl/ eh scree TOHR
author (female)	*la escritora*	lah/ eh scree TOH rah
bathroom	*el baño*	ehl/ BAHN yoh
books	*libros*	LEE bros
boss (male)	*el jefe*	ehl/ HEH feh
boss (female)	*la jefa*	lah/ HEH fah
catalog	*el catálogo*	ehl/ cah TAH loh goh
check out	*tomar prestado*	toh MAHR/ preh STAH doh
children's room	*la sala de niños*	lah/ SAHL lah/ deh/ NEEN yohs
citizenship	*la nacionalidad*	lah/ nah see oh nahl ee DAHD
director (male)	*el director*	ehl/ dee rehk TOHR
director (female)	*la directora*	lah/ dee rehk TOHR ah
driver's license	*licencia de manejar*	lee SEHN see ah/ deh/ mah neh HAHR
entrance	*la entrada*	lah/ ehn TRAH dah

exit	*la salida*	lah/ sah LEE dah
fiction	*la ficción*	lah/ feek see OHN
fine	*la multa*	lah/ MOOL tah
left	*izquierda*	ee skee EHR dah
library card	*la tarjeta*	lah/ tahr HEH tah/ deh/ bee
	de biblioteca	blee oh TEH cah
magazine	*la revista*	lah/ reh BEES tah
nonfiction	*no-ficción*	noh/ feek see OHN
novel	*novela*	noh BEH lah
overdue	*vencido*	ben SEE doh
paperback	*el libro de bolsillo*	ehl/ LEE broh/ deh/ bohl SEE
		yoh
program	*el programa*	ehl/ proh GRAH mah
reference desk	*el mostrador*	ehl/ mohs trah DOHR/ deh/
	de referencia	reh feh REHN see ah
right	*derecha*	deh REH chah
signature	*la firma*	lah/ FEER mah
story hour	*la hora de cuentos*	lah/ OH rah/ deh/ KWEN tohs
table	*la mesa*	lah/ MEH sah
telephone	*el teléfono*	ehl/ teh LEH foh noh
time	*el tiempo*	ehl/ tee EM poh

PHRASES

Good morning	*buenos días*	BWEH nohs/ DEE ahs
Good afternoon	*buenas tardes*	BWEH nahs/ TAHR dehs
Good evening	*buenas noches*	BWEH nahs/ NOH ches
Welcome to the library	*Bienvenidos a la biblioteca*	bee ehn veh NEE dohs/ ah/ lah/ bee blee oh TEH cah
The librarian can help you.	*El bibliotecario* (male) *le puede ayudar*	ehl/ bee blee oh teh CAH ree oh/ leh/ PWEH deh/ ah yoo DAHR
	La bibliotecaria (female) *le deh/ ah yoo*	lah/ bee blee oh teh CAH ree ah/ leh/ *puede ayudar* PWEH DAHR
How are you today?	*¿Cómo está usted hoy?*	COH moh/ ehs TAH/ oo STED/ oy?
Do you speak English?	*¿Habla usted inglés?*	AH blah/oo STEHD/ een GLEHS?
I do not understand.	*No entiendo*	noh/ ehn tee EHN doh
Please speak more slowly.	*Por favor hable más despacio.*	pohr/ fah VOHR/ AH bleh/ mahs/ deh SPAH see oh
Please follow me.	*Por favor sígame*	pohr/ fah VOHR/ SEE gah meh

APPENDIX 5C: DÍA DE LOS NIÑOS/DÍA DE LOS LIBROS

Día National Advisory Committee
www.ala.org/ala/alsc/diadelosninos/contact/contact.htm

Día Founders
www.patmora.com
www.reforma.org

State Web Sites:
El Paso (Texas) Public Library
www.elpasotexas.gov/kidszone/kidszone_library/diadelosninos/diadelos-
ninos.htm

Texas State Library
www.texasdia.org
www.tsl.state.tx.us/ld/projects/ninos/titlecontents.htm

State Library and Archives of Florida
www.diaflorida.com

Home of *Día*
www.ala.org/dia

Contact ALSC at dia@ala.org

Día Celebrations
Click here to read about the variety of events and celebrations that have
been organized.
www.ala.org/ala/alsc/diadelosninos/diacelebrations/diacelebrations.htm

APPENDIX 5D: BILINGUAL FINGERPLAYS

LOS ELEFANTES (THE ELEPHANTS)

(Finger play about elephants)
Un elefante se balanceaba
Sobre la tela de una araña.
Cuando veía como resistía
Fue a llamar a otro elefante.

Dos elefantes se balanceaban
Sobre la tela de una araña.
Cuando veía como resistía
Fue a llamar a otro elefante
Trés...

Cuatro...

Cinco...

LOS POLLITOS (FLUFFY CHICKS)

Los pollitos dicen	Fluffy chicks like singing
Pío, pío, pío	cheep, cheep, cheep
Cuando tienen hambre	whenever they feel hungry
Cuando tienen frío.	Whenever they feel chilly.
La mama les busca	Mama hen now brings them
El maíz y el trigo	wheat and golden corn
Les da la comida	Feeds them tasty dinners
Y les presta abrigo	blankets them with feathers
Bajo sus dos alas,	Huddled all together
Acurracaditos	under her two wings
Hasta el otro día	till the break of dawn
Duermen los pollitos	the fluffy chicks will dream.

Permission to reprint fingerplays granted by L. Zwick and O. Garza de Cortés from *Rimas y cancioncitas para niños,* and L. DeArce, *Arrorro, mi niño, Latino Lullabies and Gentle Games.* Copyright © 2004 by Lulu Delacre; permission arranged by Lee & Low Books, NY, NY 10016. Selections were made by Ms. Veronica Maciel, Spanish-language story-time coordinator, San Diego County Library, November 2006.

APPENDIX 5E: TIPS FOR PLANNING LIBRARY PROGRAMS FOR ADULTS

MAKING CONTACTS:

T   Utilize local talent when available. For example, if a neighborhood community center has a dance group that performs for events, invite the group to perform for an audience at the library.

T   Talk to your staff, friends, customers. If they know of any individuals with special talents (authors, musicians, artists, dancers, for example) that can be showcased for a library event, ask them to follow up with more information. This can be a potentially good source for a library program.

T   Conventions/conferences are good places to make contacts with authors, publishers, and illustrators, as program possibilities.

BOOKING THE PROGRAM

T   When booking a program, confirm the fee and the performer's contact information.

T   Discuss payment options; it is a good idea to ask the performer to bring an invoice on the day of program. If the program is free, this should be made clear to all parties involved.

T   Verify if there are any special needs such as audiovisual equipment or a special room arrangement.

T   Give precise directions to the library and instructions for parking.

T   Send a letter to the performer confirming time, place, and other program details.

T   Reconfirm with the performer at least one week before the scheduled program.

PUBLICIZING THE PROGRAM

T   Assure a good turnout by publicizing the program to the intended audience. Adult programs do not usually draw the large crowds that attend children's programs. But even if the audience is small, you have reached an important segment of your community.

T   Create a flyer that is attractive and gives the necessary information: who, what, when, where, contact person, length of program.

Distribute the flyer in person, if possible, to community centers, churches, shopping centers, local schools (especially adult schools offering ESL classes), senior centers, etc.

T   Talk it up to customers (and ask staff to talk it up). Record a message on the voice mail so incoming callers hear bout the event.

T   Create a display in the library that highlights the upcoming program.

T   Look for Web sites that publicize Latino events in your community at no charge and get yours listed.

T   Write a press release for local newspapers and invite reporters to cover the event. Also, send the press release to radio and television stations that do public service announcements.

T   Encourage local teachers/professors to give extra credit to their students who attend an author or other program at the library.

DAY OF THE PROGRAM

T   Have a sign-up sheet for program attendees. If you also ask for addresses, you can add these individuals to your mailing list and keep them informed of future programs.

T   During the introduction to the program, take the opportunity to highlight other upcoming programs or library services to the audience.

T   Take photos and send them to the performer as a memory of the event, add them to the library's scrapbook, include them in the library newsletter, and use them for future displays.

T   Distribute evaluations to be completed after the program. Ask attendees to let you know how they heard about the program. This will help determine the most effective methods of publicity.

AFTER THE PROGRAM

T   Review evaluations.

T   Write thank-you letters/notes.

Prepared by Linda Chavez Doyle, REFORMA President 2003/2004, for: En Vivo! Live! Library Programs for Latino Adults.

6 REACHING THE LATINO COMMUNITY

CONFRONTING THE CHALLENGES

> *Recognizing the growth of the Latino population is a first step toward developing library outreach to a target population. However, it is also important to understand what the information needs of the community are (Bala and Adkins, 2004: 120)*

This chapter focuses on two main areas. In the first, we concentrate on how to conduct effective outreach to attract Latinos in your community. In the second area, we offer advice on planning the marketing and public relations of library programs and services to the Latino community. We have included some examples of successful program flyers used by libraries we researched.

Public libraries have no uniform standard or basic outreach practice, so some libraries are funded with multiple staff that coordinate an office or department that can offer an advanced level of service. Others have no formal coordinating outreach service office or unit, but use general fund money to assertively connect with emerging ethnic user groups. Most libraries, at this time, do not have the funds to develop a comprehensive outreach services program, much less hire an outreach coordinator—although they can write a proposal for funds to develop such a program.

Funds to recruit and hire an outreach coordinator and to develop plans and services for serving your Latino community would be used to help you apply the knowledge you are gaining. We encourage you to pursue this because it is important. However, it presents a significant challenge to the library system of sustainability once the funding period expires.

How well do you know your Latino community? Keep in mind that nothing can be done in terms of outreach and marketing until your library has reviewed and designed programs and services that will attract Latinos. You need to have programs to promote that are the result of some type of Latino community analysis (see Chapter 4).

Remember that although your library already has programs and services in place that can be of interest to Latinos, there probably is no systematic outreach and marketing to attract them to your library for some of the basic services already provided. You can start at this fundamental level while you develop some specialized programs to interest them.

Here are some other challenges for you to consider:

- the language barrier
- cost factors (for example, late fees and fines for lost books)
- distrust of another white institution
- recent immigration to the United States from various Latin American countries
- undocumented immigrant status
- unfamiliarity with free library services

Dealing with all these challenges at once may seem overwhelming to you. Remember, however, that you need to take the overall challenge of reaching out and serving Latino residents step by step. Approach this challenge by attending first to those outreach efforts that are attainable and within your current staffing and funding levels.

> Approach this challenge by attending first to those outreach efforts that are attainable and within your current staffing and funding levels.

Have you come to the conclusion that you don't have funds to hire an outreach librarian or to develop and implement an in-depth outreach services plan? Don't let that stop you. There are three areas of outreach that are attainable, including:

- creating partnerships in the community;
- offering library programs and services designed particularly for the Latino community;
- marketing those programs outside the library and within the Latino community.

LEARNING EFFECTIVE STRATEGIES

If you and your current staff are solely responsible for conducting outreach to your Latino community, here are some strategies to consider:

1. Know as much as possible about the Latino community that you plan to serve.

2. Learn about the Latino culture (and any possible sub-cultures) in your community.

3. Demonstrate a sensitivity toward Latinos regardless of their socioeconomic background.

4. Discover and contact the formal and informal Latino leaders who can serve as resources in this effort.

5. Identify the organizations, agencies, and individuals with whom you can form partnerships in your outreach efforts.

6. Execute effective public relations and marketing of your services to Latinos in your community.

7. Ascertain where to promote your programs and services efficiently and effectively.

8. Develop and provide specialized Spanish-language resources for the Latino community.

Items 1–7 listed above are within your capabilities with your current staffing; the main challenge here is the time. Another item that is important to your outreach efforts is the need for you to be able to communicate with Latinos of all ages. (Abanira, 1984)

Item 8 is more problematic and a definite challenge. In Chapter 8 we will examine ways to meet this challenge, such as writing a proposal for external funds for bilingual staff or engaging bilingual volunteers for specific bilingual hours in the library and/or for assistance in selecting and acquiring bilingual or Spanish-language library materials.

PARTNERING FOR OUTREACH

The best thing you can do is to develop partnerships with organizations, agencies, and individuals who can provide personnel, program expertise, facilities, and public relations resources (see Chapter 5). Because outreach and partnerships go hand in hand, let us review those possible partners. Your partners could include social services agencies, civic organizations and clubs, churches and religious groups, government agencies, local government departments (such as police, fire, parks and recreation), educational institutions, and day care centers.

Once your partnerships are established and your joint programs and services are identified, you can determine which ones are achievable given your staff and funding constraints. Concentrate on providing those programs. Leave the more costly ones until you find external funds or until you can integrate them into your library's general programs and services. Remember, some action is better than no action.

MARKETING FOR THE LATINO COMMUNITY

Once you have developed some programs and/or services for the Latino community based on the results of the community analysis, you must market those programs to your specific audience. A very good, in-depth manual, *¡Bienvenidos! Welcome! A Handy Resource Guide for Marketing Your Library to Latinos* by Susannah Mississippi Byrd, covers this area in depth. We do not want to replicate Byrd's guide; however, we do want to include some basic tips and examples of how to market specifically to your Latino community. For our purposes, we use marketing and public relations (PR) interchangeably. Here are some effective tips on handling your PR.

PLAN WELL

Outreach and PR have a planning component, as does almost everything we suggest to you. Make sure to have a mini-PR plan for each of your programs/services. Let's take the *Día* event project mentioned in previous chapters. Simultaneously with the planning and implementation of this new program, you and your staff need to have your PR plan in place. This plan should include the following components:

- identifying your target audience (in our scenario, it would be Latino children and their families);
- identifying the most effective marketing/PR mechanism to be used for the effort (flyers describing the *Día* celebration distributed in schools and in the community, Public Service Announcements (PSAs) on the Spanish-language and English radio and television stations, presentations before school administrators and the school board);
- identifying the most effective places to reach that audience (for example, schools, health clinics, laundromats, churches, malls).

USE PROMOTIONAL FLYERS AND THE INTERNET

Promotional flyers are usually the least expensive way to advertise a program or event. They can be disseminated in many different ways, such as by hand or as posters on bulletin boards. Production costs can be very low depending on the final product. We recommend that the flyers be printed on bright-colored paper.

Create a logo or translate your library's mission statement into Spanish and make it an icon on your library Web page. This can link to programs that you are gearing for the Latino community on a monthly basis. Research the most effective *virtual* places to reach that audience (for example, discussion lists, chat rooms, free e-mail provider services). Disseminate e-copies of your program flyers as attachments via e-mail blasts, and include your partners in the distribution. They will appreciate seeing your level of activity. Perhaps they will inquire about a project that interests them. Research the most popular telecommunication methods and if the Latino community in your service area is using them, the library should as well!

USE BILINGUAL PR

All your PR pieces must be bilingual; if you cannot offer bilingual or Spanish programs because you lack bilingual staff, volunteers, or partners to present them, you should still promote your English-language programs on bilingual flyers. This allows monolingual (Spanish-language) Latinos to understand what kind of programming the library does offer. They can still share that information with others—family, friends, coworkers.

Figures 6-1 to 6-14 are some examples of bilingual flyers used to market programming to Latinos. We chose to include these examples from various public libraries because we wanted to recognize them for the excellent work they have done in marketing to and serving their Latino communities.

The flyers show a range of sophistication, from homemade, low-budget flyers to professionally produced ones. Such resources as equipment, personnel, and time will probably determine how fancy any of your PR flyers can be.

Figures 6-1 to 6-3 represent basic bilingual flyers (front and back) advertising a *Día* dance program and bilingual story hours.

Figures 6-4 to 6-6 show three different bookmark formats. These are produced as double-sided and bilingual.

Figure 6-7 and 6-8 are examples of Spanish flyers for a young adult library program and a children's library program.

Figures 6-9 and 6-10 are examples of full page (8.5" x 11") Spanish flyers for an English class and a Spanish book discussion group.

Figures 6-11 through 6-13 represent partnership programming. The first is a notice or announcement in Spanish for a community meeting soliciting input as to what services should be offered in the education center, and the next two are announcements in Spanish and English of the Reading Partners Program, a training opportunity that Dr. Schon takes to teachers and schools.

Figure 6-14 is a flyer in English advertising Spanish/English resources. Although we do not provide it for this flyer, we strongly recommend that

Figure 6-1. Día de los Niños Flyer

(Permission to adapt and reproduce granted by Jose Aponte, Director, San Diego County Public Library.)

Figure 6-2. Spanish-Language Storytime Flyer

(Permission to adapt and reproduce granted by the Athens-Clarke County Public Library System.)

all your advertising be provided in both languages on the same double-sided document or side by side on your library Web page.

Figure 6-15 (English) and Figure 6-16 (Spanish) show an Internet parental consent form. This is provided as a standard bilingual Library form.

Figure 6-17 is an example of a billboard in Spanish encouraging families to apply for library card membership.

EMPHASIZE THAT LIBRARY PROGRAMS AND SERVICES ARE FREE

It is important to emphasize in all your promotional pieces that library programs and services are free. Very few of the flyer examples we provided

Figure 6-3. Bilingual Storytime Flyer

(Permission to adapt and reproduce granted by the San Diego County Library System.)

mentioned this, but Latinos who are new to the community or new to the country need to know that public library programs and services are free.

WRITE EFFECTIVE PRESS RELEASES

Writing press releases about your library programs is another effective PR method. If you have a local or area newspaper, submit a write-up of the program. If there is a Spanish-language newspaper in your community or if the local newspaper has a Spanish-language section, submit the write-up in Spanish as well.

Figure 6-4. Electronic Catalog Bookmark

(Permission to adapt and reproduce granted by the San Diego County Library System.)

A press release includes a heading that says "Immediate Press Release" or "Please Release on (date)." It should also include:

- the name of the organization submitting the press release;
- the date of the press release;
- the contact person and his or her telephone number;
- a catchy headline or title;
- the five "Ws"—who, what, when, where, and why;
- # # # (to signify the end of the press release).

Figure 6-5. Spanish-Language Classics Bookmark

(Permission to adapt and reproduce granted by the Queens Public Library.)

¡BIENVENIDOS A QUEENS!
www.BienvenidosaQueens.org
¡Bienvenidos a Queens, NY, USA!

¡Bienvenidos a Queens! es un servicio en línea que provee acceso a información en español sobre salud, asuntos de inmigración, vivienda, clases de inglés y otros tópicos útiles para los recién llegados a este país.

Puede tener acceso a ¡Bienvenidos a Queens! desde las 63 bibliotecas de Queens Library, y desde cualquier computadora con acceso al Internet.

Otros servicios gratuitos especiales de la Biblioteca de Queens para personas que hablan español:

- Libros, videocintas, CDs, etc., en español en muchas de las bibliotecas
- Programas de destrezas para adaptarse a la vida estadounidense en español, y programas que celebran la cultura hispana / latina
- Página en español, Recursos locales hispanos / latinos y WorldLinQ™ en español
- Clases de inglés
- Centros de Aprendizaje para Adultos
- Talleres para aprender a escribir su resumé
- Ayuda con la tarea escolar

Invitamos a las agencias que ofrecen servicios en español para inmigrantes a comunicarse con la Biblioteca para incluirlos en ¡Bienvenidos a Queens! Para mas información llame al 1-718-990-0894

Queens Borough Public Library
89-11 Merrick Boulevard
Jamaica, New York 11432
www.queenslibrary.org

¡Bienvenidos a Queens!

THE BOROUGH PUBLIC LIBRARY
FOUNDED 1896
INCORPORATED

Este servicio es el resultado de los fondos de Library Services and Technology Act, donados por New York State Library.

¡BIENVENIDOS A QUEENS!
www.BienvenidosaQueens.org
Welcome to Queens, NY, USA!

¡Bienvenidos a Queens! is an online service of the Queens Borough Public Library that gives access to information in Spanish on health, immigration issues, housing, English classes, and other topics useful for newcomers.

¡Bienvenidos a Queens! is accessible from the 63 libraries in Queens, and from any computer with Web access.

Other special free services of the Queens Library for Spanish speakers are:

- Books in Spanish, videos, CDs, etc., in many libraries
- Coping Skills programs in Spanish and programs celebrating Hispanic/Latino culture
- Página en español, local Hispanic resources, and WorldLinQ™ en español
- English classes
- Adult Learning Centers
- Resumé workshops
- Help with homework

We invite agencies that offer Spanish language services for immigrants to contact us so that they can be included in ¡Bienvenidos a Queens! For more information, call 1-718-990-0894.

Queens Borough Public Library
89-11 Merrick Boulevard
Jamaica, New York 11432
www.queenslibrary.org

¡Bienvenidos a Queens!

This service is supported by Federal Library Services and Technology Act Funds, granted by the New York State Library.

Figure 6-6. ¡Bienvenidos a Queens! Bookmark

(Permission to adapt and reproduce granted by the Queens Public Library.)

Figure 6-7. Spanish-Language Flyer for a Young Adult Library Program—Taller de Repostería

¡El Club Bilingüe!

Hola

Mathilde Cubas presenta una serie de cuentos y leyendas en inglés y español para niños que tienen 5-10 años. Las presentaciones serán los sábados a las 3:30 p.m. en varias bibliotecas de la ciudad de Greensboro.

9 de agosto: **La leyenda del Lago** (Honduras): Biblioteca de Glenwood
23 de agosto: **El Cadejo** (Centroamérica): Biblioteca de Glenwood

13 de septiembre: **Las Medidas de los Flamencos** (Uruguay): Biblioteca de Guilford College
20 de septiembre: **La Mujer de Piedra** (Zapoteca): Biblioteca Central

4 de octubre: **El Lago de Oro** (Colombia): Biblioteca Central
18 de octubre: **La Xiquat/La Siguanabana** (Centroamérica): Biblioteca de Vance Chavis

8 de noviembre: **El Rescate del Fuego** (Brazil) : Biblioteca de Benjamin
22 de noviembre: **Un Pez en las Manos** (Republica Dominicana): Biblioteca Central

13 de diciembre: **Los Dos hermanos** (Bolivia): Biblioteca de McGirt-Horton

¡Por favor reúnanse con nosotros!

A World of Possibilities

Figure 6-8. Spanish-Language Flyer for a Children's Library Program

(Permission to adapt and reproduce granted by the Greensboro Public Library.)

Figure 6-9. Spanish-Language Flyer for an English Class

ARLINGTON
VIRGINIA

Arlington Central Library
1015 N. Quincy Street
Arlington, VA 22201

Free parking
Metro: Orange Line
(Ballston or Virginia Square)
General information:
703-228-5990
Special accommodation:
703-228-5715
TTY: 703-228-6320
Hablamos español:
703-228-5710
www.arlingtonva.us

Conversando Sobre Libros:

Grupo de Discusión de Literatura Latinoamericana y Española

**Jueves 17 de Noviembre, 7 pm
Biblioteca Central**

Delirio de Laura Restrepo. Ganadora del Premio Alfaguara 2004, *Delirio* es una expresión de todo lo que Colombia tiene de fascinante, e incluso de terriblemente fascinante. Un hombre regresa después de un corto viaje de negocios y encuentra que su esposa ha enloquecido completamente.

Inscríbase y pida prestada una copia de *Delirio* en el escritorio de circulación de la Biblioteca Central.

Contacto: Angélica Cofré, 703-228-5945

www.arlingtonva.us
CLICK LIBRARIES

Figure 6-10. Spanish-Language Flyer for a Spanish Book Discussion Group

(Permission to adapt and reproduce granted by the Arlington Public Library System.)

La Biblioteca y Centro Educativo de la Comunidad de Pinewoods

celebrara una reunión comunitaria, para determinar los horarios y los días que ustedes sugieran que este abierto el centro para su uso.

Lugar: Oasis Católico

Fecha: domingo 6 de febrero del 2005

Hora: 1:00 PM

Lyndon House Arts Center
ACC Leisure Services Department

Athens-Clarke
COUNTY LIBRARY

La biblioteca ofrecerá.

1. Clases de ingles.

2. Acceso a las computadoras y la Internet.

3. Acceso a 249 bibliotecas del estado de Georgia.

4. Cursos vocacionales.

5. Cursos para adultos para alcanzar los niveles de primaria, secundaria y preparatoria.

6. Ayuda con la preparación de sus impuestos.

7. Ayuda con las tareas escolares de sus niños.

Seleccione los días y las horas que a usted le gustaría que el centro este abierto.

___lunes ___martes __miércoles __jueves __viernes __sábado __domingo

Días de la semana __ 10:00AM-6:00PM __11:00AM-7:00 PM __12:00PM-8:00PM

Sábado ___9:00AM-3:00PM ___10:00 AM-4:00PM ___11:00AM-5:00PM

Domingo __1:00PM-4:00 PM ___2:00PM-5:00

Figure 6-11. Spanish-Language Notice for a Community Meeting

(Permission to adapt and reproduce granted by the Athens-Clarke County Public Library System.)

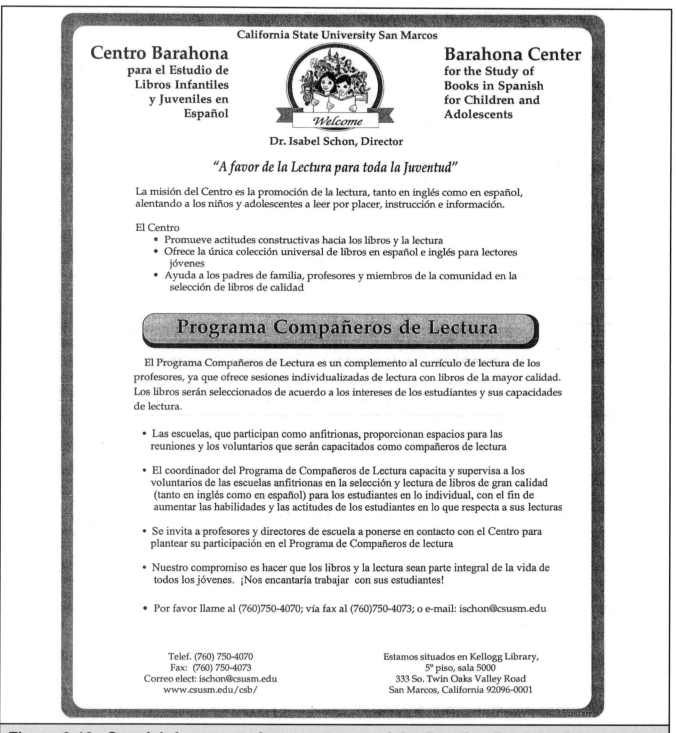

Figure 6-12. Spanish-Language Announcement of the Reading Partners Program

(Permission to adapt and reproduce granted by Dr. Isabel Schon, Barahona Center, California State University San Marcos.)

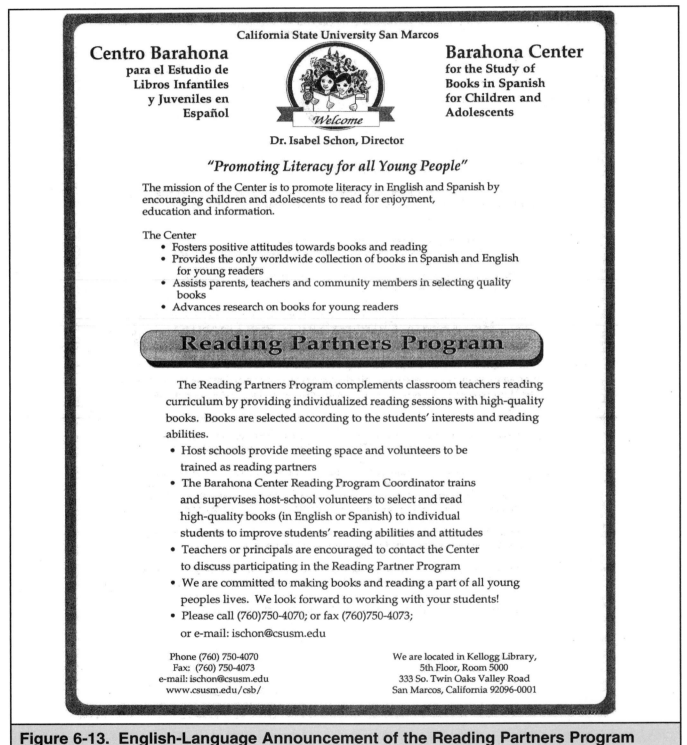

California State University San Marcos

Centro Barahona
para el Estudio de
Libros Infantiles
y Juveniles en
Español

Barahona Center
for the Study of
Books in Spanish
for Children and
Adolescents

Welcome

Dr. Isabel Schon, Director

"Promoting Literacy for all Young People"

The mission of the Center is to promote literacy in English and Spanish by encouraging children and adolescents to read for enjoyment, education and information.

The Center
- Fosters positive attitudes towards books and reading
- Provides the only worldwide collection of books in Spanish and English for young readers
- Assists parents, teachers and community members in selecting quality books
- Advances research on books for young readers

Reading Partners Program

The Reading Partners Program complements classroom teachers reading curriculum by providing individualized reading sessions with high-quality books. Books are selected according to the students' interests and reading abilities.

- Host schools provide meeting space and volunteers to be trained as reading partners
- The Barahona Center Reading Program Coordinator trains and supervises host-school volunteers to select and read high-quality books (in English or Spanish) to individual students to improve students' reading abilities and attitudes
- Teachers or principals are encouraged to contact the Center to discuss participating in the Reading Partner Program
- We are committed to making books and reading a part of all young peoples lives. We look forward to working with your students!
- Please call (760)750-4070; or fax (760)750-4073; or e-mail: ischon@csusm.edu

Phone (760) 750-4070
Fax: (760) 750-4073
e-mail: ischon@csusm.edu
www.csusm.edu/csb/

We are located in Kellogg Library,
5th Floor, Room 5000
333 So. Twin Oaks Valley Road
San Marcos, California 92096-0001

Figure 6-13. English-Language Announcement of the Reading Partners Program

(Permission to adapt and reproduce granted by Dr. Isabel Schon, Barahona Center, California State University San Marcos.)

Figure 6-14. Sample Flyer (English)

(Permission to to adapt and reproduce granted by the Boulder Public Library.)

BRANCH _____

SAN DIEGO COUNTY LIBRARY

INTERNET PARENTAL CONSENT FORM

The Internet is a vast network of computer networks linking millions of computers around the world. The networks belong to government bodies, businesses, universities, libraries, and individuals. The resources that the Internet makes available to users are, therefore, tremendous and constantly changing, in format and content.

The Worldwide Web (WWW) is a giant Internet menu system that electronically links documents that may contain not only text, but also graphics and sometimes even video and sound. The Web lets users navigate between documents by opening links that connect users directly to the site of the information, sometimes half-way around the world.

Libraries and Librarians have a responsibility to provide free access to material and information presenting all points of view. The Internet allows access to materials and information far beyond the library walls. Some parents, however, may believe that certain information available on the Internet is inappropriate for their children. The Internet may contain material that may be considered controversial or offensive. Because resources on the Internet are constantly changing, it is not possible for Library staff to control or monitor specific information that children or youth may locate on the Internet.

Parents or guardians of minor children, not the San Diego County Library, are solely responsible for their child's use of the Internet at the Library. Parents must read and sign this Internet Parental Consent Form to authorize their children under the age of 18 to use the Internet. In addition, children under the age of 18 must sign the "Responsible User" statement at the bottom of this form. Parents are encouraged to explore the Internet *with* their children.

****

PARENT OR GUARDIAN OF INTERNET USERS UNDER THE AGE OF 18: I have read the above explanation of the Internet and the San Diego County Library Internet Policy. I give permission for my child named below to use the Internet at any San Diego County Library Branch.

Print Parent's First and Last Name _____

Parent's Signature _____ Date _____

CHILDREN UNDER THE AGE OF 18: I have read the above explanation of the Internet and the San Diego County Library Internet Policy. I agree to use the Internet in a safe and responsible way. If I do not use the Internet in a safe and responsible way, my Internet privileges will be suspended.

Print Child's First and Last Name _____

Child's Date of Birth _____/_____/_____

Child's Signature _____ Date _____

LIB 08-03 (Rev. 02-01-2002)

Figure 6-15. Internet Parental Consent Form (English)

(Permission to adapt and reproduce granted by the San Diego County Library System.)

SUCURSAL_____

SAN DIEGO COUNTY LIBRARY

PERMISO PARA USAR EL INTERNET
(para menores de edad)

El Internet es una gran red que conecta a millones de sistemas de computadoras en todo el mundo. El sistema le pertenece al gobierno, a los negocios, a las universidades, a las bibliotecas y a los individuos. Las Fuentes que el Internet les pone al alcance a sus clients son de gran volumen y siempre están cambiando su formato y contenido.

El Worldwide (WWW) es un menu gigante que electrónicamente conecta documentos que no sólo contienen texto, sino también información gráfica y a veces, hasta videos y sonido. El Web les facilita a sus clients el "navegar" de un documento a otro y conectarse directamente con una fuente de información, quizás a medio mundo de distancia.

Las bibliotecas y los bibliotecarios tienen la responsabiblidad de proveer el acceso gratuito a todo tipo de materials e información. El Internet permite el acceso a los materials y a la información que se encuentra muy lejos fuera de las paredes de la biblioteca. Algunos de los padres creen que la información que se adquiere a través del Internet no es apropiada para sus hijos. El Internet puede contener información que sea considerada controversial u ofensiva. Debido a que las Fuentes del Internet cambian constantemente, no es possible que el personal de la Biblioteca pueda controlar o vigilar el tipo de información que los niños y adolescents encuentran en el Internet.

Los padres o guardiances de los niños menores de edad, y no la Biblioteca del Condado de San Diego, son responsables por sus hijos y el uso del Internet en la Biblioteca. Los padres deben leer esta planilla (Internet Parental Consent Form) y completar las dos primeras líneas para autorizar a sus hijos menores de 18 años de edad a que usen el Internet. Además, los niños menores de 18 años de edad deben leer la sección "Responsible User" y firmar las últimas dos líneas de esta planilla. Les sugerimos a los padres que exploren el Internet *con* sus hijos.

****

PARA LOS PADRES O GUARDIANES DE NIÑOS MENORES DE 18 AÑOS DE EDAD: He leído la explicación de las reglas del Internet y de la Biblioteca del Condado de San Diego. Le doy permiso a mi hijo(a) cuyo nombre aparece en las últimas dos líneas de esta planilla para que use el Internet en cualquier Biblioteca del Condado de San Diego.

Imprima el primer nombre y apellido del Padre (Madre) _____

Su firma _____   Fecha _____

PARA LOS NIÑOS MEMORES DE 18 AÑOS: He leído la explicación de las reglas del Internet y de la Biblioteca del Condado de San Diego. Usaré el Internet de una manera segura y responsable. Si no uso el Internet de una manera segura y responsable, el privilegio de usar el Internet se me suspenderá.

Imprima el primer nombre y apellido del niño (a) _____

Fecha de nacimiento del niño _____/_____/_____

Firma del niño _____   Fecha _____

LIB 08-03 (Rev. 02-01-2002)

Figure 6-16. Internet Parental Consent Form (Spanish)

(Permission to adapt and reproduce granted by the San Diego County Library System.)

Figure 6-17. Billboard Encouraging Families to Apply for Library Card Membership

(Permission to adapt and reproduce granted by the Tulsa Public Library System and "Lamar Tulsa Billboard Artwork — "Somos miembros.")

UTILIZE PUBLIC SERVICE ANNOUNCEMENTS

Remember to use the media for public service announcements (PSAs). The only cost here is the time to write the PSA and submit it to the appropriate media (radio and/or television). If your local or area radio station has a Spanish-language listening segment, you can also submit the PSA in Spanish. Public service announcements should be an average length of 30 seconds and include a telephone number for further information.

GIVE EFFECTIVE PRESENTATIONS
IN THE COMMUNITY

Most library administrators are excellent at presentation and persuasion. These skills are essential, especially during budget hearings. Remember to use these skills in your PR efforts. You can set up presentations and/or interviews with radio and television stations as well as with schools, civic organizations, and community groups.

DEVELOP A DISTRIBUTION LIST

We suggest that you develop a PR distribution list. Oxnard Public Library (California) gave us this idea when the first edition was written and it is still valid today. The list would include all the different organizations (partners) who have assisted the library in its PR efforts within the Latino community and should be referred to each time you are ready to market a particular program or service to Latinos. The list should include the categories listed below.

- Flyer distributions—include all the organizations, agencies, and individuals who are willing to distribute library flyers and other PR information to the Latino community (at no charge). If at all possible, include the number of flyers they are willing to distribute each time.
- Flyer and poster postings—include all the organizations, agencies, and businesses that have agreed to post PR materials on their bulletin boards and windows for the Latino community.
- Publications distribution—include all publications in your local community and region that are willing to provide free news releases and/or PSAs of your special programs designed to attract the Latino audience. This list should be subdivided by categories such as newspapers, magazines, organization newsletters, church bulletins, and radio and television stations.
- Unable to help—list organizations that have been unable to help. Make sure to include the last date they were contacted. The list is important because it helps prevent any embarrassment to the library and irritation for the organization. However, it does not hurt to call them once in a while. Sometimes the leader or manager changes, and with that personnel change may come a positive philosophical change toward helping organizations like the public library.

- Freebies—although this category is not directly related to PR, we suggest you still include it. List retail businesses that will consider providing donations of food, gifts or gift certificates, books, facilities, and other services (such as printing, daycare, or transportation).

INCLUDE ESSENTIAL INFORMATION IN THE DISTRIBUTION LIST

Essential information for the distribution list includes:

- contact person
- address
- telephone and fax numbers
- e-mail address
- Universal Research Locator (URL) for their Web site
- a checklist of what the organization is willing to do
- number of copies for distribution
- requirement to call ahead
- last date of list compilation.

Figure 6-18 is a sample form to use or adapt for compiling this list. You may find some of the same organizations, agencies, or businesses are listed on your partnerships form. Remember that your PR list can be printed and/or entered into a database to allow for easy and continuous updating. We also suggest that you start a partnership blog for local service agencies and non-profit organizations interested in serving Latinos.

MAKING OUTREACH WORK

Outreach not only includes the development of programs designed to interest this underserved community but also includes your marketing efforts to reach out and get them to attend library programs—at the library or at other partnership sites. You must reach out to let the Latino community know you are determined and excited to serve them and meet their information needs. You need to attract the Latino community to your library, and that is your challenge.

Programming, partnerships, outreach, and marketing/public relations are all interrelated. When developing programs and services for your

1. Organization/ _____

   Agency Name _____

2. Contact person _____

   _____

3. Address _____

   _____

   _____

4. Telephone _____ Fax Number _____

5. E-mail Address _____

6. We are willing to help the library accordingly (please check *all* that apply):

   _____ Post flyers

   _____ Hand out flyers

   _____ Deliver flyers door-to-door

   _____ Mail flyers

   _____ Publish news release

   _____ Announce PSAs

   _____ Link to our Web page

   _____ Sorry, unable to help

7. Please send us _____ (number of) copies.

8. _____ Yes _____ No   Please call us before you bring materials
                              over for distribution.

9. _____ Contact our webmaster for content guidelines and to submit Library
           logo. Contact info:

Figure 6-18. Publicity Distribution Form

underserved Latino community, it is difficult to consider one of these components without considering the others.

Keep in mind that you already have a lot of experience in all of these components. The challenge for you now is to apply those marketing/PR experiences designed for your general library users and then to design programs and services for a new and growing clientele—the Latinos in your community.

You have to start somewhere and sometime; remember that sooner is better than later, and something is better than nothing. As you begin to meet this service challenge, it should only get easier with more experience under your belt. It is important to acknowledge success, whether big or little, when trying to reach out to a relatively new constituency. Celebrate your successes!

7 ESTABLISHING A LATINO COLLECTION

In this chapter we will provide some guidance on how to start a Latino collection and how to provide access to it. It is clear that the traditional methods of collection development and technical services must be modified in order to meet the information needs of Latinos.

Even if you follow our tips, you will still find this task to be frustrating at times. There are many questions, and no one has all the answers. You are to be commended for taking on this challenge. What a luxury it would be if you had unlimited resources to purchase all the library materials you want for all your patrons, and unlimited resources to catalog, process, and provide access to such a collection!

An approach to collection development that incorporates different sensitivities and skill sets, such as cultural competency, is crucial to building a relevant collection of materials to be used by and to be about Latinos in your community. Unfortunately, published reviews of Latino materials are not abundant; although traditional book jobbers are making some progress, they are not able to supply everything that your library needs, and linguistic problems (of the translated materials and/or lack of availability of materials from the country of origin) can cause delays in your collection development work. The challenge you face is that Latinos in your community have pressing needs now.

To meet these needs today, you will want to adjust your collection development practices. By all means, gain allies in the Latino community by publicly advertising that you are responsibly and enthusiastically attempting to develop a collection that will meet the needs identified in your community analysis. Make it a shared goal to provide physical and intellectual access to library services in your community. Las Vegas-Clark County Library District incorporates diversity of collections in two critical documents in Figures 7-1a and 7-1b (pages 155–156).

The main challenge is that this approach can be very time-consuming and often frustrating for those in your library responsible for collection development and acquisitions. We hope that the practical tips and advice offered in this chapter will make your efforts to develop a collection appealing to Latinos a bit easier and more rewarding.

ADDRESSING MANAGEMENT ISSUES

Certain management issues will have a significant impact on your collection development efforts, and the way in which your library system handles them is important. In some cases they involve a challenge to traditional collection development practice of selection and evaluation. When selecting books from a Latino perspective, the same skills are necessary but one must be flexible in their application. (Mestre and Nieto, 1996)

The following are management issues pertaining to collection development:

- reviewing collection development policies and practices
- linking collection development to the results of the needs assessment
- establishing advisory groups
- dealing with the lack of Spanish-language skills among collection development staff
- encouraging the development of support systems

REVIEWING COLLECTION DEVELOPMENT POLICIES AND PRACTICES

If you have a formal collection development policy, you need to review it to identify practices and procedures that are potential barriers to your multicultural collection development efforts. Some well-meaning policies unintentionally impede the development of collections for Latino users.

Your policy should clearly indicate that your library collections are for the benefit of everyone in your service area and that some information needs in your community can only be met by purchasing library materials that are bilingual or in languages other than English. Including this idea in your collection development policy is a clear signal that you are serious about meeting the information needs of all your citizens. Additionally, a policy statement will give you much-needed backup in case any members of your community complain about the noticeable increase in the number of Spanish-language materials in your library.

Some libraries require that two positive reviews of proposed materials be found before they can be acquired, or they favor purchasing from one or two major vendors, discouraging the purchase of items from small or specialty presses in the United States, publishers and distributors outside the country, neighborhood bookstores, or conferences and book fairs. These entrenched library policies add complications to the collection process. (Marquis, 2003)

LAS VEGAS-CLARK COUNTY LIBRARY DISTRICT
DIVERSITY VISION STATEMENT

The Las Vegas-Clark County Library District is committed to a workplace in which all people are respected as individuals and are valued for their contributions in accomplishing the District's mission. The District will foster an inclusive, supportive, open, challenging and innovative work environment to enable employees to be positive, creative and reach their full potential.

Why Diversity?

American Library Association Key Action Report #4

The following is taken from the American Library Association's action report regarding diversity.

> *"Diversity is one of five key action areas adopted by the American Library Association to fulfill its mission of providing the highest quality library and information services for all people. The Association actively promotes equal access to information for all people through libraries and encourages development of library services for diverse population.*
>
> *The strength of our nation is the diversity of its people. How we deal with this diversity continues to be a challenge.*
>
> *Diversity applies to more than race and ethnicity. It applies to physical disabilities, sexual orientation, age, language and social class.*
>
> *Democracy is rooted in respect for all people. Respect is based on understanding. Librarians believe that education is key to building communities and a nation based on understanding and respect.*
>
> *Libraries are an American value. They offer people of all ages and backgrounds the resources they need to learn and grow and achieve their dreams.*
>
> *The strength of libraries has always been the diversity of their collections and commitment to serving all people. Libraries of all types – public, school and academic – provide a forum for diverse ideas and points of view that can help us learn about and better understand ourselves and each other.*
>
> *If libraries are to be their best, their services and staff must reflect both the people they serve and the larger global community. Today's libraries provide a wide range of opportunities for people with diverse needs and interests. These include cultural heritage collections, materials in alternate formats such as large print, also multilingual Internet training, bilingual story hours, English as a Second Language classes and many other creative and resourceful programs.*

Adopted: February 8, 2001   5

Figure 7-1a. Las Vegas-Clark County Library District Diversity Vision Statement

(Permission to adapt and reproduce granted by Las Vegas-Clark County Library District.)

As a profession, librarians are committed to providing information and resources that serve the diverse needs of their communities and reflect the diversity of human knowledge and experience".

Diversity and the Las Vegas-Clark County Library District's Mission Statement

The Las Vegas-Clark County Library District's mission is "*to provide the community with materials, services, and facilities to satisfy the need for information; to facilitate lifelong learning; and to promote use of the library. Its aim is to promote the value of information, reflecting the diversity of cultures and viewpoints; and to enhance the community's awareness of services which aid in the development of individual and community creativity and excellence.*"

In order to successfully achieve the District's mission, we need to attract and retain a skilled, competent and diverse workforce and foster a positive work environment with opportunities for advancement, training and challenges for all.

The ALA Diversity Action Report states that to effectively serve an ever-growing diverse population our workforce needs to be reflective of the Nation and of our communities' diversity. A diverse workforce is inherently more productive. Implementing strategies that encourage diversity such as empowering employees, enhancing the quality of work life, forming labor-management partnerships, and fostering a positive work environment with opportunities for advancement, training, and challenges will strengthen the District's mission.

An organization that accepts diversity and recognizes the contribution of all employees is a healthier and more productive organization than one that does not. Understanding and recognizing diversity enables an organization to capitalize on the differing views and contributions that each of its employees bring to the workplace. Such an organization provides for a richer work environment and ensures that employees work more closely with one another in carrying out organizational goals and objectives. Understanding and recognizing the contribution of diversity enables an organization to better adapt to change.

Managing diversity is important. Whatever the diversity, in people or systems, the benefits of factoring a myriad experiences, insights and approaches into decision making can only enhance the viability of solutions, and our ability to forecast potential consequences. Integrating diversity into an organization's management practices provides opportunities to facilitate organizational change, harness employee potential, achieve performance goals, and enhance internal and external customer satisfaction, thus furthering the mission of the District. The District's greatest assets are its employees.

The District's Diversity/Competitive Workplace Committee realizes that pursuing the objectives of a diversity initiative will require new ways of thinking and doing business. These new ways of thinking can be accomplished if the District's policies and vision are supported by the organizational culture. The District's commitment to the principles and legal obligations of Equal Employment Opportunity objectives remains firm and unchanged, and in fact, is enhanced and strengthened through its ability to manage diversity.

Adopted: February 8, 2001   6

Figure 7-1b. Las Vegas-Clark County Library District Diversity Mission Statement

(Permission to adapt and reproduce granted by Las Vegas-Clark County Library District.)

"Librarians must make every effort to identify and acquire Spanish-language, culturally sensitive materials for their Latino users in order to accomplish the mission of serving communities regardless of language, cultural background, and economic status." (Marquis, 2003: 106) As a manager, your role should be to remove barriers and to facilitate Latino collection development.

LINKING COLLECTION DEVELOPMENT TO INFORMATION NEEDS

You will gain much-needed support and assistance from the Latino community by showing that your attempts to meet their identified needs are sincere. A second management issue is making certain that your collection development efforts are linked very closely to the results of the Latino community demographic analysis and needs assessment. Since each Latino community's needs are unique and since each library is unique, it is not possible for us to tell you specifically what should be in your collection, nor can we provide any formula that can tell you what percentage of your collection development budget to devote to Latino material collection. You and your staff are ultimately responsible for developing a collection that meets the unique blend of needs identified in your Latino community assessment.

Latinos in one community may want you to concentrate on improving the English reading skills of their young children. In another community, there may be an overwhelming concern about providing more recreational materials for young adults. Latinos in still another community may want you to purchase mostly newspapers and magazines from various Central and Latin American countries, rather than books. Perhaps Latinos in your community will want you to devote most of the available resources to purchase Spanish-language, self-help materials for adults. These are just a few of the many possibilities.

Fortunately, your analysis of Latino demographics and your local needs assessment will help you determine where the greatest needs are—and will enable you to develop the library's collection for Latinos, based not on any preconceived ideas of what might be needed, but on the needs expressed by members of the Latino community during the needs assessment.

As an administrator, you will need to develop a plan that shows how your library will allocate collection development funds to meet these needs. This plan need not be lengthy to be good. It should be readily understood by managers, library employees, the board of trustees, the media, leaders in the Latino community, and the general public, and it should include a list of needs identified by the community (see the Latino needs/wants statements described in Chapter 4). This list should be accompanied by library strategies to meet each of the identified needs with budget allocations assigned to each strategy. Figure 7-2 provides two examples of a needs/wants statement with a collection strategy and a budget allocation.

1. Specific need/want example:

Need/Want Statement:	Latino young adults in our community want Spanish-language magazines.
Collection Strategy 1:	Library will purchase 10 Spanish-language magazines for Latino YA males.
Budget Allocation:	10 Spanish-language magazines at $40/each = $400.
Collection Strategy 2:	Library will purchase 10 Spanish-language magazines for Latino YA females.
Budget Allocation:	10 Spanish-language magazines at $40/each = $400.
Total Budget:	$800

2. General need/want example:

Need/Want Statement:	Latinos in our community want their elementary school children to read and have an appreciation for both English and Spanish.
Collection Strategy:	Library will purchase bilingual recreational books for elementary school children.
Budget Allocation:	100 books at $30/each = $3,000.
Collection Strategy:	Library will purchase bilingual language instructional DVDs for children.
Budget Allocation:	50 DVDs at $25/each = $1,250.
Total Budget:	$4,250

Figure 7-2. Sample Needs/Wants, Collection Strategies, and Budget Allocations

It is impossible to obtain everything that is needed all at once; nonetheless, it is essential that you make a good-faith effort to allocate resources where they are needed most. In the end, you will be thankful that your library devoted the necessary time and energy toward the Latino community needs assessment. Now you can channel your limited funds to the areas that are considered to be a high priority by the Latino community.

ESTABLISHING AND LISTENING TO A LATINO ADVISORY GROUP

A voluntary Latino advisory community group may be helpful in developing a collection for Latinos. You can share your ideas on the allocation of resources with members of this advisory group to get feedback on and support for your library strategies and budgetary allocations. Consider establishing an advisory group of Latino teens (young adults) to give you ideas on library materials that will help attract this hard-to-reach clientele.

Members of advisory groups can provide direct assistance in any number of ways:

- They can peruse appropriate publisher or distributor catalogs and make recommendations to the selectors.
- When new books are processed, they can prepare bilingual handouts or bibliographies publicizing the new arrivals.
- They can review the newly acquired materials and write bilingual articles about them for your library newsletter.
- They can be involved in organizing Spanish book clubs based on the new arrivals.

Your local situation will inspire you to think of other possible uses for this advisory group. Remember that this advisory group can also serve as one of your political action groups when needed.

HANDLING SPANISH AND BILINGUAL MATERIALS

Your staff (selectors) who are unfamiliar with Spanish will have difficulty choosing Spanish library materials that are the most appropriate for Latinos in your community. This is a management issue that is important to address when developing a collection for Latinos. Just as an English-speaking American might have a little difficulty with British English or with English from several hundred years ago, so too might an American Latino have some difficulty reading books in Spanish from different Central or South American countries. If the language barrier is too great, the material will not be used or enjoyed. Generally speaking, the selector should try to select materials that are closest to the vernacular used by Latinos in the community, but this is not an absolute rule.

Bilingual materials also present a problem to English-monolingual selectors, as they will not be able to judge the quality of books that contain inferior translations. One solution is to have bilingual and bicultural library staff who can make these quality judgments. The next best solution is to provide opportunities and incentives for your selectors to learn Spanish. Also, you can encourage your selectors to interact with and get advice from bilingual individuals in the community. Even if all the above steps are taken, every now and then a few unwanted books will still make their way into the library collection. When this happens, acknowledge it, accept it, use it as a learning experience, and then move on.

A significant number of English-speaking Latinos have very limited Spanish speaking and reading skills. Consequently their preference will be for English-language materials on a wide variety of subjects. You cannot assume that all Latinos want or need Spanish or bilingual resources.

Make sure that your collection includes English-language materials about the history of Latinos in the United States, with particular emphasis on the history of the particular subcultures represented in your service area. It should also include a selection of literary works by U.S. Latino authors writing in English, as well as English translations of major literary works from the Spanish-speaking world. Your collection probably already addresses many of the needs of Latinos whose first language is English but remember to utilize the community analysis data, your Latino advisory members, and teen advisory group members as sources of suggestions and trends.

SUPPORTING SELECTORS

You need to provide a supportive atmosphere to ensure that your staff can develop skills and confidence in these new endeavors. As the final management concern, we would like to address the development of a support system for your collection development staff. Most likely, starting a Latino collection from scratch will necessitate change, some of which could be drastic. Some of your staff will respond quite well; others may have a more difficult time. Useful strategies include the following:

- Establish in-house teams to discuss Latino collection development issues and resolve any problems that arise.
- Support attendance at national, regional, and state conferences and workshops where Latino collection development issues are discussed.
- Provide opportunities for staff to meet and interact, formally and informally, with others in the immediate area who are dealing with similar issues or who have special skills.
- Cooperate with other libraries and library associations to bring outside speakers and experts to local workshops and conferences.
- Provide funds, opportunities, and incentives for employees to learn Spanish.
- Encourage collection development staff to interact with the Latino community and solicit ideas on improving the library's collections.

Being aware of these issues and dealing with them constructively will establish and nurture a positive framework. Your library's overall success in collection development may very well depend on how effectively staff can respond and adapt to the needs of customers.

FINDING SELECTION RESOURCES

A growing number of American publishers and distributors are making it easier for small and medium-size libraries to obtain recommended titles for Latinos in each of the various age groups. The availability of and access to materials, especially books, for Latinos of all ages has greatly improved. Consequently, these publishers and distributors are able to supply many of the materials needed by many small and medium-size libraries that are beginning to develop collections for Latinos. In this section, we provide tips for selectors who are responsible for developing your library's collection for Latinos.

BOOK DISTRIBUTORS

Listed in Appendix 7A at the end of this chapter are the major U.S.-based distributors that are experienced in Latino book distributing. These distributors realize they are dealing primarily with English-speaking selectors, and their catalogs are written in English. Probably no single distributor will be able to meet your diverse needs. We suggest that you contact each one and they will gladly send you a catalog and put you on their mailing list. By reviewing the offerings of a number of competitors, you will be able to do comparison shopping. Reviewing catalogs, Web sites, and other mailings from a variety of distributors will give a broad view of the available materials.

When you start to receive and review these catalogs, you will find that each company is unique. Some are very general in scope, offering materials for all age groups, in all formats, including English, Spanish, and bilingual titles. Some distributors are much more specialized. Some have strengths in certain areas (such as children's literature) or formats (for example, reference books in Spanish). Some distributors offer special services to attract business from libraries. For example, some offer volume discounts to libraries, and some even have approval plans. Some distributors can provide MAchine-Readable Cataloging (MARC) records for you to enter into your catalog for a small additional fee.

This segment of the book industry has been and will continue to be dynamic. Some companies will respond better or more quickly than others to market demands. New, specialized distributors could emerge to capture untapped markets.

Because changes in this industry can and do happen quickly, it is impossible for us to recommend any particular distributor for specific types of material. Instead we provide a chart (see Figure 7-3) that you can use to track distributor offerings. When you receive catalogs and mailings from

Company	Provides books for which ages?			Provides nonprint materials? (Check all that apply)				Provides magazines?	Provides fotonovelas?	Catalog contains informative English annotations?
	Children	YA	Adult	Audio	Video	Kits	Software	Yes/No	Yes/No	Yes/No
1.										
2.										
3.										
4.										
5.										
6.										
7.										
8.										
9.										
10.										
11.										
12.										
13.										
14.										
15.										

Figure 7-3. Latino Distributor Tracking Chart

the various companies, we suggest that you review them and make notations on the tracking chart.

Here is a list of questions to ask yourself when reviewing a catalog from a distributor:

- Does the distributor sell materials for all different age groups, or does it specialize?
- Does the distributor sell materials in different formats (such as DVDs, recordings, videotapes, CDs and other electronic formats, kits)?
- Does the distributor offer core collections? A number of distributors offer core collections that can contain up to several hundred books, primarily for children and young adults, at a less expensive price than if each title in the collection were purchased separately. Some distributors

develop their Latino core collections based on officially adopted lists of titles that are endorsed by public agencies. Other distributors have developed their own core collections based not on officially adopted lists but on such market factors as expected library demand, availability, price, quality of material, and reputation of publisher. Purchasing a core collection is a relatively inexpensive way to develop immediately a beginning collection for Latino children and young adults. Depending on the size of your library, you may even consider purchasing multiple sets of these core collections.

- Does the distributor sell specialized materials, such as *fotonovelas*? *Fotonovelas* are pulp-magazine books in comic-book style published in Mexico that are very popular among some Latino young adult and adult immigrants. Many Latinos come to the library only for *fotonovelas* at first, but they may eventually begin to use other library materials and services.

- Does the distributor sell magazine subscriptions?

- Does the distributor offer special services to libraries, such as approval plans or library discounts?

- Does the distributor offer MARC records?

- Does the distributor's catalog contain informative English-language annotations?

- Does the distributor have a local sales representative for your area?

We highly recommend the use of distributors because they are able to supply many of the needs of small and medium-size libraries. However, in the box below we have listed some of the possible problems selectors will encounter when relying on distributor catalogs (whether hard copy or on the Internet).

Problems Stemming from Relying on Catalogs:

- Some distributors do not provide informative English-language annotations in their catalogs.
- Since distributors are in business to sell products, the catalogs do not provide objective reviews.
- A few distributors do not provide the date of publication information in their annotations.
- With some distributors, it is difficult to identify the age group for which an item is intended.

For these reasons, it is helpful to view the materials in person. Some distributors have approval plans that give you the opportunity to review items and to return them if you decide they do not meet your needs. If your library is within reasonable driving distance of one or more of these distributors, the sales representatives are often willing to show you samples of their products right in your library. If possible, attend these sessions with members of your Latino advisory group; they can review the materials and make recommendations.

Another way to get firsthand exposure to a wide range of materials is to meet with the distributor representatives at conferences. Feria Internacional del Libro (FIL) or the Guadalajara International Book Fair is considered one of the most accessible of the international book fairs that are held annually in Argentina, Puerto Rico, and other countries. Many of these distributors are exhibitors at American Library Association conferences and at other library association conferences around the country. These are great opportunities to make professional contacts and to review personally the materials they have on hand.

AUDIO AND VIDEO DISTRIBUTORS

The matrix chart in Figure 7-4 can be used to keep track of the strengths of a particular company. Many of the Latino book distributors listed in Appendix 7A at the end of this chapter also provide a variety of audio and video materials; other companies specialize in providing an assortment of audio and video materials for Latinos. There are instructional, educational, and recreational resources on a variety of topics. Each of these companies is unique. One may have a strength in providing materials to a particular age group. Another may have strong collections in recreational video recordings, but little in educational material. Appendix 7B lists the distributors of specialized audio and video Latino materials. We recommend that you obtain a current catalog from each of these specialized distributors or download a copy from the distributor's Web site.

PUBLISHERS

In this chapter we have emphasized distributors because they can provide a wide range of materials from domestic and international sources. In addition to distributors, a number of U.S.-based publishers are interested in Latino materials, and they are also eager to sell you their products. You can find a directory of these publishers in Appendix 7C. We recommend that you obtain catalogs from each of these publishers or visit their Web sites. Some publishers primarily publish Spanish materials; others concentrate on publishing English works by or about Latinos. Most are in the private sector, but a few are affiliated with universities, and several are nonprofit.

Directions:

Distributors offer audio and video materials for a wide variety of Latino language and age groups. When reviewing a distributor's catalog, note the type of material offered for the various Latino groups, and enter the company name in the appropriate cell on the chart.

When completed, you will have a handy reference chart of companies that provide materials for specific Latino language/age groups.

	Types of Materials			
	Audio		Video	
Latino Group	**Recreational**	**Educational**	**Recreational**	**Educational**
Spanish-speaking Children				
English-speaking Children				
Spanish-speaking Young Adults				
English-speaking Young Adults				
Spanish-speaking Adults				
English-speaking Adults				

Figure 7-4. Audio/Video Distributors Matrix

Some offer more academic titles, while others are more interested in the mass market. Each has something valuable to contribute to your Latino materials collection.

EVALUATING MATERIALS FOR LATINO CHILDREN AND YOUNG ADULTS

In this next section we provide some useful criteria for selecting or evaluating Latino materials for children and young adults. Factors typically considered in this process are value, need, format, price, and availability. These are useful criteria, but they do not specifically address Latino materials. Your collection development policy most likely addresses general evaluation or selection criteria, but unless you have revised it lately, it will be too narrow for the work you are embarking on.

"When evaluating materials for Latino children, language and cultural issues arise. It is important to understand the cultural heritage, language, socioeconomic backgrounds, preferred learning modes, and socialization patterns of your target before providing effective service." (Mestre and Nieto, 1996: 27)

> What are the language issues? It may be important to iden-tify books written by an authority in the area of preference, for example Puerto Rico, when purchasing books in the Spanish language. If the book is primarily in English, with some Spanish phrases thrown in, the terminology should be checked for mistakes or in the event that it demeans a par-ticular ethnic group in the attempt to characterize it. Lan-guage mixing (or code switching) cannot be placed simply at random within a text but rather the author should be comfortably familiar with how Latinos mix languages in their daily speech. Librarians looking at children's materi-als may take a word out of context by using its literal trans-lation, attribute a negative connotation to it, and reject an otherwise excellent book. (Mestre and Nieto, 1996: 27–28)

What are the cultural issues? Consider the portrayal of the cultural group and the general accuracy of the material presented. It is difficult to write convincing and accurate literature if the author is removed from the cultural or ethnic experience, so the author's perspective is important. Ac-cording to Mestre and Nieto, children's books "should present Latinos with the same variety, humor, dignity and skill that is seen in books about others. They should be careful not to perpetuate stereotypes." (Mestre and Nieto, 1996)

When evaluating materials for Latino young adults, one valuable re-source that provides some general guidance to selectors is the Center for the Study of Books in Spanish for Children and Adolescents (Centro para el Estudio de Libros Infantiles y Juveniles en Español), based at California State University, San Marcos. Since 1991 the center has sponsored annual conferences on Spanish books for children and young adults. Dr. Isabel Schon, director of the center, is a leading authority on the subject of Span-ish books for young readers, and she has authored many articles and works that can serve as references in developing your collection. Her biblio-graphic tools appear regularly in *Booklist* and *VOYA*. Another reason to contact the center is that for a small fee it provides recent bibliographies of recommended children's and young adult materials. Further information on the center can be found in Chapter 10.

Another source can be professional newsletters from organizations such as REFORMA and the American Library Association, which publishes an

Ethnic Materials and Information Exchange Roundtable newsletter, as well as from the members of the REFORMA listserv. (Immroth and McCook, 2000)

> Works by distinctive authors that represent the ethnic origins or the audience in your geographical setting are important. Materials that appeal to Latino teens on the West Coast might be very different from those that appeal to Latino teens on the East Coast. Latino authors that are appearing on high school reading lists with more frequency are Claribel Alegria, Manuel Alonso, Sandra Cisneros, Laura Esquivel, Esmeralda Santiago, Nicolosa Mohr, Mary Ellen Ponce, and Judith Ortiz Cofer. (Immroth and McCook, 2000:111)

In your day-to-day practice of collection development, it is impossible to inspect personally each and every title before selecting it. We hope that these collection development tips will help you get started. Your desire to serve the Latino community is important but the selection of materials that reinforce positive self-image and reflect the culture and language of our youth will be critical at any library.

PROVIDING COLLECTION ACCESS

You have learned how to purchase some wonderful materials to reach out to your Latino community. The next challenges arise from trying to link the materials to your public. Plan—again the mantra for those of you reading this manual—with staff, volunteers, and advisory boards on how best to give visibility to your efforts.

SELECTING A SITE

First, you will need to select a site in your library for the new materials. To focus attention on the new collection, you need to designate an area in your library that is as attractive as other areas of the library. Be sure to include proper bilingual signage to direct users to the collection. If you want to name this area, you should use words in Spanish—or at the minimum in both English and Spanish. We advise you not to use "Foreign Language" in any part of the signage. You have just created a non–English language collection and your advisory group should be consulted with suggestions on naming and publicizing.

PROCESSING MATERIALS

One problem you will encounter is that some of the materials you purchase may not be shelf-ready when they arrive in technical services. Some of the bindings will not be of the quality that is typically found in the United States. Similarly, the paper quality may not be as good. Be prepared to spend more on processing time and supplies than you would with traditional materials. When you start receiving materials, it will be easier to judge how much of a challenge this will be. You will then be better able to budget for this extra activity.

CATALOGING MATERIALS

What may seem to you like an ordinary, everyday matter—performing a subject search in an online catalog—can be a frustrating experience for others with limited English skills. In an ideal world, every library would first have an automated library system with a multilingual interface that would be easy for all patrons to use. Second, the bibliographic database that your library uses to obtain cataloging records would have an accurate and complete MARC record for each item you purchase, no matter the original language of the item. Third, the bibliographic records for all Spanish-language items in your library would contain both Spanish and English subject headings.

Among the libraries that have developed catalogs that are user-friendly to Latinos are the San Antonio (Texas) Public Library and the Queens (New York) Borough Public Library. CARL Corporation, Inc., and the San Antonio Public Library have jointly developed a Spanish-language interface to its children's catalog. "Catalita" has been operational since May 1997. Queens Borough Public Library allows users to search the library's catalog in Spanish (and other languages) and to access its community services database.

Like most libraries, yours will probably not have a Spanish-language catalog interface for quite some time. Since you will be relying on your English-only catalog for the foreseeable future, you need to make some adaptations so that you can provide access to Spanish materials.

One of your major challenges will be to catalog the Spanish-language materials that you have purchased. Be prepared to spend more on this activity than you do with traditional materials. You will find that no matter which database you use to obtain bibliographic records, there will be a significant number of Spanish-language items for which there are either no cataloging records available or for which the records will need modification. For many Spanish-language items, this means you will have to modify existing records, do your own original cataloging, find some alternative methods for obtaining the needed bibliographic records, or a combination of all three.

As we have mentioned before, the best solution is to have bilingual individuals on your staff; they are best able to review and understand Spanish-language materials, search for matching records in whatever source your cataloging department uses to obtain bibliographic records, make modifications to bibliographic records if necessary, and do any original cataloging that is required.

If such staffing is not possible, there are some alternatives:

- Purchase MARC records from the specialized Latino distributors. The distributors realize that cataloging Spanish-language materials is difficult for the smaller libraries, and they are able to sell MARC records for the items they carry at a reasonable price.

- Contract with a nearby source (for example, an academic library, library consultant, or library cooperative) who has experience in cataloging Spanish-language materials.

- Review the cataloging records for the same or similar Spanish-language items in the databases of larger, metropolitan libraries that have larger Spanish collections.

- Hire a bilingual person or recruit a bilingual volunteer from the community (such as a local Spanish teacher) who can assist the cataloger.

A major decision you will have to make, and an added expense, is whether or not to add Spanish subject headings to the bibliographic records of Spanish materials. In the long run it may be the best option because if your integrated library system vendor provides a Spanish-language version of the Online Public Access Catalog (OPAC) in the future, Spanish-speaking patrons will be able to search the catalog in their native language. Until then, including Spanish-language subject headings in your bibliographic records for Spanish materials will provide better access. If your catalog is Web-based, the keyword searching feature can alleviate the lack of Spanish interface by providing access by means of particular search features.

Another way to improve access is to produce attractive bibliographies written in Spanish, describing the Spanish-language materials in a wide variety of topics that are of current or lasting interest. These guides to the collection can be placed near the collection itself and also near the reference desk, and they can also be used as public relations pieces when you go out into the Latino community. This is a project that can be undertaken by the Latino advisory group. Another inexpensive way to improve access is to provide a Spanish-language overview of the Dewey Decimal System near the collection (see Chapter 5, Figure 5-1).

Although an online catalog with English-language commands or menus can be an impenetrable barrier to access for Latinos, it does not have to be. Every library is struggling with access issues, but state libraries, regional library systems, and state library associations do their part by providing practical workshops on these challenging technical services issues. There are creative ways to make it work for Latinos.

APPENDIX 7A: LATINO BOOK DISTRIBUTORS

Adler's Foreign Books
915 Foster Ave.
Evanston, IL 60201
(800) 235-3771
fax (847) 864-0804

AIMs Foreign Langauge Books, Inc.
    and Another Language Press
7709 Hamilton Ave.
Cincinnati, OH 45231
(800) 733-2067
fax (513) 521-5592
www.aimsbooks.com

Arte Público Press
Piñata Books
University of Houston
M.O. Anderson Library, Rm. 2
Houston, TX 77204
800-633-ARTE
(Fax) 713-743-2847

Bilingual Educational Services
2514 S. Grand Ave.
Los Angeles, CA 90007
(800) 448-6032
(213) 749-6213
fax (213) 749-1820
www.besbooks.com

Bilingual Publications Co.
270 Lafayette St., Suite 705
New York, NY 10012
(212) 431-3500
fax (212) 431-3567
e-mail:LindaGoodman
    @juno.com

Chullain Publishing Corp.
28625 Kennedy Gulch Rd.

Conifer, CO 80433
(303) 838-4375
fax (303) 838-4791

Continental Book Co., Inc.
Western Division
625 E. 70 Ave., Suite 5
Denver, CO 80229
(303) 289-1761
fax (800) 279-1764

Continental Book Co.
80-00 Cooper Ave., Bldg. #29
Glendale, NY 11385
(718) 326-0560
www.continentalbook.com

Donars Spanish Books
P.O. Box 808
Lafayette, CO 80026
(800) 552-3316
(303) 666-9175

Downtown Book Center, Inc.
School and Library Division
247 S.E. First St.
Miami, FL 33131
(800) 599-8712
(305) 377-9939
fax (305) 371-5926
www.libros-direct.com

Fiesta Book Company
P.O. Box 490641
Key Biscayne, FL 33149-0641
(305) 858-4843

Fondo de Cultura Economica
    USA
2293 Verus St.

San Diego, CA 92154
(619) 429-0455
fax (619) 429-0827
www.fceusa.com

Ingram Library Services, Inc.
P.O. Box 3006
One Ingram Blvd.
LaVergne, TN 37086-1986
(800) 937-5300
www.Ingrambooks.com

Latin Trading Corp
539 W. H St., Suite B
Chula Vista, CA 91910
(619) 427-7867
fax (619) 476-1817

Lectorum Publications, Inc.
205 Chubb Ave.
Lyndhurst, NJ 07071-3520
(800) 345-5946
(201) 559-2225
www.lectorum.com

Libros Latinos
P.O. Box 1103
Redlands, CA 92373
(800) MI-LIBRO
(909) 793-8423
fax (909) 335-9945
e-mail:Libros@concentric.net

Los Andes Publishing, Inc.
P.O. Box 2344
La Puente, CA 91746
(800) 532-8872
www.losandes.com

Mariuccia Iaconi Book Imports
970 Tennessee St.
San Francisco, CA 94107
(800) 955-9577
(415) 821-1216
fax (415) 821-1596
www.mibibook.com

Multi-Cultural Books and Videos,
   Inc.
28880 Southfield Rd., Suite 183
Lathrop Village, MI 48076
(800) 567-2220
www.multiculturbv.com

NTC/Contemporary Publishing
   Group
4255 W. Touhy Ave.
Lincolnwood, IL 60646
(800) 323-4900
www.ntc-cb.com

Santillana Publishing Company,
   Inc.
2105 N.W. 86th Ave.
Miami, FL 33122
(800) 245-8584

Spanish Book Distributors, Inc.
8200 Southwestern Blvd. #1316
Dallas, TX 75206-2180
(800) 609-2113
www.sbdbooks.com

T.R. Books
822 N. Walnut Ave.
New Braunfels, TX 78131-0279
(800) 659-4710

APPENDIX 7B: LATINO AUDIO AND VIDEO DISTRIBUTORS

LATINO AUDIO DISTRIBUTORS

Audio Forum: The Language Source
96 Broad St.
Guilford, CT 06437
(800) 243-1234
http://agoralang.com/audioforum.html

LATINO VIDEO DISTRIBUTORS

Facets Video
1517 W. Fullerton Ave.
Chicago, IL 60614
(800) 331-6197
www.facets.org

Latin American Video Archives
124 Washington Pl.,
New York, NY 10014
(212) 463-0108
www.lavavideo.org

Multi-Cultural Books and Videos, Inc.
28880 Southfield Rd., Suite 183
Lathrup Village, MI 48076
(800) 567-2220
www.multiculbv.com

APPENDIX 7C: LATINO PUBLISHERS

Arte Público Press
Univ. of Houston
M.O. Anderson Library, Rm 2
Houston, TX 77204-2090
(800) 633-2783
(713) 743-2841
fax (713) 743-2847
fax (602) 965-8309

Children's Book Press
246 First Street, Suite 101
San Francisco, CA 94105
(415) 995-2200
fax (415) 995-2222

Children's Press
Grolier Publishing
90 Old ShermanTurnpike
Danbury, CT 06819
(800) 621-1115

Chulainn Publishing Corp.
244 Wagon Tongue Rd.
Bailey, CO 80421
(888) 525-2665
www.newpublications.com

Corona Publishing Co.
P.O. Drawer 12407
San Antonio, TX 78212
(210) 341-7525

Curbstone Press
321 Jackson St.
Willimantic, CT 06226
(860) 423-5110
fax (860) 423-9242
www.connix.com/~curbston/

Floricanto Press
16161 Ventura Blvd., Suite 830
Encino, CA 91436-2504
(818) 990-1879

Fondo de Cultura Economica
    USA
2293 Verus St.
San Diego, CA 92154
(800) 532-3872
(619) 429-0455
fax (619) 429-0827

Los Andes Publishing Inc.
P.O. Box 2344
La Puente, CA 91746
(800) LECTURA
fax (562) 531-0799

Santillana Publishing Co.,
    Inc.
2043 N.W. 87th Ave.
Miami, FL 33172
(800) 245-8584

8 LATINOS: PLANNING FOR A SKILLED, COMPETENT WORKFORCE

> Latino librarians can communicate effectively with Spanish speakers and direct them to materials designed for them. "Imagine the difference between the resources an English speaker receives from a librarian compared with those received by a [native] Spanish speaker," says Elizabeth Martínez, a library science educator and former executive director of the ALA. "I am still amazed at the belief that a smile will suffice when communicating with Spanish-speaking Latinos. Doesn't every library user get a smile? We need equitable service for Spanish speakers." (Espinal, 2003)

All library personnel, volunteers, and trustees you might have—both of Latino origin and not—are crucial to your library's success in attracting and serving your underserved Latino community. The library workers set the tone for your library. Probably the most serious mistake any library can make is fail to sensitize its workers to cultural awareness and ethnic diversity issues.

Latinos in your community might be at your library for a diverse range of reasons, and every effort must be made to serve them competently. Potential patrons will keep coming to the library or be deterred depending on the people they meet and how they are made to feel. (Moller, 2001)

Library personnel are the focus in this chapter, from the best-case scenario of an ethnically-diverse workforce (and ways to obtain it) to the realities of an all-White staff and how to help them. Tips on the recruitment of minority personnel will be offered, and Latino library trustees and internal Latino advisory committees also will be discussed.

LATINO TO LATINO: THE BEST-CASE SCENARIO

The need for bilingual staff continues to be a pressing point in libraries. Much of the work that needs to be done to attract Latinos in your community to the library requires the ability to speak their language and to understand the Latino culture. Therefore, having a bilingual and bicultural Latino workforce is obviously the best-case scenario. One could argue that a non-Latino who is bilingual could be as effective. We are not denying that such staff members can be effective, but the best-case scenario for the workforce is to have some bilingual Latino workers on the team. Why? For the most part, Latinos that work in the library have the following characteristics that would be hard to match by a non-Latino:

- Latino library workers grew up with and know the local Latino culture (albeit there are many subcultures among the Latino population in this country)
- They are acutely aware of the cultural differences between the predominant white culture and the Latino culture and can adjust to those differences
- They are visible and easily identifiable among the Latino community you are striving to serve
- Latino staff offers a sense of commonality (for example, physical characteristics, heritage, etc.) that automatically establishes a sense of trust between them and the Latino community.
- They know and speak the local vernacular Spanish language
- They are familiar with and often live in the Latino community
- Latino library workers bring a sense of purpose and commitment to serving the local Latino community
- They can be good role models for Latino children and teens

How else can bilingual/bicultural Latino library workers serve the library and the community? Latinos can reach out effectively to the Latino community and know Spanish-speaking individuals in the community who can assist the library with bilingual programs. They, themselves, can offer bilingual programming, such as children's story hours in Spanish, as well as design and write the bilingual flyers that advertise the various bilingual programs being offered. They can do effective collection development and processing of Spanish-language materials. Additionally, they can serve as public-relations liaisons to the Spanish-language media. (Hispanic Services Committee, 1990)

> There are very few Latino library professionals relative to the 42.7 million Latinos living in this country.

RECRUITING LATINO LIBRARIANS

Let's assume that you were successful in getting some extra librarian positions funded to help you concentrate on developing services to your Latino community. Your recruitment efforts demand planning a strategy that will be successful, and we have some tips for planning that strategy.

One of the most difficult challenges is recruiting Latino librarians. This is a challenge no matter the type of library. First of all, there are very few Latino library professionals relative to the 42.7 million Latinos living in this country. This is where the challenge begins.

Write your job announcement to allow for the expansion of the pool of candidates. That is, write the job announcement so that the minimum qualifications are indeed the minimum. If someone with two years experience can do the job as well as someone with five years of experience, then require only two years of experience. (Peterson, 1996) On the other hand, if the position requires a special skill, then be specific. If you want a librarian who can communicate with the Latino community, do Spanish-language programming, and buy Spanish-language materials, then you need to make fluency in Spanish a requirement. You should also provide added compensation to employees who have these special bilingual abilities.

Once the job announcement is ready to go, you need to plan strategically where to advertise. Depending on the size of your community, you might be successful in finding some Latinos with MLS degrees. Usually your chances are much greater in finding Latino paraprofessionals from your local community. Nonetheless, it does not hurt to advertise the professional position locally.

Word of mouth is another effective local strategy. Ask your local Latino residents—business people, educators, community leaders, government employees—for referrals. You never know who might have a second cousin with an MLS who just might be interested.

We recommend that you contact the placement officers at the library and information studies programs in areas that have some concentration of Latinos. These officers can usually provide names and addresses of Latino alumni and current Latino students. A list of such library programs is included in Appendix 8A at the end of this chapter.

REFORMA (National Association to Promote Library and Information Services to Latinos and the Spanish-Speaking), an American Library Association (ALA) affiliate, distributes a biannual newsletter to its 700-plus members. You can advertise your position there. REFORMA also manages an Internet discussion group (called REFORMANET) that posts job announcements. You can find more information on REFORMANET in Chapter 10.

Cultivating your own staff is a very effective way to increase the number of Latino professional librarians. Although this is a long-term solution, it is still doable. The strategy is to support Latino paraprofessionals already on your staff in getting their MLS degrees. Once they achieve that goal, they should be next in line for assuming professional positions as librarians. (Peterson, 1996)

There are a variety of ways to encourage Latinos to earn their MLS degrees. Providing tuition reimbursement or incentives is one way; the other is to provide release time for your employees to attend classes that are only offered during the workday. Scholarship opportunities are still another way for recruiting Latino MLS graduates. For example, the Colorado State Library's advisory board has provided scholarship funds to attend library school. The recipients must have demonstrated a commitment to working with minorities. On the national level, the American Library Association's Spectrum Initiative is providing scholarships for minorities who study information science at the masters and doctoral level.

RECRUITING LATINO PARAPROFESSIONALS

In addition to locating Latino librarians, put time and effort into finding, hiring, and training Latino paraprofessionals. When developing the job description for a paraprofessional staff position, we recommend that you make bilingual ability in Spanish a requirement. That is the only way to attract someone who meets your library's primary need—bilingual competency. Your commitment to serve Latinos will be demonstrated and solidified when you follow through with this bilingual requirement and are able to hire a bilingual Latino paraprofessional.

In developing the job announcement and in order to get Latino residents to apply, do not make experience in a library a requirement. This requirement will automatically eliminate almost all Latinos. Also, understand that the more requirements you list, the more Latinos you eliminate. For example, there may be a Latino individual who can help in bilingual translation of programs, services, and promotional materials; who can canvass the Latino community in the library's outreach efforts; and who can be trained to offer story hours and work various service desks. However, if you make "typing 50 words per minute" or "experience with personal computers and/or word-processing software" a requirement, you might eliminate many qualified Latino applicants.

Remember that you are making an investment when you hire a Latino paraprofessional. That person will bring special characteristics to the library—bilingual ability and inside knowledge of the Latino community and culture. In return, you must commit to the time it will take to train this individual in the library-related duties and responsibilities that will make him or her successful in the library.

We recommend that you advertise in the local and area newspapers. If there is a Spanish-language newspaper, advertise in it. See if you can get someone to translate the job announcement into Spanish for that newspaper. If there are Spanish-language radio or television stations in the area, advertise there too.

We have one other advertising tip: Put the job announcement in a flyer format and distribute the flyers throughout the Latino community. You need to get the information directly to the community from which you want to draw your applicants.

Last but not least, rely on word-of-mouth referrals. Ask staff, Latino library users, educators, Latino business people, and others for referrals. People will usually only refer others to you who are capable, dependable, and responsible.

RECRUITING LATINO VOLUNTEERS

Volunteers are vital to most libraries. There is no reason for the scope of your volunteer base not to include bilingual Latino individuals. This is definitely the next best thing to hiring permanent Latino staff. Latino volunteers can help you in providing services to their community. Most public libraries, especially in smaller communities, do not have a high staff turnover rate. Consequently, very few permanent staff positions—professional or paraprofessional—become vacant. This aspect, along with budget limitations, is a real barrier in hiring additional permanent staff—Latino or not—and it is beyond the library's control to rectify.

Latino volunteers should come from the Latino community, and speaking Spanish should not be their only responsibility. The library needs to train them to work adequately in the library and to do outreach for the library in the Latino community.

How and where do you find Latino volunteers? Here is where a lot of time and dedication takes place. First of all, how do you regularly enlist non-Latino volunteers from your community? Try using similar methods in the Latino community as you would use in any other. Following are some tips for recruiting Latino volunteers to help you in your efforts to serve the Latino community:

- Check among your current staff. They may know of Latinos who might be willing to volunteer or who might be able to help you find Latino volunteers.

- Find out who the formal and informal Latino community leaders are. Enlist their help. Some may have friends or relatives who might be willing to volunteer in the library.

- Check with church leaders and religious organizations most frequented by the Latino community for volunteer referrals.

- If you already have Latino users in your library, ask them for referrals. In fact, if some of them are adults or young adults, see if they would be willing to volunteer some time.

- Check with other organizations and government agencies that provide services to Latinos. They can help with referrals.
- Don't forget to check with the local junior high and high schools. If the high school has Spanish classes or a Spanish club, members may be willing to volunteer to do bilingual story hours or translate after school during scheduled hours.
- If your community has a recreational center that is frequented by Latinos, go there to recruit volunteers.
- If your community has a senior citizen's center, recruit Latino senior citizens as volunteers. Libraries, in general, have real success with senior volunteers.
- Cooperate with your local judicial system and use community service workers.
- Advertise in the local media for bilingual volunteers. If there are any Spanish-language media, make sure to advertise there also.
- Invest in your teens (young adults). They are a great source for building a volunteer base. They can effectively assist in your bilingual story hours and your summer reading programs.

> Latino volunteers should come from the Latino community, and speaking Spanish should not be their only responsibility

We know from personal experience of many success stories of volunteer programs using young adults. Not only is there a certain vitality with this age group, but they also are full of ideas. A word of caution, however: If your professional and paraprofessional staffs are represented by unions, be careful about how you use your volunteers. Otherwise, bilingual volunteers are a source that can be very important to the services you offer or want to offer to your Latino community.

We acknowledge that all this takes time and that you need to be aggressive about your volunteer development efforts. However, it will pay off one way or another. For example, if you already have an established group of Latino volunteers, you also have a pool of potential employees when a position does become vacant. You already have a good sense of the Latino volunteer's work ethic, sense of responsibility, attitude, capabilities, and community reputation.

Even with a pool of Latino volunteers, you are still faced with the fact that your current permanent staff is 100% non-Latino. How do you handle the challenge of preparing them to serve your underserved Latino community?

WHITE TO LATINO: REALITIES OF NON-MINORITY STAFFING

It was during a workshop in Kansas, a White librarian from a very small farming community in Kansas explained why she was attending our workshop. Her community had experienced an influx of Latino immigrants who were working in the local meat-processing plants. The Latino immigrants brought their families, and the community's population increased by 25% as a result of that influx.

Her challenge began when the Latino immigrant children started coming into the library with their mothers, and no one on her staff felt they were offering adequate services—not to mention that they did not speak Spanish. Providing that scenario, the librarian said that her all-White staff was very small and that they had been with her for years and would probably retire from the library.

This is the reality that many of you may be facing. So what can you do? You cannot lay off or fire a longtime employee because that employee does not have the characteristics (such as Spanish-speaking ability) you so desperately need. In this case, you do the next best thing, which is to work with your staff to help them understand the importance of serving Latinos in your community. This alone is not an easy task, and it is especially difficult if you are dealing with institutional racism.

Some of you will understand the realities of institutional racism. Institutional racism is embedded in the institution—school, library, organization, or community. Institutional racism occurs when the values, customs, behaviors, and attitudes of one group are so fixed that the institution becomes intolerant of any group different from itself.

Do not be surprised if this occurs in your library; you need to be prepared to deal with it. Because a library staff is so instrumental in the success of a library, you have to work with your staff so that they understand the purpose and rationale for needing to serve the Latino community.

STAFF DEVELOPMENT AND TRAINING

Staff development becomes an important part of what you do. Here are some tips for getting your staff prepared:

1. Use the same rationale for your staff that you prepare for your external groups (see Chapter 3). In fact, you have to convince your staff before you can convince others in the community.

2. Involve your staff in all aspects of developing these services. This process will make your life easier because you have the necessary staff buy-in to be successful.

3. If the opportunities are available, have your staff sign up for conversational Spanish classes at your local community college or college/university. Provide release time for them to attend classes, as well as tuition reimbursement. If funds are an issue, write a proposal for funding (see Chapter 9) that includes such items as tuition reimbursement and staff training to converse and work with Latino users.

4. If there are no colleges nearby that offer Spanish-language courses, bring someone in to teach your staff relevant Spanish words and phrases necessary in a library environment. Again, include this staff training component in your proposal to acquire funds to begin serving Latinos in your community.

5. If some staff members have developed some fluency in Spanish, offer a pay differential for that expertise.

6. If tips 3–5 are impossible, adapt a phonetic Spanish manual of library phrases. Appendix 5B at the end of Chapter 5 provides some library-related, Spanish-language words and phrases.

7. Strongly urge your state library or regional library systems office (if you have regional systems in your state) to provide appropriate staff training to help your library serve your Latino community. Chicago Public Library developed the following workshops that enabled library staff to serve their Latino communities better (Hispanic Services Committee, 1990):

   - developing library services for Latino children
   - developing a reference collection in Spanish
   - using bilingual concepts in storytelling
   - training staff on cultural awareness and sensitivity
   - developing a core collection of Spanish adult fiction
   - training staff on various Latino cultures

8. Most of the time, the American Library Association's (ALA) Annual Conference and other specialized conferences (for example, REFORMA) will have various programs dealing with library services to Latinos and minorities, ranging from the aforementioned types of topics to recruitment and retention of minority personnel.

If you and your staff do not normally attend these conferences, it would be a good investment to send someone who can attend all the relevant programs and then return and share the information. Better yet, the person can provide some internal staff training based on the conference programs. *American Libraries*, the ALA professional journal, also provides a synopsis of the various conference programs by subject category in the issue published just before the ALA Annual Conference.

9. Use Latino personnel from other organizations, as well as city and county agencies, to assist you in staff development, especially with cultural sensitivity and ethnic awareness matters.

10. Enlist volunteers from the Latino community to help you with staff development. Organize a panel of local Latino citizens to discuss their Latino culture (music, food, celebrations, and dance, for example) with your staff. Latinos, like all minority groups, are willing to share their culture in efforts to help the predominant group understand and accept them more.

Preparing staff to serve your Latino community is a must, whether you have bilingual staff or not. The tips we have provided should help you get started in relevant staff development.

RECRUITING LATINO TRUSTEES

Latino representation on your board of trustees can be one of the best ways for your library to have the leverage to encourage, develop, and implement the necessary services for Latinos in your community. Additionally, one of the best ways for any public library to know and serve its minority community is to ensure minority representation on its decision-making body. Latinos should be encouraged to apply or should be recommended to the authority that appoints library trustees.

INFORMAL RECRUITING

Canvass your churches, social organizations, and government and social services agencies for recommendations. In every Latino community, there are formal and informal leaders. Some of your formal leaders may be minority business owners, directors of agencies and organizations, educators, or government employees. Informal leaders can also be effective trustees. These may be parents, church activists, or members of the Parent Teacher Organization, all of whom have demonstrated leadership capabilities in their everyday lives and have genuine interest in the well-being of their Latino community and the whole community in general. Also look for adult Latino library users who have attended and actively participated in library programs you have offered.

In addition, your library staff may have recommendations for Latino representation. Those recommendations could include any of the categories of people just mentioned.

FORMAL RECRUITING

Use your local newspaper, radio station, promotional flyers, or a combination of media sources, to announce board openings. However, you need to be specific in encouraging members of the Latino community to apply for board positions. Distribute the flyers to popular spots in the Latino community—minority businesses, church bulletin boards, local grocery stores, gas stations, and daycare centers, for example. Human nature is such that people who read the advertisements will think of formal and informal leaders who would be excellent candidates. They, in turn, will contact those leaders and encourage them to submit their names as nominees.

If a library sincerely wants Latino board representation and follows some of the tips mentioned, there will be a response from the Latino community. A word of caution, however: Make sure that the names that go forward are indeed the names of Latino individuals who would take the position of a trustee seriously and would do a good job for the library and the Latino community.

This process of identifying Latino nominees is no different from the process you use in finding non-Latino nominees to fill board positions, except that you may have the limitation of not knowing many Latino community members. Nonetheless, it is probably in your library's best interest to identify and submit several Latino candidates to the appointing authority whose responsibility it is to select the best candidate for the board.

LATINO TRUSTEE SUCCESS

Getting a Latino on your library's board of trustees is only half the challenge. It is in everyone's best interest for the library administration to nurture, respect, inform, and educate that Latino trustee. What you already have is a leader by virtue of reputation or position in the Latino community. You need to continue to develop the leadership skills of that Latino trustee.

Your Latino trustee is the lifeline to your Latino community. That trustee will be the liaison who will assist the library in such matters as:

- identifying potential Latino staffing prospects
- recommending effective programs to attract your under-served Latino community
- working on good pubic relations between the library and the Latino community
- developing library and Latino partnerships/networking with individuals and organizations

INTERNAL LATINO ADVISORY COMMITTEES

An internal Latino Advisory committee can enhance your total library or-ganization and help recruit new Latinos and retain the ones already em-ployed. If you eventually are able to hire a number of Latino staff members, then we strongly recommend that you encourage them to estab-lish an internal Latino advisory committee. We are personally aware of a number of internal Latino advisory committees throughout the country. We mentioned two in the first edition, Chicago Public Library's Hispanic Services Committee and Denver Public Library's (DPL) Hispanic Steering Committee. Both of these pioneering committees have changed with the passing of time.

Chicago Public Library's internal Latino advisory committee is one of several that are responsible for developing and marketing library services, resources, and programs to an ethnic community. (The ethnic community groups included are African American, Asian American, Hispanic Ameri-can, and Polish American.) Collection development is included as the committee members work to identify materials that would be relevant to the target group and evaluate databases that they recommend be made available to customers. The name of the committee has changed as well—it is now known as the Hispanic Heritage Committee. The members in-clude both Latino and non-Latino library staff members, with all of them serving the Latino populations in the Chicago Public Library service area. The committee meets regularly, utilizes an internal e-mail discussion list called *hispserv*, and provides minutes from their meetings. More informa-tion on the committee can be found on the library Web site's "Celebrating Diversity" section at: www.chipublib.org/003cpl/diversity/cd_intro.html. The responsibilities of this committee also include promotion and under-standing of the heritage and culture of Latinos to all Chicagoans, regard-less of their ethnic background. They are responsible for strengthening the relationships between organizations that serve Latinos in Chicago and the Chicago Public Library. (Wilson, personal communication, 2007)

The Denver Public Library (DPL) Hispanic Steering Committee has been created with the support of the DPL administration and DPL's Library Commission, involved in all aspects of library services to Denver's Latino community, and truly demonstrated leadership in the area of community collaboration. This committee is no longer active. In Appendix 8B at the end of this chapter, we have included the mission, goals, and bylaws of the former DPL Hispanic Steering Committee to give you an example of the structure of an internal Latino advisory committee.

Other groups that we learned about include: The Alliance for the Bi-Cultural Community of South Carolina (Comunidad), The Tulsa City-County Hispanic Resource Center Advisory Committee, White Plains Library Hispanic Outreach Group, and San Mateo Public Library's Latino Advisory Committee.

In the Westchester Library System (New York), the White Plains Library formed a Hispanic Outreach Group comprised of two bilingual librarians, assistant library director, community liaison librarian, and literacy librarian. This committee meets every two months to discuss programming (some programming is outsourced in addition to one bilingual staff member providing Spanish programming in-house), marketing, services to Latinos, and topics for the bi-monthly newsletter. A bi-monthly newsletter is produced, and the Spanish version is entitled *Noticias*. It can be found online at: www.whiteplainslibrary.org/espanol/noticias.shtml. (Canuelas, personal communication, 2007)

If your library has adequate Latino staffing, we recommend that you encourage the development of such a committee. With encouragement and proper guidance, this type of advisory group can assist your library in achieving and enhancing its goal of providing library services to Latinos in your community.

CONCLUSION

Staff members, more than library materials, have the profound effect on library users. How staff members treat people who walk in the door can determine whether or not those people will return to use the library.

Outreach to the Latino community in your service area can be greatly enhanced when you employ bilingual/bicultural staff. You need to recognize the importance of staff training and to develop partnerships with others to help provide that training. Remember to apply for external funding to help pay for the personnel costs associated with the design and implementation of programs and services for Latinos in your community and to do outreach into that community. Even if those funds are temporary, you can at least get started on this important feature of your overall library services.

APPENDIX 8A: ACCREDITED LIBRARY AND INFORMATION STUDIES PROGRAMS LOCATED IN GEOGRAPHICAL AREAS WITH LATINO POPULATIONS

California State University, San Jose
Emporia in the Rockies, Denver, Colorado (Emporia State University, Emporia, Kansas)
Florida State University, Tallahassee, Florida
Pratt Institute, Brooklyn, New York
Queens College, Queens, New York
Texas Woman's University, Denton, Texas
University of Arizona, Tucson, Arizona
University of California, Los Angeles, California
University of Denver, Denver, Colorado
University of North Texas, Denton, Texas
University of Puerto Rico, Rio Piedras, Puerto Rico
University of South Florida, Tampa, Florida
University of Texas at Austin, Texas

APPENDIX 8B: DENVER PUBLIC LIBRARY HISPANIC STEERING COMMITTEE

Mission Statement

To assist the Denver Public Library in its Mission "to inform, educate, inspire, and entertain," by exploring and implementing ways to bring about increased use of the Library and its branches by the Hispanic community,

> > Explore outreach opportunities and techniques.
> > Explore ways to better serve the Hispanic community.
> > Explore ways to make the Library more "user friendly" to the Hispanic community.

Goal 1: To assist the staff in bringing about increased involvement of the Hispanic community in all programs and activities.

A. Create Hispanic focus groups, posing up-to-date questions.
B. Increase the number of volunteers through recruitment of Hispanics of all ages.
C. Meet with Hispanic community groups and leaders.
D. Work with the schools in Hispanic communities.
E. Establish ties with the Branch Library staff to learn from their successful cultural programs, implementing their strategies in customer service to the Hispanic community.

Goal 2: To assist the staff in understanding, realizing, and capitalizing on the potential of the rich diversity of the Hispanic community.

A. Explore staff development in the areas of cultural awareness, diversity of the Hispanic community, Hispanic community activities, organizations, and the Spanish language.
B. Explore ways to make knowledge of a second language an asset.

By-Laws of the Denver Public Library Hispanic Steering Committee

Article I

The official name of this organization shall be "Hispanic Steering Committee" and shall be abbreviated as HSC throughout these by-laws.

Article II—Business and Purpose

1. To enhance library service to the Hispanic community.

2. To serve as a link of communication between the Hispanic community, the Hispanic staff, and local Hispanic organizations with DPL.

3. To represent Hispanic staff members of DPL and promote advocacy on Hispanic issues.

4. To promote Hispanic staff development through training, recruiting, and promotion.

Article III—Membership

1. HSC will have five officers.

2. Terms for all officers shall be two years. To ensure leadership continuity, the Chairperson and Secretary will be elected for terms beginning in even-numbered years; the other three officers will serve two years, beginning in odd-numbered years. Elections shall be held in October and terms will begin and end the first of January. No officer shall serve two consecutive terms.

3. Membership is open to ALL staff members—attendance of at least three-quarters of the meetings held per year must be met in order to maintain voting privileges.

Article IV—Officers

1. Officers of the HSC shall be: Chairperson, Vice-chairperson, Events Coordinator, Historian, and Secretary.

2. Nominees must be present in order to be eligible for office.

3. All officers shall be elected in October by the members of the HSC. All officers' terms shall be two years.

4. Voting procedures shall be as follows:

   A. Option to have a closed ballot.

   B. Option to vote by show of hands.

5. Duties of officers:

   A. Chairperson—calls and presides over meetings and appoints committees.

   B. Vice-Chairperson—presides when Chairperson is absent or when Chairperson gives up the Chair to the Vice-Chairperson.

   C. Events Coordinator—calls and presides over meetings of the Events Committee, plans and coordinates special events.

   D. Secretary—takes roll call and reads minutes. Prepares, signs, and distributes minutes to members prior to meetings.

   E. Historian—handles all correspondence and maintains archive of documents re: HSC activities.

Article V—Meetings

1. Meetings shall be held once a month, first Wednesday of each month.
2. The Chairperson shall call special meetings as needed.
3. Quorum—in order to have a meeting, there must be half of the total officers (three or more) attending.
4. Meetings are open to ALL staff members. Any person wishing to make a statement on any issue of concern must be recognized by the Chairperson in advance of meeting.

Article VI—Order of Business

1. Call to order
2. Roll call
3. Minutes of previous meeting
4. Chairperson's report
5. Old Business
6. New Business
7. Committee reports
8. Notification of next meeting
9. Adjournment

Article VII—Change in By-Laws

These by-laws may be changed at any regular meeting, or special meeting of the membership called for that purpose, by a majority vote of HSC, provided that notice of such proposed change is given at the preceding regular or special meeting, and a copy is made available to every HSC officer.

Permission to reprint granted by Carol Sandoval, last chair of the Denver Public Library Hispanic Steering Committee.

9 OBTAINING FUNDING

Latinos in your community, in one way or another, contribute to the tax base that funds city and county services provided by such departments as fire, police, and library. You will find yourself saying this over and over to other residents in your community. In fact, it will become second nature to you as will your rationale for serving Latino residents.

The one issue that you will constantly have to address, externally and internally, is that of funding. Serving Latinos in your community might indeed be new for your library; what is not new is the fact that Latinos in your community have already been paying for those library services through their tax dollars. For whatever reasons, they have not become library users.

We hope this chapter will give you some ideas of where and how to pursue funding from external sources. Additionally, we include grant-writing tips to get you started in developing some creative projects, and we showcase a few externally funded library projects designed to serve the Latino community.

ALLOCATING INTERNAL FUNDING

We define general funds as monies generated from a tax base. Internal funding is the money provided to the library on a yearly basis from its funding agency through general funds.

You will find that you have a lot to do to implement services to the Latinos in your community, but everything cannot be done at once. Your planning is absolutely crucial for any funding issue. By planning to deal with today's realities and to project for future needs, you will be able to provide a broader range of services for Latinos. We strongly recommend a phase-in process using the following three questions as a guide:

- What can you do right now without taking additional funds from your library's current general fund budget?
- In priority order, what do you plan to do to integrate services to Latinos in your community within your library's general fund budget?

- For the future and in priority order, what do you plan to do to secure and use external funds for the library?

When developing your plan, first identify the services you want to provide. These may include programs, materials, and personnel for Latinos in your community—a wish list of sorts. At this stage, don't get bogged down and overwhelm yourself by worrying about *how* you are going to provide those services, just list all the services you would like to offer to Latinos.

Second, delineate the services that are already available to Latinos under your current budget. You will need to sit down with your managers and/or staff to determine this. For example, services such as circulation, general reference, readers' advisory, meeting rooms, children's programming, and adult programming are already available to those Latinos who are either bilingual or monolingual in English. These services are already covered in your current budget at no extra cost.

Third, add to this list those low-cost items that will make Latinos want to come into and use your library. Items could include funds for bilingual signs, outreach activities, some special children's programming, and so on. Again, prioritize those items, asking such questions as:

- Is it important to the Latino community (for example, a program on income tax advising)?
- Will it be popular and of high interest (for example, a bilingual puppeteer)?
- Is it doable and expedient?
- Can you share resources (for example, forming a partnership with a social service agency to provide some relevant programming)?

Next, plan to integrate into your general fund some of the services you have listed for Latinos in your community. This calls for rethinking the use of some of your general funds. For example, let us say that your library has earmarked funds from your general fund for eight years to develop your children's collection. You have just completed your fifth year and still have three more years in that collection development project. You might want to take two-thirds of the next three years' funds and devote them to purchasing Spanish and bilingual children's materials to enhance your children's collection. Remember that bilingual materials are as useful to English-speaking children as they are to Latino children.

Another example includes sharing the funds available for adult general programming. Let's assume that you have budgeted a specific amount to offer adult programming each year. You can take a percentage of those allocated funds to offer bilingual programs to all adults. Again, depending on the general nature of those topics (for example, wills, hospice care, teenage pregnancy prevention), these bilingual programs can be beneficial to those Latino adults who are monolingual in Spanish as well as to those non-Latino adults who are monolingual in English.

These are examples of how you can begin to offer services using current general fund moneys to attract Latinos. However, don't forget that original list of Latino services. You may have listed services that have not fallen in the planning and funding schedule just provided. Although those are the services that, most likely, will take extra funds not available through your general fund budget, you at least have a plan for providing services to Latino residents in different phases and you know where you need to apply your current funds. You will need some planning, rethinking, redesigning, and initiative to know when to seek external funds to augment your general budget.

PURSUING EXTERNAL FUNDING

Most public libraries will not be able to develop and provide all services needed by Latinos solely relying on general fund, tax-based dollars. If you want to do more than what can be done within your existing budget, you will have to think of other ways to fund some of your projects. One of the best ways to supplement your general funds is to pursue external funding aggressively.

We define external funding as any moneys coming from any source outside of your tax-supported general fund. These external funds could come from private sources (such as corporations, foundations, individuals); from government entities other than the one that funds your library; from your Friends of the Library or your library foundation, if you have one; or they could come from library money-making projects. We even consider library discretionary funds—money from fines, lost books, or copier services—as external funds. However, you will have to check on your funding agency's fiscal rules to make sure there are no restrictions on the use of such funds.

Many people are intimidated by proposal writing. Writing grant proposals, working with your Friends group or library foundation, contacting external private and public funding agencies will take time and effort; however, the payback in getting a project funded can be substantial. For example, if it took a total of $960 (48 hours of total staff time at an average of $20 per hour from beginning to end) to submit a proposal for funding, and if you received funding based on that proposal for $38,000, you will have increased your investment nearly 40 times! When you look at fund-raising from that perspective, it becomes well worth your time.

We know that it is difficult to handle rejection. Unfortunately, that is a fact of life in fund-raising. However, when you do get a proposal funded or a project supported by an external group, you tend to forget your last rejection.

WRITING PROPOSALS

We want to focus on grant writing as a major method for obtaining external funds. There are many books on proposal writing; we suggest you refer to some of them if you need a more in-depth discussion. This is a quick lesson in Grant Writing 101.

Many different organizations—private, public, and nonprofit—provide funds for other organizations, usually through a competitive process. Funding organizations will often specify general guidelines such as:

- The applicant organization must be nonprofit
- They may restrict the use of their funds if they are scheduled to supplant your general fund budget
- They may restrict the use of their funds to support only an existing project or service
- They may ask you to specify pilot projects that will be supported by the library or the library's internal funding body after the external funds run out
- They may provide topical guidelines dealing with funding specific subjects areas (such as science, humanities, art)
- There may be funding and time limitations
- They may have very specific proposal guidelines and format (such as page restrictions) for preparing the application

We would like to share our philosophy as to the kind of proposal that is attractive to funding organizations. First of all, after you determine that you have met all the general guidelines and criteria, you need to start thinking about other criteria, such as:

- demonstrated need
- creativity
- buzz words or words *du jour*

For the sake of this grant-writing discussion, let us offer a hypothetical situation: Your library has committed to reach out aggressively to Latinos in your community. You have completed your planning process and one of your priorities is service to Latino children and young adults. You have incorporated some services for them into your general fund budget but now are pursuing external funding sources.

The first thing to consider is identifying a special need—in this case something to do with serving Latino children and young adults. You can probably identify something right this moment off the top of your head.

Let us start with demonstrating *the need*. In many cases, need is related to problem solving. That is, you recognize a problem and can also define a response to solve it. It is important to show and verify how your library, community, Latino residents (or a combination) fit into *the need* category. Any data and studies, for example, that can be presented are essential to demonstrate *the need*.

Again in our hypothetical scenario, you are bothered by the reports and articles you have been reading concerning the high Latino youth dropout rate in your community and in the state. You are also concerned about the growing illiteracy rate among teenagers. You know that there is a strong correlation between literacy and educational success. You also know that public libraries should work closely with schools to assist in providing supplementary library services. You have therefore decided to create an after-school, bilingual, homework help center sponsored by the library.

To illustrate your point concerning need, use whatever published data you can find on local and national educational attainment levels that will allow you to draw inferences about the literacy rates of Latino young adults in your community (see Chapter 3). You have also conducted some focus groups in your Latino community and have the summaries of those group discussions that overwhelmingly show that the community is concerned about its children and teenagers and would like your library to assist them in some way. Having shown sufficient need for your proposed service, you can move on to creativity.

Most funding organizations do not want to fund something that does not seem creative or that is already part of a current project. You are convinced that something needs to be done to help solve a problem; however, you need a *creative idea* to help solve the problem. The concept of a homework center in a library, you have found, is new to the state. In fact, the school districts have been unable to fund such a service. Your idea is therefore a creative one from a library service point of view.

Even more creative is the fact that you have chosen to locate this homework center where it is most needed—in the Latino neighborhood—and to make it bilingual. Now you have really mastered creativity!

So far, you have shown a strong need in your proposal; and you have come up with a creative idea to meet that need. Now you need to build in the *buzz words* or *words du jour*. Using such words will effectively strengthen your proposal.

In our hypothetical scenario, buzz words you would use throughout your proposal could be *illiteracy*, *dropout rates*, *graduation success*, *children at risk*, *teenagers at risk*, and *crime prevention*. Because your idea shows commitment to serving the Latino children and young adults in the community, don't be afraid to use those buzz words.

1. Title Page	7. Project Activities
2. Introduction/Background	8. Activities Time Line
3. Demonstration of Need	9. Budget
4. Purpose	10. Evaluation/Assessment
5. Description of Project	11. Support Letters
6. Goals and Objectives	

Figure 9-1. Sample Proposal Format

Demonstrating a strong need coupled with a creative idea or solution to solve a problem are the basics for a proposal. Now you are ready to move on to the next steps. Other parts of a proposal tend to follow conventions specific to proposal writing. However, we want to make sure you understand the importance of each part of a proposal. Figure 9-1 provides you with a sample proposal format. Following is a brief discussion of each item in that proposal format.

1. Title Page
   The title page includes the title of the proposal, the name of the organization submitting the proposal, and the contact person. We recommend that the title describes what the project is—but try to make it catchy. For our hypothetical scenario, the title might be "From Dropout to DropIN: A Library HomeworkHELP Center."

2. Introduction/Background
   The introduction can be brief. Here you identify the *local problem* (for example, high dropout rate of Latino youngsters). If you did any preliminary research on the proposed topic, you would include it here. For example, you could cite an article that describes the success rate of a minority tutoring project.

3. Demonstration of Need
   The demonstration of need tells the reader *why* you need to do the project. For example, you could elaborate on the problem of Latino high school dropouts—how it affects illiteracy, the economy, and so forth. Use your local demographic data here.

4. Purpose
   For the purpose of your project, you need to tell the reader what you want to accomplish in order to help solve a problem. For example: *The purpose of the HomeworkHELP Center is to provide academic assistance to*

at-risk Latino students, thereby increasing the high school graduation rate of Latinos in the community.

5. Description of Project
Describe the proposed project in layperson's terms. Make the description succinct but effective; use your buzz words.

6. Goals and Objectives
The goals will include much of what was stated in the "Purpose" text; goals are usually in numerical format. The objectives tell how you will accomplish each goal. We strongly recommend that each objective be measurable. In the broadest sense, this means that if something is achieved, you can prove it. See Figure 9-2 for an example.

7. Project Activities
A list of activities is optional. However, the more information you can provide without overwhelming the reader, the better you will demonstrate your careful thought and planning and the fewer questions the reader will have. We recommend that you follow the same format as the one used under "Goals and Objectives." Figure 9-3 shows an example that includes goal, objective, and activities.

Goal 1. To provide a site where Latino children can come in to get help with their homework.

Objective A. By November 2012, a site will be selected and prepared to house the HomeworkHELP Center.

Figure 9-2. Sample Project Goal and Objective

Goal 1. To provide a site where Latino children can come in to get help with their homework.

Objective A. By November 2012, a site will be selected and prepared to house the HomeworkHELP Center.

Activity 1. Prepare the specifications for the HomeworkHELP Center site.

Activity 2. Work with City Facilities Department to find an appropriate site.

Figure 9-3. Sample Project Goal, Objective, and Activities

8. Activities Timeline

 Some people prefer to use a chart that shows the term of the project in months and then lists the activities. Software applications such as Microsoft Project can provide a time line schematic; an outline also works well. This time line gives the proposal reader a clear indication of a carefully planned project that recognizes specific time frames for completing each phase of the project.

9. Budget

 Include whatever costs it takes to complete the project. Sometimes external funding organizations will have guidelines that you need to be aware of, such as:

 - Dollar for dollar match—This means that if they fund you for $38,000, the library must match these funds with $38,000. Usually the external funding organization does not care where you get the money, just as long as there is a match, either a cash match, an in-kind match, or a combination of both.

 - In-kind costs—Some external funding agencies will allow you to show your in-kind contributions. For example, you can show the percentage of the salary of anyone donating time to the project or you can show the amount of non-cash match the library will provide (such as books or equipment).

 - No support for indirect or overhead costs—The external funding organization wants to make sure that every dollar it awards goes to funding the project and does not go to supplementing fixed costs of the library or salaries of individuals not working on the project.

 - No support for any type of equipment or salaries—Usually the funding organization does not want to buy library equipment or pay for salaries.

 Figure out what it will take to complete the project down to the last activity and dime. Remember that most proposal readers are very astute. Do not "pad" the project budget—they will figure it out.

 One of us was once on a reading team for an external funding agency that received a proposal from a library that wanted funds for starting a literacy program. Its budget costs seemed in line until, at the very end, the library requested 10 desktop computers. Nowhere in the proposal did the library say how or where those PCs would be used to do any literacy-related activities or what kind of computer software would be needed. The project was funded, but funds were denied for nine of the ten PCs.

In this budget section, we recommend that you err on the side of too much information rather than not enough. For example, enter a budget item accordingly:

1,000 Spanish/bilingual children's/YA books
[$20/book x 1,000 books] $20,000
Rental of HomeworkHELP Center facility
[700 sq.ft. @ $15/sq.ft. x 5 years] $52,500

10. Evaluation/Assessment

After you have set down what you want to do, how and when you are going to do it, and how much it is going to cost, you are now ready to tell the agency how you will evaluate whether or not the project has been successful.

Most external funding agencies usually require the applicant to address evaluation/assessment, but one of the most common mistakes made by libraries submitting proposals at the local, state, and national levels is providing a weak evaluation component or none at all. If you follow the process we outlined in the goals, objectives, and activities sections, it is not difficult to design an equally strong evaluation component. Again, this is a step-by-step process. Following are some suggested evaluation measures:

- Meeting goals and objectives—If your objectives are measurable, then half of the assessment process is done. Part of your project evaluation will be showing whether or not each goal and objective was met and how.

- Evaluation from participants—This is another effective evaluation procedure. Devise a sample evaluation form that could be completed by the Latino students using the HomeworkHELP Center. Tell how and when you plan to use it.

- Evaluation from project staff—Although this step can be perceived as subjective and possibly self-serving, it is still a viable way to evaluate the project. Most people are honest in sharing the successes and setbacks of a project.

• External evaluation—Either your library or the external funding agency may want to bring in an external evaluator(s). If you decide to take this option and there are costs related to this method of evaluation, build the those costs into your proposed budget.

11. Support Letters
We strongly recommend that you include support letters in the appendices of your proposal. Using our scenario of the HomeworkHELP Center, we recommend including letters from members of the Latino community—Latino students who would benefit, your local school administration and teachers, community agencies, and parents. Make sure to enclose a copy of the proposal when you write to an organization or individual asking for a support letter. If the proposal is not finished, then send a brief summary highlighting the proposal components.

Ideas for external funding need not be as elaborate as a HomeworkHELP Center. An idea could be as simple as asking for funds to develop a collection of Spanish and bilingual children's books. Our point is that it is often necessary to pursue outside funds to get special projects started for Latinos in your community.

FINDING EXTERNAL FUNDS

One of the most common library funding sources for years has been LSCA (Library Services and Construction Act), now named LSTA (Library Services and Technology Act). Most states receive LSTA funds that are administered by the state library in each state. Some state libraries have restricted how LSTA funds can be used, but for the most part LSTA funds have been available to fund creative projects.

At one time there were funds from the Major Urban Resource Library (MURL) for those public libraries that served populations over 100,000. Consider what Denver Public Library and Oxnard (California) Public Library did with their MURL funds. Denver allocated all of its MURL funds for a certain number of years to develop a very strong children's collection of Spanish and bilingual materials. Oxnard Public Library used a combination of MURL and LSCA funds to build its Spanish/bilingual collection, and it now has the largest collection of Spanish materials between Los Angeles and San Francisco!

There are other possible external sources. Research the private philanthropic organizations based in your state. Contact them to find out their funding cycles and the guidelines for submitting proposals. Ask them to send the appropriate information to you.

Next check the service organizations in your area and their regional headquarters. For example, the Rotary Clubs in Colorado, in conjunction with Pizza Hut, funded a statewide Read-Aloud program that encouraged any nonprofit organization, including libraries, to apply for funds to promote reading to children.

Check the corporate sector as well. It does not matter, for instance, that the corporation is located in the city and your library is in a small rural community, as long as the corporation does statewide marketing. If the corporation has a community relations or philanthropic department, it may be willing to fund a much-needed program for your local community. Such a program is great public relations for the corporation. Don't be timid about approaching nationwide businesses. Many national corporations have regional or state offices, and that is the place to start.

Look at other nonprofit organizations at all levels—local, state, and national—that fund outside projects. For example, a state humanities council can be approached by a library in a rural part of the state. Such a library could request funds to bring minority humanities scholars and/or authors residing in the state to offer some bilingual, Latino-related humanities programming to its community.

Other national government agencies, such as the Department of Education through LSTA funds and the Institute of Museum and Library Services (IMLS), provide funds for innovative projects. Check their RFP (Request for Proposal) guidelines. Perhaps your library can design an innovative project partnership to serve Latino residents with another agency closely related to the department issuing the RFP.

Don't forget your local Friends of the Library, if you have one. They can designate a particular fundraising effort to help your library meet the needs of Latinos in the community.

EXAMINING SUCCESSFUL IMLS PROPOSALS

The following are just some projects that were funded based on proposals submitted to increase the number of librarians in the profession. The common goal of these projects was the desire to diversify the library workforce. Please note that the libraries are collaborating with other organizations in submitting these project proposals.

A consortium in West Texas, El Paso Area Libraries (EPAL), received an IMLS grant to involve Latinos in the field of librarianship. Luis Chaparro, the chair of EPAL, explained that the focus of the proposal is recruiting students to apply for graduate school and mentoring them throughout their studies. (L. Chaparro, personal communication, November 2006)

In 2006, the University of Missouri received two IMLS grants to educate doctoral students. Denice Adkins stated that their need to diversify, both ethnically and intellectually, is in the professoriate. The students are awarded a stipend, and all tuition is paid for four fully-funded years. (D. Adkins, personal communication, November 2006)

Building on a successful IMLS grant award, Denver Public Library is writing another grant that will involve the REFORMA Colorado chapter as well as the University of Denver. The grant will provide scholarships and other types of assistance to graduate students in the metro-Denver area and includes mentoring and professional development. The REFORMA chapter, according to Orlando Archibeque, President of Colorado REFORMA chapter, will recruit, interview, and select candidates for the process.

Fountain of Youth, a project of the Houston Public Library, seeks to recruit bilingual candidates (who speak Spanish, Chinese, Vietnamese) to earn their graduate degrees in library science and to work at the Houston Public Library in the Youth Services department for two years after graduation. Aside from a strong commitment to youth librarianship, the candidates must be accepted to the University of North Texas' online degree program and maintain a "B" average in all course work. The incentives, funded by the IMLS grant, include full in-state tuition; paid membership in the Texas Library Association, Public Library Association, and American Library Association (as well as travel and registration to their respective conferences) for two years; and a stipend for books and expenses.

PERSERVERING TO FIND FUNDING SOLUTIONS

Internal and external funding are the major emphases in this chapter. For public libraries, funding is a constant challenge. Many compete with other local government agencies for limited available funds. Consequently, there are never enough dollars to provide every needed program. There is no excuse, however, for not aggressively looking for external funds and for not integrating some library services for Latinos.

For those of you who are novices to the grant-writing process, the outline we provided delineating the proposal mechanics should get you started. You will never experience the joy and satisfaction of being notified that your project was funded unless you submit a proposal!

Reading teams will usually let the library know of a proposal's weaknesses. Deal with their suggestions and resubmit the proposal or submit the same proposal to another external funding source as well. Think positive, be more assertive, and don't let any rejection deter you.

10 RESOURCE DIRECTORY

In Chapter 4, we stressed that Latinos in your community must be represented in any sampling technique used to assess information needs. Likewise, keep this in mind as you develop programs, collections, services, and partnerships. The list of resources that you utilize should be relevant to Latinos in your neighborhood.

For example, for some Latino families, the need for a storyteller or a *narrador de cuentos* is not relevant. They want a job first, or health care assistance. Storytelling is not a concept that makes sense to them, especially if they were not read to as children. Education does not rank near the top of the priorities list for some low-income families. Participation on the part of the children or the presence of these families at the library is never going to be achieved unless there is a clear understanding of how reading and education could be an advantage for them if they were involved. (Patterson, 1998)

This chapter includes the names of selected publications, library organizations, library committees, training programs, and conferences that deal directly with library services to Latinos. The Web sites included should serve as examples of the type of information that will assist in providing referrals, background, or starting points for you, your staff, and of course the Latino community in your service area.

Remember that these universal resource locators (URLs) are current as of our publication date. By the time this book is available, many of the URLs may be out of date or may no longer exist. We trust that as experienced library workers, you will make an effort to do some research to update the URLs and perhaps the data provided before making it available to customers.

PUBLICATIONS

Library Services for Latinos

Byrd, Savannah Mississippi. 2005. *¡Bienvenidos! ¡Welcome! A Handy Resource Guide for Marketing Your Library to Latinos*. Chicago, IL: American Library Association.

Castillo-Speed, Lillian. 2001. *The Power of the Language—El Poder De La Palabra: Selected Papers from the Second Reforma National Conference*. Englewood, CO: Libraries Unlimited.

Güereña, Salvador, ed. 2000. *Library Services for Latinos: An Anthology*. Jefferson, NC: McFarland.

Güereña, Salvador, and Edward Erazo. 2000. "Latinos and Librarianship." *Library Trends 49* (Summer): 131–181.

Immroth, Barbara Froling, and Kathleen de la Peña McCook, eds. 2000. *Library Services to Youth of Hispanic Heritage*. Jefferson, NC: McFarland.

Luévano-Molina, Susan. 2001. *Immigration Politics and the Public Library*. Westport, CT: Greenwood Press.

Marquis, Solina Kasten. 2003. "Collections and Services for the Spanish-Speaking: Issues and Resources." *Public Libraries 42* (March–April): 106–112.

Marquis, Solina Kasten. 2003. "Collections and Services for the Spanish-Speaking: Accessibility." *Public Libraries 42* (May–June): 172–177.

Moller, Susan Chickering. 2001. *Library Service to Spanish Speaking Patrons: A Practical Guide*. Englewood, CO: Libraries Unlimited.

National Endowment for the Arts. 2004. *Reading at Risk: A Survey of Literacy Reading in America*. Washington, D.C. Available: www.nea.gov/research/ResearchReports_chrono.html.

Schon, Isabel, and Lourdes Gavaldón de Barreto, eds. 1994. *Contemporary Spanish-Speaking Writers and Illustrators for Children and Young Adults: A Biographical Dictionary*. Translation from the Spanish by Jason Douglas White. Westport, CT: Greenwood Press.

Shapiro, Michael. 2003. "Developing Virtual Spanish-Language Resources: Exploring a Best Practices Model for Public Libraries." *Oregon Library Association Quarterly 9* (Summer): 15–19.

U.S. Citizenship and Immigration Services. 2006. *Library Services for Immigrants: A Report on Current Practices*. (March) Available: www.uscis.gov/files/nativedocuments/Library_Services_Report.pdf.

Resources Listing Recommended Materials for Latinos—Children/Young Adults

Saroj Ghoting. "Early Literacy Guides in Spanish." Saroj Ghoting Early Childhood Literacy Consulting. Available: www.earlylit.net/readytoread/indexS.html

Schon, Isabel. 2000. *Recommended Books in Spanish for Children and Young Adults: 1996 through 1999*. Lanham MD: Scarecrow Press.

_____. 2003. *The Best of the Latino Heritage 1996–2002: A Guide to the Best Juvenile Books about Latino People and Cultures*. Lanham, MD: Scarecrow Press.

_____. 2004. *Recommended Books in Spanish for Children and Young Adults: 2000 through 2004.* Lanham, MD: Scarecrow Press.

Schon, Isabel, ed. 1994. *Contemporary Spanish-Speaking Writers and Illustrators for Children and Young Adults: A Biographical Dictionary.* With the collaboration of Lourdes Gavaldón de Barreto; translation from the Spanish by Jason Douglas White. Westport, CT: Greenwood Press.

Treviño, Rose Zertuche, ed. 2006. *The Pura Belpré Awards: Celebrating Latino Authors and Illustrators.* Chicago, IL: American Library Association.

Wadham, Tim. 2006. *Libros Essenciales: Building, Marketing, and Programming a Core Collection of Spanish Language Children's Materials.* New York: Neal-Schuman.

Wadham, Tim. 1999. *Programming with Latino Children's Materials: A How-To-Do-It Manual for Librarians.* New York: Neal-Schuman.

Great Web Sites for Children, *Lugares en espanol para ninos.* ALA ALSC. Available: www.ala.org/gwstemplate.cfm?section=greatwebsites& template=/cfappsgws/displaysection.cfm&sec=20

Recommended Materials for Latinos— Magazines for College Students

Saludos Hispanos
www.saludos.com/saludosmagazine.html

El Andar
www.elandar.com/

Caoba-revista para la mujer afrolatina
www.caoba.org

Recommended Materials for Latinos—Agricultural Workers

Commission for Labor Cooperation. *Protection of Migrant Agricultural Workers in Canada, Mexico and the United States.* Washington, D.C. (2002). Available: www.naalc.org/english/pdf/study4.pdf
In Spanish: www.naalc.org/spanish/pdf/migrant_workers_spanish.pdf

Commission for Labor Cooperation. *Guide to Labor Laws and Employment Laws for Migrant Workers in North America.* Washington, D.C. (2002). Available: www.naalc.org/migrant/english/pdf/mgintro_en.pdf
In Spanish: http://www.naalc.org/migrant/spanish/mgtab_sp.shtml

Recommended Materials for Latinos—Hispanic Heritage Month Subject Guide

This Web site, produced by Arlington County Public Library, is a great example that provides a listing of events, local contacts, local organizations, and eSources for Latinos. A well-done and comprehensive guide, it can serve as both a model of a successful Web site and an effective tool for practitioners. Available: www.arlingtonva.us/departments/libraries/info/HispanicHeritage/LibrariesInfoHispanicHeritageMain.aspx

INTERNET RESOURCES

The following is a selective list of World Wide Web sites that are of particular interest to Latinos and to those developing Latino library services. There are so many resources on the Internet pertaining to Latinos that it is impossible to list all of them.

Virtual Tools for You

CRÍTICAS
A product of *Library Journal*, this magazine began publication in 2001. It is subtitled, "an English speaker's guide to the latest Spanish language titles." In June 2005, *Críticas* went from a bimonthly print issue to a monthly online magazine. Two print issues a year are distributed as supplements to *Library Journal* subscribers only. Also available is a free e-newsletter, *Críticas Connections*.

The resources page includes the Spanish-Language Publishing Marketplace Directory and How-To Articles, which are mandatory destinations for library workers serving Latino and immigrant communities. www.criticasmagazine.com/community/894/Resources/43349.html

Barahona Center for the Study of Books in Spanish for Children and Adolescents

The center is a resource center of books in Spanish and in English about Latinos, for children and young adults. The center publishes bibliographies, offers workshops each summer and the center's director, Isabel Schon, is a leading authority on the subject, with many books, articles, and book reviews to her credit.

Dra. Isabel Schon, Director
California State University San Marcos
Kellogg Library, 5th Floor
333 S. Twin Oaks Valley Road
San Marcos, CA 92096-0001
Fax (760) 750-4073; Phone (760) 750-4070
ischon@csusm.edu
www.csusm.edu/csb/

SOL

Spanish in Our Libraries (SOL) is an electronic newsletter and discussion list. www.sol-plus.net/index.htm

PLUS

Public Libraries Using Spanish (PLUS) is a searchable research bank that provides excellent publicity and signage to address the linguistic gap in our branch libraries. www.sol-plus.net/plus/home.htm

Both SOL and PLUS sister sites are the work of Bruce Jensen. They are a refreshing source for practical tools and philosophical renewal of the role we play in delivering service and impacting lives. All authorship resides with Mr. Jensen, and as his small print reads: "not-for-profit use encouraged."

Finding Non-English Books

Ethnologue.com
This site offers the most comprehensive listing of information about the currently known languages of the world. www.ethnologue.com/info. asp#contact

Howard Karno Books

Specializing in Latin Americana, this site can provide new, out-of-print, and rare books, original materials, photography, and documents. Strong emphasis on history, archaeology, and the arts. www.karnobooks.com/cgi-bin/karno/aboutus.html?id=4S3H5QiY

America Reads Spanish

Aimed at increasing the use and reading of the Spanish language in the United States, this campaign was developed by the Spanish Institute for Foreign Trade and the Spanish Association of Publishers Guilds. Among the many partners and collaborators are professional associations, bookstore chains, public and private libraries, and prominent Hispanic associations in this country, in Spain, and in Latin America.

Features include "The Essential Guide to Spanish Reading," at www. americareadsspanish.org/es/guia_esencial.asp, and a list of Spanish-language books/materials distributors in the United States, at www.americareadsspanish.org/es/distribuidores-inicio.asp. From this list, you can find companies that provide sourcing of books for your multilingual needs, such as Baker & Taylor or Brodart en Español. The Web site also provides a newsletter, new releases in Spanish, and information on authors and upcoming conferences/events.

In English: www.americareadsspanish.org/en/default.asp

In Spanish: www.americareadsspanish.org/es/default.asp

Web site for free downloadable books in Spanish:
http://ar.groups.yahoo.com/group/librosgratis/

Pew Hispanic Center

Founded in 2001, the Pew Hispanic Center is a nonpartisan research organization supported by The Pew Charitable Trusts. Its mission is to improve understanding of the U.S. Hispanic population and to chronicle Latinos' growing impact on the entire nation. The center conducts and commissions studies, and regularly conducts public opinion surveys that aim to illuminate Latino views on a range of social matters and public policy issues. The center focuses on eight key subject areas: demography, economics, education, identity, immigration, labor, politics, and remittances.

> Pew Hispanic Center
> Pew Research Center
> 1615 L Street, N.W., Suite 700
> Washington, DC 20036-5610
> www.pewhispanic.org
> info@pewhispanic.org
> (202) 419-3600 main telephone
> (202) 419-3608 fax
> (202) 419-3606 media and information line

Latinos in the United States

This Web site from Centros Communitarios de Aprendizaje provides useful tools for improving basic life skills and relevant information. www.cca.org.mx/portalcca/comunidades/hispanos.htm

LIBRARY ORGANIZATIONS AND COMMITTEES

REFORMA

REFORMA (National Association to Promote Library and Information Services to Latinos and the Spanish-Speaking) was founded in 1971. This affiliate of the American Library Association encourages membership from both individuals and institutions. There are 26 REFORMA chapters in cities across the country. REFORMA publishes a biannual newsletter, *REFORMA Newsletter*, and sponsors REFORMANET, an electronic discussion group open to members only and the premiere group in this country working to provide services to Latinos locally and globally. As the officers change each year, the Web site will provide you with the means to contact the current leadership of REFORMA.

> National REFORMA Office
> Office Manager: Sandra Rios Balderrama
> E-mail: REFORMAoffice@riosbalderrama.com
> URL for REFORMANET info page:
> lmri.ucsb.edu/mailman/listinfo/reformanet
> URL for REFORMA Web page:
> www.reforma.org

Latino Literacy Now

A nonprofit organization that supports and promotes literacy and literacy excellence within the Latino community, Latino Literacy Now created the International Latino Book Awards in 1999 in recognition of the many positive contributions being made to Latino literature by writers and publishers worldwide. These awards are given annually at the BookExpo America. The organization, in association with actor, director, and activist Edward James Olmos, hosts the Latino Book & Family Festival series. (See Figure 10.1) For more information contact:

> Jim Sullivan
> jim@LBFF.us
> Latino Literacy Now
> 2777 Jefferson St. Suite 200
> Carlsbad, CA 92008
> (760) 434-4484
> Fax: (760) 434-7476
> www.lbff.us/home/about-us/index.htm

American Library Association (ALA)

Association for Library Service to Children, Committee on Selection of Children's Books and Materials from Various Cultures

This committee encourages libraries and librarians to meet the variety of language and cultural needs of children.

> Contact:
> ALSC Committee on Selection of Children's Books and Materials from Various Cultures
> c/o American Library Association
> 50 E. Huron St.
> Chicago, IL 60611
> (800) 545-2433, ext. 2163

Association for Library Service to Children/REFORMA, Pura Belpré Award Selection Committee

This joint ALSC/REFORMA committee annually honors and recognizes a Latino writer and illustrator whose work best portrays, affirms, and

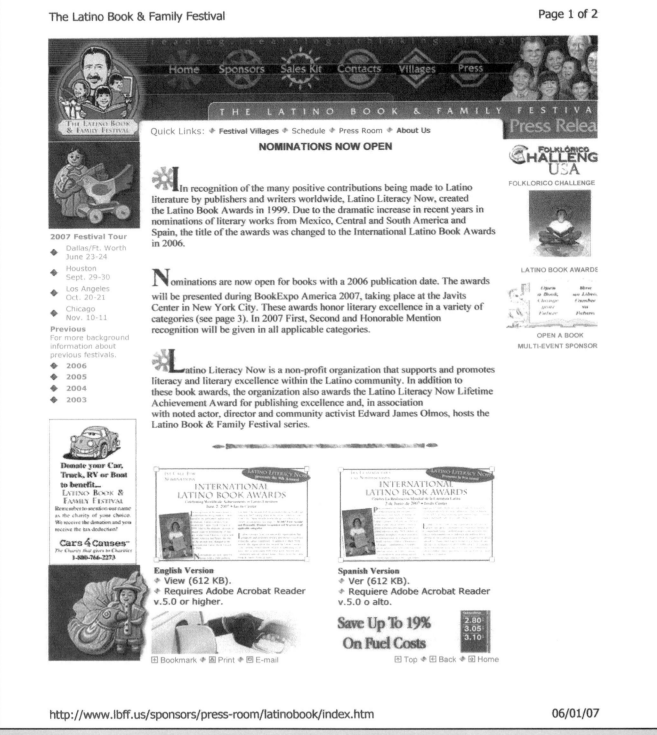

Figure 10-1. Latino Book and Family Festival Web Page

celebrates the Latino cultural experience in an outstanding work of literature for children and youth.

Contact:

ALSC-REFORMA, Pura Belpré Award Selection Committee
c/o American Library Association
50 E. Huron St.
Chicago, IL 60611
(800) 545-2433, ext. 2163

Committee on Diversity

Formerly known as the Council Committee on Minority Concerns and Cultural Diversity, the charge of the committee is to provide a forum to research, monitor, discuss, and address national diversity issues and trends. The committee will analyze and address the impact of diversity issues and trends on the profession, and analyze the relevance and effectiveness of library leadership, library organizations, and library services to an increasingly diverse society.

Contact:

Committee on Diversity
ALA Office for Diversity
50 E. Huron St.
Chicago, IL 60611
(800) 545-2433, ext. 5020

Ethnic Materials and Information Exchange Round Table (EMIERT)

This ALA roundtable serves as a source of information on ethnic collections, programs, and services. It develops and offers programs that deal with the many aspects of ethnicity and librarianship at the ALA annual conference. EMIERT awards the Coretta Scott King Award annually to an African American author and an African American illustrator for an outstandingly inspirational and educational contribution.

Contact:

Ethnic Materials and Information Exchange Round Table
c/o American Library Association
50 E. Huron St.
Chicago, IL 60611
(800) 545-2433, ext. 4294
www.ala.org/emiert

Office for Diversity (OFD)

This office serves as a key resource and link to the professional issues that speak to diversity as a fundamental value and action area of ALA. The Office for Diversity serves as the liaison to the Committee on Diversity and its subcommittees. Additionally, this office administers Spectrum, a scholarship program designed to improve library service through the development of an ethnically diverse workforce.

Contact:
ALA
Director of the Office of Diversity & Spectrum
50 E. Huron St.
Chicago, IL 60611
(800) 545-2433 ext. 5048
diversity@ala.org
www.ala.org/diversity

Office for Literacy and Outreach Services (OLOS)
The Office for Literacy and Outreach Services (OLOS) supports, serves, and promotes adult literacy, and it promotes equity of information access initiatives for traditionally underserved populations through training, information resources, and technical assistance.

Contact:
ALA, Office for Literacy and Outreach Services
50 E. Huron St.
Chicago, IL 60611
(800) 545-2433, ext. 4294
Fax: (312) 280-3256
olos@ala.org
www.ala.org/olos

Reference and User Services Association (RUSA), Management and Operation of Public Services Section, Library Services to the Spanish-Speaking Committee
This RUSA committee works to improve library services for Latinos at both the local and national levels. They provide the Guidelines for Library Services to Hispanics at www.ala.org/ala/rusa/rusaprotools>/referenceguide/guidelineslibrary.htm

Contact:
RUSA Library Services to the Spanish-Speaking Committee
c/o American Library Association
50 E. Huron St.
Chicago, IL 60611
(800) 545-2433, ext. 4398
rusa@ala.org
www.ala.org/rusa

Young Adult Library Services Association (YALSA), Outreach to Young Adults with Special Needs Committee
This YALSA committee (in 1997 a merger between the Special Needs Committee and the Outreach Committee) addresses the needs of young adults who face barriers of access to libraries because of economic, social, cultural, physical, or legal factors.

Contact:
YALSA Outreach to Young Adults Committee
c/o American Library Association
50 E. Huron St.
Chicago, IL 60611
(800) 545-2433, ext. 4390
Fax: (312) 280-5276
YALSA@ala.org

Seminar on the Acquisition of Latin American Library Materials (SALALM)

SALALM is an international organization concerned with the control and dissemination of bibliographic information about Latin American publications, the development of library collections of Latin Americana to support educational research, and the development of library materials for the Spanish- and Portuguese-speaking populations of the United States.

Hortensia Calvo, Executive Secretary
SALALM Secretariat
The Latin American Library
422 Howard Tilton Memorial Library
7001 Freret St.
Tulane University
New Orleans, LA 70118-5549
salalm@tulane.edu
www.library.cornell.edu/colldev/salalmhome.html

National Library of Medicine-Medline Plus en Español

The Web site for the National Library of Medicine offering a Spanish-language version of the resource tool used by the public to find answers to questions related to health. MedlinePlus also offers information on prescription medication, an illustrated medical dictionary, interactive patient programs, and up-to-the-minute health news. Features a tour in Spanish for first time users, which can be taken in eight minutes or less.
www.nlm.nih.gov/medlineplus/spanish/aboutmedlineplus.html

Other Recommended Health-Related Web Sites

Offering resources in Spanish: www.pulevasalud.com

Red Cross Web site in Spanish:
www.cruzrojaamericana.org/index.asp

Universal health symbols to assist customers with limited English proficiency:
www.hablamosjuntos.org/signage/symbols/default.using_symbols.asp

U.S. Department of Agriculture Web site in Spanish:
www.usda.gov/EnEspanol/

U.S. Environmental Protection Agency Web site in Spanish:
www.epa.gov/espanol/

U.S. Health & Human Services Web site, with links to carefully selected information and Web sites from over 1,500 health-related organizations:
http://www.healthfinder.gov/espanol/

LIBRARY TRAINING

WebJunction

WebJunction was developed pursuant to a grant from the Bill and Melinda Gates Foundation. It is an online community geared toward library staff and under the auspices of Online Computer Library Center (OCLC).

WebJunction's Spanish Language Outreach Program helps equip local library staff with knowledge and resources to reach out to Spanish speakers in their communities and increase their access to technology (See Figure 10.2). Recently, they partnered with the Colorado State Library and made a video entitled *Bridging the Digital Divide in the Spanish speaking Community* (2004), available on the Web at www.webjunction.org/do/DisplayContent?id=8579.

Features of the WebJunction's Spanish Language Outreach Program that will serve as great resources are offerings of monthly "In Depth Webinars," and their case studies. Available on the Web at www.webjunction. org/do/Navigation?category=10555

State Associations

Many state library associations and state libraries offer the support you will need in your quest for tools and techniques. Check out your regional library community.

The Utah State Library offers "Serving Spanish Speaking Communities" as part of their Web site. This provides a virtual one-stop resource for library workers. At the bottom of each page in this section there is a fact provided as a tip entitled, "Did you know?" Available at www. library.utah.gov/library_services/spanish_speaking/ index.htm

In Ohio, librarians can refer to the Ohio State Library's page for "Services to Hispanic/Latino Community Members," which can be found at http://winslo.state.oh.us/services/LPD/tk_latino.html

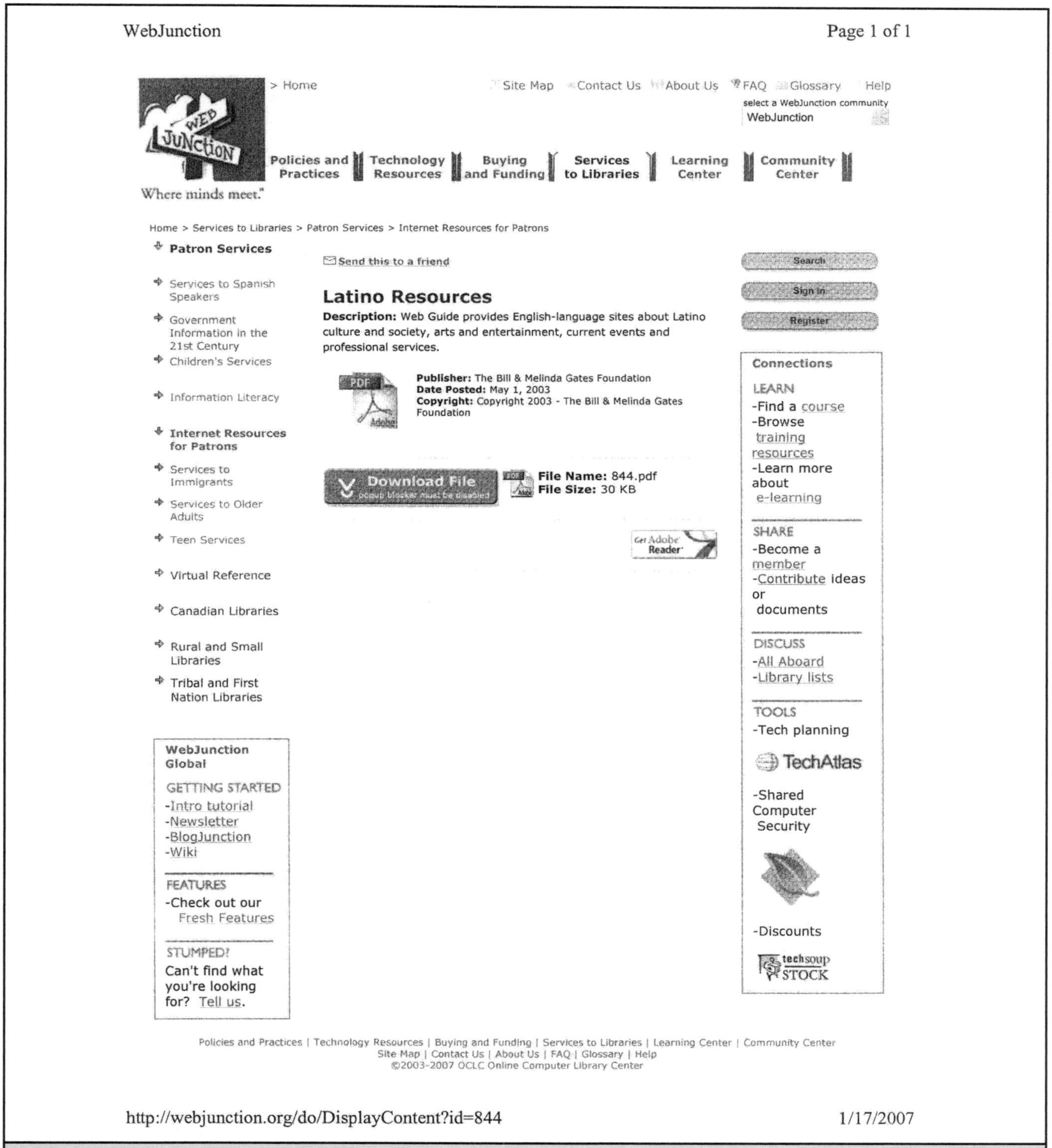

WebJunction   Page 1 of 1

> Home   Site Map   Contact Us   About Us   FAQ   Glossary   Help

select a WebJunction community
WebJunction

Where minds meet.

| Policies and Practices | Technology Resources | Buying and Funding | Services to Libraries | Learning Center | Community Center |

Home > Services to Libraries > Patron Services > Internet Resources for Patrons

⇓ **Patron Services**

✤ Services to Spanish Speakers

✤ Government Information in the 21st Century

✤ Children's Services

✤ Information Literacy

⇓ **Internet Resources for Patrons**

✤ Services to Immigrants

✤ Services to Older Adults

✤ Teen Services

✤ Virtual Reference

✤ Canadian Libraries

✤ Rural and Small Libraries

✤ Tribal and First Nation Libraries

WebJunction Global

GETTING STARTED
-Intro tutorial
-Newsletter
-BlogJunction
-Wiki

FEATURES
-Check out our Fresh Features

STUMPED?
Can't find what you're looking for? Tell us.

✉ Send this to a friend

Latino Resources
Description: Web Guide provides English-language sites about Latino culture and society, arts and entertainment, current events and professional services.

Publisher: The Bill & Melinda Gates Foundation
Date Posted: May 1, 2003
Copyright: Copyright 2003 - The Bill & Melinda Gates Foundation

Download File popup blocker must be disabled

File Name: 844.pdf
File Size: 30 KB

Get Adobe Reader

Search
Sign In
Register

Connections

LEARN
-Find a course
-Browse training resources
-Learn more about e-learning

SHARE
-Become a member
-Contribute ideas or documents

DISCUSS
-All Aboard
-Library lists

TOOLS
-Tech planning

TechAtlas

-Shared Computer Security

-Discounts

techsoup STOCK

Policies and Practices | Technology Resources | Buying and Funding | Services to Libraries | Learning Center | Community Center
Site Map | Contact Us | About Us | FAQ | Glossary | Help
©2003-2007 OCLC Online Computer Library Center

http://webjunction.org/do/DisplayContent?id=844   1/17/2007

Figure 10-2. WebJunction Web Page

Also in Ohio, there exists the Ohio Library Council's Diversity Awareness and Resources Committee. These colleagues have designed a very attractive Web site as just one of the ways that they continue to provide timely, excellent programs, Web resources, and other educational opportunities to promote inclusion and diversity awareness. For starters, visit their section "Language Resources" at www.olc.org/diversity/lang.html

In California, the Infopeople Project is supported by the U.S. Institute of Museum and Library Services under the provisions of the Library Services and Technology Act. Administered by the California state librarian, Infopeople Training is offered in a variety of formats: There are all-day and half-day workshops as well as online learning courses.

You don't always have to be a member of the California library community to register for an Infopeople training. For information about training, or using materials found on the Web site, contact the Infopeople Project assistant by e-mail at assist@infopeople.org or by phone at (650) 578-9685. One example of a training program that was targeted to improve services to the Latino Community can be found at www.infopeople.org/workshop/311.

Perhaps one of their best known resources on this subject, "Survival Spanish for Library Staff," a CD and accompanying materials produced by Infopeople and the State Library of California, can be obtained for your system at www.infopeople.org/training/

Check also your state offices of education for tools that they have developed/utilized to work with the families of bilingual children. You could probably use these very same resources.

In Colorado, for example, the Office of Education's Web site has a section entitled "Spanish Resources," available at www.cde.state.co.us/cdelib/technology/spanish.htm

In conjunction with the Colorado State Library, major Web sites containing Children's Literacy information in Spanish are summarized at www.cde.state.co.us/cdelib/ethnic.htm

Learning Light

If you are going to offer in-house training, Spanish-language training has been developed by the Learning Light. Materials are specifically designed for organizations that are in need of training staff to converse with Spanish-speaking patrons. Reproducible kits are made available through licensing, and more information can be obtained by contacting the Learning Light at www.thelearninglight.com/STWLibrary.html

CONFERENCES

REFORMA (National Association to Promote Library and Information Services to Latinos and the Spanish-Speaking)

REFORMA's third national conference is scheduled for September 2008. Look for this conference to be held biannually in even-numbered years.

For workshop proposal submissions and details visit www.reforma.org.

Guadalajara International Book Fair/Feria Internacional del Libro (FIL)

This annual book fair in Guadalajara, Jalisco, Mexico (usually held in late November and early December) brings together over 9,000 professionals and representatives from over 900 Spanish-language publishing houses, distributors, and booksellers from all over the world. The American Library Association organizes a delegation of American librarians to attend FIL and provides significant financial support.

> David Unger, U.S. Coordinator
> FIL/New York
> Division of Humanities NAC 5/225
> The City College of New York
> New York, NY 10031
> Voice: (212) 650-7925
> Fax: (212) 650-7912
> E-mail: FILNY@aol.com

Foro Transforterizo de Bibliotecas/Transborder Library Forum (FORO)

FORO, the Transborder Library Forum, is a volunteer organization that cultivates a venue for the cooperative exchange of ideas and the discussion of experiences and efforts concerning the provision of library services in the border regions between the United States, Mexico, and Canada. www.asu.edu/lib/foro/

Trejo Foster Foundation Institute

The Trejo Foster Foundation (TFF) was established to bring to the forefront issues concerning library and information services for people of Hispanic heritage in the United States. TFF sponsors biannual educational institutes to bring together leaders, practitioners, and students in the library and information fields to discuss and advocate for issues, policies, and practices that affect Hispanic/Latino communities and individuals.

Trejo Foster Foundation
13462 N. Holly Grape Dr.
Marana, AZ 85653
Phone: (520) 572-2264
E-mail: Ninfa.Trejo@pima.edu
www.tffoundation.org

Joint Conference of Librarians of Color

Anyone can participate and network at the Joint Conference of Librarians of Color. The first conference held in October 2006 was organized and sponsored by the American Indian Library Association (AILA); the Asian/Pacific American Librarians Association (APALA); the Black Caucus of the American Library Association (BCALA); the Chinese American Librarians Association (CALA); and REFORMA, the National Association to Provide Library and Information Services to Latinos and the Spanish-Speaking. The conference presents issues, concerns, and information that will assist in serving communities of color and supports and encourages library workers from those populations and communities.

ALA, Office for Literacy and Outreach Services
50 E. Huron St.
Chicago, IL 60611
(800) 545-2433, ext. 4294
Fax: (312) 280-3256
E-mail: olos@ala.org
www.ala.org/ala/olos/jointconferenceoflibrariansofcolor/geninfo.htm

IFLA

IFLA is the International Federation of Library Associations and Institutions. The IFLA World Library and Information Congress is traditionally held annually in varying parts of the globe. The organization is in the hands of IFLA Headquarters and the national committee.
www.ifla.org/IV/index.htm

National Association of Bilingual Educators (NABE)

The National Association of Bilingual Educators is the only professional organization at the national level wholly devoted to representing both English language learners and bilingual education professionals. Conferences are held annually in February.
www.nabe.org

BIBLIOGRAPHY

Abanira, Marsha. 1984. "Outreach Services to the Spanish-Speaking Community." Paper presented at the First Bi-national Conference of Librarians in California and Baja California, Tijuana, Baja California, Mexico.

Bala, B., and D. Adkins. 2004. "Library and Information Needs of Latinos in Dunklin County Missouri." *Public Libraries* (March/April): 120.

Buck, K., K. Millikan, C. Rider, and S. Smith. 2004. Library Services for Hispanic Patrons. *Indiana Libraries* 23: 23–29

Burgess, H., and G. Burgess, eds. 2003. "Stereotypes/Characterization Frames." *Beyond Intractability*. Conflict Research Consortium, University of Colorado, Boulder. (October 2003) Available: www.beyondintractability.org/essay/stereotypes/

Byrd, S. M. 2005. *¡Bienvenidos! ¡Welcome! A Handy Resource Guide for Marketing your Library to Latinos*. Chicago, IL: American Library Association.

Camarillo, A. 1979. *Chicanos in a Changing Society: From Mexican Pueblos to American Barrios in Santa Barbara and Southern California, 1848–1930*. Cambridge, MA: Harvard University Press.

Constantino, R. 1994. "It's Like a Lot of Things in America: Linguistic Minority Parents' Use of Libraries." *School Library Media Quarterly* 22 (Winter): 87.

"Día Celebrates 10th Anniversary in San Antonio." *Críticas*. (February 15, 2006) Available: www.criticasmagazine.com.

Espinal, I. 2003. "Wanted: Latino Librarians." *Criticas Magazine*. (October 1) www.criticasmagazine.com/article/ CA323763.html

Garza de Cortés, O. 2006. "Celebrate Día's 10th Anniversary." *Críticas*. (April 15) Available: www.criticasmagazine.com.

Güereña, S. 1990. "Community Analysis and Needs Assessment." In *Latino Librarianship: A Handbook for Professionals*, edited by S. Güereña (17–23). Jefferson, NC: McFarland.

Guzman, B. 2001. *La Poblacion Hispana*. Washington, DC: U.S. Census Bureau. Available: www.census.gov/prod/2001pubs/c2kbr3sp.pdf

Hispanic Services Committee. 1990. *Hispanic Services: A Practical Manual for the Public Librarian*. Chicago, IL: Chicago Public Library.

Howrey, S. 2003. "De Colores: The Universal Language of Bilingual Storytime." *American Libraries* (October): 38–43.

Immroth, B., and K. McCook, eds. 2000. *Library Services to Youth of Hispanic Heritage.* Jefferson, NC: McFarland.

Kochhar, R. 2007. "Latino Labor Report 2006." *Pew Hispanic Center Report.* Available: www.pewhsipanic.org/reports/print.php?ReportID=70

Lyman, Rick. 2006. "Census Shows Growth of Immigrants." *New York Times* (August 15). Available: http://nytimes.com

Margolis, R. 2001. "The Best Little Library in Texas: Run-down Branch of Austin Public Library Turns Around and Wins Giant Step Award." *School Library Journal* (January): 54–58.

Marquis, S. K. 2003. "Collections and Services for the Spanish-Speaking: Issues and Resources," Pt. 1. *Public Libraries* 42 (March–April): 106–112.

Marquis, S. K. 2003. "Collections and Services for the Spanish-Speaking: Accessibility," Pt. 2. *Public Libraries* 42 (May–June): 172–177.

Mestre, L. S., and S. Nieto. 1996. "Puerto Rican Children's Literature and Culture in the Public Library." *Multicultural Review* (June): 26–38.

Moller, S. C. 2001. *Library Service to Spanish Speaking Patrons.* Englewood, CO: Libraries Unlimited.

Mylopoulos, C. 2004. "Programming for Participation: Building Partnerships with the Immigrant Newcomer Community." *Multicultural Review* 13 (Summer): 39–42.

Neumiller, M. 1997. "Bilingual Story Times in North Central Washington." *ALKI* 13 (December): 29.

Patterson, I. M. 1998. "Charlotte Public Library Speaks Español: Approaching the Hispanic Community through Storytelling." *North Carolina Libraries* (Winter): 145–147.

Pavon, A., and D. Borrego. 2003. *25 Latino Craft Projects.* Chicago, IL: American Library Association.

Peterson, R. E. 1996. *Recruitment and Retention of Minority Personnel and Trustees in Public Libraries.* Denver, CO: Colorado Dept. of Ed.

Pisano, V. H., and M. Skidmore. 1978. "Community Survey—Why Not Take an Eclectic Approach?" *Wilson Library Bulletin* 53 (November): 253.

Ramirez, R., and G. P. de la Cruz. 2003. *The Hispanic Population in the United States: March 2002.* Washington, DC: U.S. Census Bureau.

Stavans, Ilan. 1995. *The Hispanic Condition: Reflections of Culture and Identity in America.* New York: HarperCollins.

Talbot, C. 1990. "What Is a Multicultural Library Service?" *Library Association Record* (July): 501–503.

U.S. Census Bureau. *Facts for Features, Hispanic Heritage Month 2006: Sept. 15–Oct. 15.* Available: www.census.gov/Press-Release/www/2006/cb06ff-14.pdf

U.S. Census Bureau. 2004. "U.S. Interim Projections by Age, Sex, Race and Hispanic Origin—Summary Tables, Table 1a. Projected Population of the United States, by Race and Hispanic Origin: 2000 to 2050" (March 18, 2004). Available: www.census.gov/ipc/www/usinterimproj/natprojtab01a.pdf

U.S. Census Bureau. *Census 2000, Summary File 3 (SF 3)*; generated by Jacqueline Ayala using American Factfinder (August 8, 2006). Available: www.factfinder.census.gov

Wadham, T. 1999. *Programming with Latino Children's Materials: A How-To-Do-It Manual for Librarians*. New York: Neal-Schuman.

Wexler, S. 2001. "Fantastic Fiestas in the Library: Florida Florida Teens Connect with their Caribbean and Hispanic Roots." *VOYA* (October): 247–249.

INDEX

ABOUT THE AUTHORS

Dr. Camila Alire is Dean Emerita of University Libraries at the University of New Mexico and Colorado State University. She has presented workshops on library services to Latinos throughout the United States. She is past president of REFORMA (National Association to Promote Library and Information Services to Latinos and the Spanish-Speaking) and past president of the Association of College and Research Libraries.

Jacqueline Ayala is a Senior Library Consultant with the firm of Ron Baza and Associates, Inc., and has worked in public, academic, legal, and non-profit libraries. She has provided business and legal research and has a national track record of proven leadership. Serving as President of REFORMA (National Association to Promote Library and Information Services to Latinos and the Spanish-Speaking) in 1998–1999 is one of her accomplishments. She is active in various local Library Associations, has participated on committees, is active in her local REFORMA chapter of LIBROS, takes part in National Library Legislative Day, and has presented at numerous conferences and workshops.